rewriting

the sexual contract

Edited by

Geoff Dench

INSTITUTE OF COMMUNITY STUDIES

Contents

FUTURE MODELS & OPTIONS

APPENDICES

ACKNOWLEDGEMENTS

This book would not have appeared without the support of the Joseph Rowntree Foundation, which both funded the original research that fed my interest in the issues explored here and has helped to support the production of this subsequent collection. Special thanks are due to Barbara Ballard for her patience and encouragement.

Colleagues at the Institute have given me a lot of back-up during the preparations for publication. Kate Gavron in particular has been typically generous with a whole range of editing and sub-editing advice and assistance.

Finally, though it may not be the usual thing to do, I would like to thank the contributors to this volume. They have submitted themselves to a very tight schedule, and put up with a good deal of harassment from me. In addition to delivering their own pieces, mostly on time, they have done more than they probably appreciate, through their conversations with me, to help develop the overall form and compass of the book. They have made it possible for a rather vague initial concept to take eventual shape.

Introduction

Geoff Dench

In a world changing rapidly on almost every front, nothing appears to have been transformed more fundamentally or decisively than our ideas about how men and women should be expected to relate to each other - whether personally, within families, or in the public sphere. Only one generation ago it was still taken for granted by most people, and by state policy, that men and women were inherently different and needed each other's distinctive mutual support. Both the durability of their desire for each other and the wider social order were seen as underpinned by this inter-dependence. Many people no longer feel this, and social policies have ceased to rely on it. There is instead a widespread assumption that social progress has rendered superfluous all of the social imperatives and conventions which previously constrained gender roles and sexual relations. Complementarity has been replaced by an assumption of personal autonomy and interchangeability. Each of us feels that we can be what we like, and construct our own biographies. If we want to have a new sort of template for society, in which gender does not have to entail what it used to, or indeed to mean anything at all, then that is what we can now choose.

Maybe we can, and will. But I suspect that this libertarian prognosis does go rather against the grain of most people's everyday practical experience. Behind the modern rhetoric of personal independence, old ideas about the importance of sexual differences and divisions of labour in the constitution of society may survive largely unaltered for many people. Popular book sales are perhaps a better index than articles in cutting-edge journals of what people really think. We should not forget that Barbara Cartland continues to set new records with the sales of her resolutely romantic novels. Old ways may also be resurfacing in new guises. In the US, which is usually five to ten years ahead of us in testing new lifestyle cultures, the best-seller lists over the last few years have contained a stream of books spelling out the rules of how to catch your man and, having done so, how to understand and hold on to him. Although often dressed up in neologisms and phrased as psychoanalytic revelations, these manuals are devoted to discovering and celebrating notions of sexual difference and interdependence which our grandparents would have regarded as commonplace.

There have been similar shifts lately in Britain, including I think some revival of tolerance towards men in writing on gender issues. For some years until quite recently men were subject to regular doses of advice from commentators, such as Harriet Harman (1993 and Patricia Hewitt (1993), telling us sternly that we had failed to earn our passage to the future, and so were being left behind by women. Now books are emerging from the same intellectual stable, by Adrienne Burgess and others (1996: 1997), which although ostensibly still urging that men need to progress, are much more likely to present the journey as a joint adventure for men and women. Even more significantly perhaps, not far below the surface they also betray a discernible hankering after the comfortable virtues of the traditional family man. Alongside this a whole new genre of books by feminists rediscovering motherhood has evolved.

Some of this may represent only passing fads or flutters of lifestyle nostalgia. It is too early to say. But it does indicate that we should not assert too confidently that conventional prescriptions for relations between men and women have been torn up and thrown away for ever. Scepticism is permitted again. It has become possible to ask whether the drive towards strict gender symmetry is actually producing the benefits for women and society which it has promised, *without* being dismissed out of hand as a misogynist or carpet-bombed with accusations of being 'afraid' of feminism.

Assessing the evidence for change

The accumulating evidence from social research, although tangled and notoriously difficult to interpret, does I believe reinforce the case for caution. The immediate impetus for this book derives from a small study of my own into the changing position of men in British family life (1996b). This investigation turned up a number of findings of a very paradoxical nature, which seem to conflict with the conclusions of much other current research in Britain, and raise serious questions about how research findings are best interpreted. Although its conclusions are necessarily tentative, given the small scale of the study, they are potentially very significant and impressed on me the need for some wider discussion of how to arrive at better understandings of what is currently going on in domestic relations.

My findings highlighted in particular the importance of examining very closely the nature of the link between what people say and what they do. Thus they confirmed, in line with many current attitude surveys, that a substantial minority of all men, and a majority of younger men, offer verbal support for more 'egalitarian' gender roles. What they also showed, paradoxically, is that those men who do actually share domestic work with partners may in fact be more inclined towards *traditional* gender attitudes. Most 'caring' men saw their own major family role as earning the basic family income. They were happy to help out in the home, to enable their partners to enjoy the stimulus of having a paid job themselves; but they did not regard themselves as sharing equal responsibility for domestic work. It seemed more a matter that, having successfully fulfilled a traditional male role, they had the confidence to take on other roles *as well.*

By contrast, those men who strongly supported the androgynous ideal, and rejected conventional sexual divisions, were among the least likely to be involved in actual family work themselves - either by sharing domestic labour or even, indirectly, by serving as breadwinners. Such men had much higher rates of living alone, absent fathering, and socially marginal lives. Thus the declared pursuit of egalitarian sex roles by men seemed to be associated in practice not with new harmony and equality so much as with a growing separation and even *polarisation* between the lives and lifestyles of men and women. This involved a liberation of men from family duties and domestic drudgery, and a corresponding over-burdening of women with greater responsibilities, both at home and at work.

There appears to be a basic *asymmetry* here between men's and women's lives and experience which is generally glossed over. For men, being a carer may usually be *complementary* with being a family provider, not an alternative or even competing activity as it is for many women.

Corresponding paradoxes emerged in the responses by women. A clear majority of younger women (though, as for men, only a small minority of older) supported the libertarian emphasis on couples negotiating between themselves their division of labour, rather than just 'accepting conventional rules'. But the way in which they organised their own lives actually seemed to follow very closely a 'conventional' model, in that most of these respondents who were living with partners did actually divide up tasks with them in traditional ways. They then *justified* it however on such grounds as that this allocation happened to suit their respective inclinations and skills. They did not see themselves as following convention, but as exercising their free personal choice. So it was alright!

The message which seemed to be coming out of this study was that much of the recent libertarian revolution is very superficial. To the extent that it *does* exist it may also be counterproductive in its own terms, as it fails to recognise differences between men and women which have implications for the successful organisation of family life. The domestic lives of modern women may not have been improved so much as we suppose. What has changed very visibly is their attitudes, and above all their rules for legitimising behaviour.

Against this, the domestic lives of some men seem to have gone through considerable reconstruction, but in many cases away from rather than in the direction of gender symmetry. And those men who are adapting positively to new patterns of family life and employment are *not* the ones most strongly influenced by egalitarian ideas. They may even be responding sympathetically to women's new needs *because* they do still believe in difference, and do not really think that sexual divisions can change very much. New man; new chivalry.

Towards a neo-conventional consensus?

It would follow from this analysis that the best option for the future might well lie in seeking reforms *within* a conventional framework, through a refinement and up-dating of traditional sexual relations. This may actually bring us nearer to symmetrical behaviour than an approach which attempts to promote identical attitudes and motivations as well. Pushing for radical restructuring of sex roles, by repudiating interdependence and celebrating autonomy, may delay new accommodations by encouraging that selfish, yobbish behaviour among men which modern women find such a turn-off.

This paradoxical conclusion does moreover, from my own findings, seem to have a lot of backing already among many ordinary people. In spite of great public emphasis on the radical dismantling of traditional sex roles, most people seem to be looking for rather small changes in the behaviour of people around them. They want more flexible divisions of labour. But most of them, including most women - and not least many who were themselves hostile to conventional families when they were younger - seek this within a framework of 'neo-conventional' relationships, that is where there is still a broad assumption that women have primary responsibility for managing family life, while men have greater overall commitment to economic activities. There is I suspect a widespread acceptance not only that within this context there is more than enough space to change people's - that is men's - behaviour, but that it does in reality offer the *surest* means of achieving the flexibility they desire.

I have however found very little other research in Britain which allows itself to be pulled in a similar direction. This may be because public values and behaviour are changing fast here at the moment. I have recently moved into this area of investigation, and I may have done so just as the field itself has started to move. It may also or instead be that many researchers and analysts are being slow to pick up what is going on. Either way it seemed to me that my newcomer's eye might have been quicker to detect that a fresh popular consensus on sexual divisions was in the making.

The purpose of this collection of essays is to explore how far this may be true, or have gone, by bringing together in one place the opinions of a wider range of views than is generally found together in a single volume, around the questions of what is currently happening to gender relations in Britain and what can or should be done by social policy to help these develop in a desirable direction. If any sort of real consensus is taking shape among opinion leaders in this area, this should pick it up.

The contributors are all people whose work as social researchers, commentators and practitioners involves them in analysing and influencing public attitudes in this area. Although writing from a wide range of occupational and moral perspectives, and with a variety of political orientations, they all have in common a finger on some important part of the national pulse. What they see and think as individuals may differ profoundly, but between them they represent a wide selection of the contemporary views to be found in the community.

Guide to the chapters

This book is structured around the idea of a sexual contract. The term is used here to encompass any conventional set of rules about the nature of proper exchanges that men and women can expect to engage in, and which constrain and shape their personal relations and the respective roles they can play in wider society. It does often have a narrower reference. In the work of Carole Pateman, who coined and first publicised the concept (1988), it refers to an inherently patriarchal set of institutions which legalise male sexual access to women and control over them. This approach has prompted many insights into the character of our political and legal fabric. But it is arguable that its emphasis on rights and *formal* statuses allows us only a partial view of sexual relationships in the operation of human society, and of the balances of power involved.

Popular concepts do have a way of losing their sharpness though, as they evoke or come to have ascribed a whole range of extra meanings. And it is in this catholic spirit that the concept of sexual contract has been adopted for this book. What we need here is a flexible boundary to encompass some broad questions about the sexual divisions of labour, and reciprocity between men and women, which lie at the heart of both public roles and family life. The term is very suitable for this purpose. It draws attention to the nature of mutual accommodations which take place within partnerships. It also raises questions about the relationship between individual choice and the framework of group conventions or ground rules, rooted in long-term, collective considerations, which regulate and set *limits* to purely personal negotiation.

The collection is organised into three sections. The first deals broadly with the 'past', in the form of the traditional sexual contract we have left behind and the forces within society which led to change. The next looks at how we are living now. The third considers possibilities and hopes and policy options for the future. This tripartite division is to some extent artificial, as most contributions to the book have something to say in all tenses. Some pieces indeed could have fitted equally well into any part of it. But most have more relevance in one section than the others, and overall the division and ordering adopted does serve, I think, to place related topics together, and to move the argument along.

In the first piece of the collection *Carole Pateman* reminds us of her original usage of the idea of the sexual contract, as part of an emerging awareness of structured inequality in the political realm. She argues that changes in women's status in recent years have not reduced the validity of the questions it prompts. *David Phillips* takes a very different line, by proposing that there were implicit deals underlying conventional marriage which gave moral advantages to women over men. The transition since the middle of the century to more direct involvement of women in the public realm is then explored by *Miriam David*, using the career of Margaret Thatcher as a key marker. *Geoff Dench* suggests that this process needs to be understood as linked to the circulation of political elites. While producing greater individual freedom it has entailed statist encroachments on family life.

Opening the section on present-day lifestyles, *Roger Scruton* observes that the notion of a sexual contract embodies telling implications about the transience and shallowness of relationships in contemporary society. *Ros Coward* surveys the current state of family life and notes that although it is good to have witnessed the demise of authoritarian patriarchy, the consequences are perhaps more complicated than feminists expected, especially for children, and not least in poor families. *Patricia Morgan* then looks closely at the problems which may be experienced by children, and in parenting relationships, as a result of changes in the sexual division of labour.

Focusing more specifically on men, *Sebastian Kraemer* sees them as in the process of developing new roles in response to the changing expectations of women, and argues that culture should be aimed at surmounting rather than just reflecting basic sexual differences. *John Griffiths* gives an account of the difficulties facing

men who take on 'mothering' roles in our society, and makes a plea
for greater tolerance and flexibility. *John Baker* takes this point
further by suggesting that movement of women into the public realm
is not yet properly matched by an acceptance of fuller male
participation in parenting. *James Jones* considers the idea of
fatherhood in Christian theology, which he believes is still an
important force in contemporary society for encouraging men to take
their family roles seriously.

The last chapters in this section assess evidence for change in
relationships, attitudes and behaviour. *Jacqueline Scott* analyses
shifts in support for different models of gender roles, and concludes
that attitudes will continue to change unless social policy hinders
corresponding changes in behaviour. Next *Jonathan Gershuny*
demonstrates that men are still slow in taking on more domestic
activities. But he concludes that the process is continuing steadily
in the right direction. *Rosie Styles* shows how the endorsement of
shared parenting through new forms of ritual, may already be
encouraging construction of new types of inter-personal bonds and
commitment, around the provision of a secure home for children.

The third part of the collection starts with *Catherine Hakim*'s
discussion of the discrepancy between popular preferences and
official policies. European Commission policy is based on the
premise that all women want equal participation with men in the
labour market, whereas there is evidence that the majority of people
favour a modernised sexual division of labour. Against this, *Ruth
Lister* argues that it is important, for the sake of personal autonomy
and genuine interdependence, that government policy should
promote and support female economic independence. *Shirley Dex*
and *Robert Rowthorne* then make a case for co-ordinating public
policies around the needs of families as a whole, and all their
members, *rather* than prioritising the interests of women.

Angela Rumbold, writing as someone who came into parliament
as an established and committed mother, questions how far
politicians, as commonly selected, are the best people to formulate
policies relating to family life. *Clive Soley* points out that it is very
dangerous for politicians, especially men, to say too much about
family values, and proposes that the best course is to support
measures allowing diversity. *Michael Young*, futurologist as well as

parliamentarian, senses that a new age is dawning in which there can be more co-operative relations between men and women, with stronger public support for the family life of both.

His confidence is not fully shared by *Jack O'Sullivan*, who proposes that for their part men are too negative at the moment. They need to give themselves a shake and realise that this is the time to take control of their own destinies. *Fay Weldon* writes that to some extent women get the men they deserve. She sees the shift in what women require from men leading towards new forms of masculinity in the future. *Helen Wilkinson* argues that among young people now there is already evidence of movement away from separate sexual roles, values and characteristics. The sexual contract will need to be thoroughly modernised in this direction if it is to accommodate this and subsequent generations.

The two final contributions both indicate that moving forward successfully can involve preserving (or even retrieving) elements of the past, and also giving due attention to feelings. *Sharon James-Fergus* suggests that life in Britain may have undermined relations between African-Caribbean men and women. Members of that community are now having to recreate for themselves conventional family life and interdependence. The last word goes to *Barbara Cartland*, who has the longest vantage-point of any contributor, which has given her a first-hand view of both the movement for women's suffrage *and* seventies feminism. Her message is that women still want love, and that this is what holds families together.

Consensus regained?

The purpose of this collection was to see whether any new public consensus is emerging on sexual relations. In the event, only a rather limited amount of agreement emerges here, certainly on specific questions. This is of course partly because of the deliberate selection of people with contradictory views. To some extent, and less obviously, it may also be a result of the variety in *style* of pieces. There has been an attempt to balance detailed, closely documented presentations with a mixture of shorter personal views. This enlarges the range of the debate; but it may also operate to conceal common themes.

When all of this is allowed for, I do think that some movement is discernible. Although there is still much evident disagreement, the battle-ground itself has shifted. For example, most contributors accept that there are important sexual differences which have a biological base, and diverge mainly over how culture and social policy should best deal with them. Until recently many people regarded the idea of difference itself as highly contentious.

Thus there is a greater measure of actual agreement here on some broad questions than would have been found only a year or so ago. There is a general willingness to recognise both that conventional sexual divisions of labour had become outmoded, and also that the more utopian projects for reconstructing society have not been and perhaps cannot be achieved. Some gains have been made, notably in personal freedom. But this may have been at the price of triggering off different problems which now need attention in their turn. Closely related to this, there is I think a growing readiness to look back more positively at 'conventional' families and marriage, as holding some answers (though not all) to these newly diagnosed ills. Overall this adds up to a pulling back from extremes - both the sexual radicalism of the seventies and the fierce traditionalist backlash to this - and a common movement towards compromise.

Where there is, above all, a consensus in this volume is over the importance of the issues discussed. And at the end of the day what may be most significant is the willingness of people with very different orientations to collaborate in the production of a book on this topic. We are starting to come out of our bunkers. This surely is a sign of the times, and a very auspicious one, as it suggests that a full opening-up of the debate, long delayed by intense mutual suspicions, is now imminent.

WHERE WE ARE COMING FROM

Beyond the Sexual Contract?

Carole Pateman

I coined the term 'the sexual contract' a decade ago in response to, and in criticism of, a long tradition of argument in political philosophy (Pateman, 1988). The argument holds that the best way to appreciate why government and major social and political institutions are legitimate is to suppose that they were agreed to in an original contract. All the potential inhabitants of a new political order, it is supposed, have come together to decide upon the assumptions and principles that should guide the creation of their society. This mode of argument became important from the seventeenth century onward, but it has gained a vigorous new lease of life since the 1970s, and become very influential in contemporary political theory. Its present-day adherents do not all agree about exactly what institutional form and structure follows from an original contract. Typically, however, they share a (tacit) assumption; that one form of government or power, the patriarchal form exercised by men over women, is irrelevant to their arguments.

The Sexual Contract contains a discussion of the famous texts in political theory (by, for example, Hobbes, Locke and Rousseau) in which theories of an original contract were first formulated, and a discussion of some central institutions in our society, in particular, marriage, employment and prostitution. I have been interested in questions about democracy and democratization for the whole of my academic career and, although *The Sexual Contract* is not explicitly framed in terms of democratic theory, it is part of my contribution to this field.

Public discussion of issues related to sexuality, marriage and the sexual division of labour, has grown since I wrote the book, but their political significance for the creation of a more democratic society is still not taken seriously enough.

Original contracts and marriage contracts

Interpretation of the classic texts is fundamental to any assessment of institutions based on the theory of an original contract. In my re-reading of the classic theories I showed that standard interpretations leave out half the argument. Arguments about masculinity, femininity and relations between the sexes, are ignored, even though the classic theorists drew conclusions about the proper place of men and women in social and political life, and thus conclusions about the proper shape of institutions, from their claims about the natures of the sexes.

Standard readings of the texts, therefore, present only a partial picture of the original contract. Indeed, theories about original contracts are commonly referred to as 'social contract' theories. This label itself demonstrates that one dimension of the original contract - the sexual contract - and thus one dimension of social and political institutions, is omitted. The idea of a social contract is a way of discussing government in the state. The sexual contract calls attention to men's power over, and government over, women; that is, to the patriarchal structure of major institutions.

Theories of an original contract rest on the premise that men or individuals are born free and equal to each other, or by nature are free and equal. The question immediately arises of how the term 'men' in 'men are born free' is to be interpreted. Is this a universal term, so that 'men' means everyone? Or does it refer only to masculine beings, so that women are excluded from the categories 'men' and 'individuals'?

Most contemporary political theorists fail to acknowledge the existence of this problem and treat 'men' as if its meaning were obvious. The reason for this vital omission is that they silently pass over the arguments of their famous predecessors about women and men. The latter (except for Hobbes) claimed that women were born into subjection, and by nature were fit only for government by men. Thus no agreement was required from women for men's patriarchal rule to be legitimate.

Or so it would seem. But another neglected feature of the texts is that, while denying women's freedom, the classic theorists affirm their freedom too. If the (ostensibly) universal language of freedom was not immediately to be compromised by an embarrassing anomaly, then women, had, in some sense, to be shown to be capable of entering into contracts, of giving agreement or consent. This is one reason why the marriage contract occupies a pivotal role. Women as well as men enter the marriage contact, and so women can be said to consent to their subordination as wives. At the same time, however, they are held (by nature) to lack the capacities required for participation in the public world of politics, of rights, of contract and citizenship, which is constructed as a masculine preserve.

The universalism of 'men are born free and equal' was immediately seized upon by all those, including women, excluded in practice from natural (today, human) rights. Universalism provided, and continues to provide, an invaluable political weapon. But women faced a major problem. In terms of logic and reason their arguments are impeccable - though that has proved no obstacle to the general refusal to take them seriously. In terms of practical politics, it was very difficult to make headway, precisely because major institutions were built around men's government, and because rights and citizenship were constructed in the masculine image.

Another reason why the marriage contract has a pivotal political place is that it is central to the problems that women have faced in gaining equal citizenship, in entering employment on the same footing as men, and obtaining protection and security for their persons. The problems are bound up with the complex inter-connections between (ideas about) masculinity and femininity, marriage and the structure of public institutions - that is, the problems involve the sexual contract. Unfortunately, when women's position becomes an issue, discussion usually turns to the family, rather than to marriage. But marriage and the family (though, of course, closely related) are not the same. The common failure to distinguish between marriage and the family helps to obscure the questions I discussed in *The Sexual Contract.* The political significance of laws, social policy and beliefs surrounding marriage is not yet fully acknowledged in either political theory or public debate.

I paid particular attention in my book to coverture, part of English common law. Under coverture, a woman lost any independent civil and legal existence when she became a wife; her person, property, earnings and children all belonged to her husband.

The connections between a wife's lack of public standing and women's exclusion from the franchise and other civil and political rights, from higher education, the professions and many areas of employment, were better understood a century ago than today. Marriage and the reform of marriage law and practice was at the heart of the campaigns of the organized women's movement from the mid-nineteenth century onward. Only very recently were the last vestiges of coverture eliminated. In Britain, for example, until the 1990s the law assumed that a woman relinquished her right of consent when she became a wife (i.e. that a husband could not rape his wife), and the Inland Revenue did not recognize wives as individuals for tax purposes.

Work and citizenship

The heyday of the modern patriarchal institutions with which I was concerned in *The Sexual Contract* (as I note at the end of the book) was from about the 1840s to the 1970s. It was during this period that the institutions now praised under the slogan of 'family values' were consolidated. Twenty years ago the conditions under which they flourished began to change, and the relationships I discussed are now much less stable.

Beliefs about the tasks appropriate for men and women, and the (lack of) legal and civil standing of wives, has bound together marriage, employment and citizenship for nearly two centuries. The assumptions central to the sexual contract and coverture were presupposed in the development of employment. The 'worker' was assumed to be a husband; he was a breadwinner who earned a family wage sufficient (in principle) to support his 'dependants', one of whom was another able-bodied adult, a wife. A wife's proper place lay outside of the public workplace. Her domain was domestic service - in the phrase used by feminists in the seventeenth and eighteenth centuries, she was the 'upper servant' in the household. The sexual division of labour mandated by the sexual contract runs through private and public life, through economics and politics as well as the household.

One consequence of this social and political structure was that the unpaid work of wives in 'the family', in private workplaces, has never had the same status or value as the paid work of male breadwinners - it has never been seen as 'work' in the same sense as paid employment.

There has been a great deal of talk about its value, but it has never counted as a contribution relevant to citizenship (although since the 1790s feminists have argued that it should count). The devaluation of this work was clearly revealed in the twentieth century when wives' status as 'dependants' of their husbands was built into the Anglo-American welfare state.

The tasks undertaken by women in their homes are part of the work of social care necessary for the well-being of all societies, and the welfare state has always depended on a good deal of social care being provided, unpaid, by wives who look after infants, the aged, the sick and infirm - and husbands - as part of 'women's work'. Yet the welfare state was established upon the principle that, unlike male breadwinners, most wives would not contribute, and would not receive benefits in their own right as citizens, but, rather, as a consequence of their marital relationship to contributing citizens.

Women's democratic standing

But is all this now of merely historical interest? According to one view - perhaps summed up by the appearance of the term 'post-feminism' - the sexual contract is obsolete. An independent standing for wives, and equal formal rights for women have been won. Employment opportunities for women have expanded, while many of the industries that provided jobs for male breadwinners have disappeared under the tide of economic transformation and globalization.

Women have begun to move into positions of authority in a number of areas. The impact of the women's movement over the past thirty years has transformed public opinion. As a consequence of these changes, this view holds, talk of the sexual contract is now out-dated.

Certainly, the changes of the past two decades have undermined the supports of familiar patriarchal structures. But it does not necessarily follow that the sexual contract has left no legacy. Notwithstanding that the 'logic' of the universalist language of theories of an original contract has prevailed, and women's equal freedom has been acknowledged in civil and political rights and in legal and social reforms, there are a number of indications that the sexual contract could be rewritten once again in a late twentieth century form.

The problems facing women are still not seen as problems for democracy. There is a tendency for anything connected with women to be bundled under the heading 'women's issues', and then treated as a matter of a special or sectional interest, an interest that demands privileges. In the debates leading up to the elections in California in November 1996, for example, in which the state's affirmative action policies for women and ethnic minorities were abolished, the proponents of abolition presented the policies in just this light. Rather than a means to remedy historical exclusion and masculine privilege, the policies were deemed to confer special advantages on women.

This approach to the problem forgets that women are half the population and half the citizen body, not a minority or sectional interest. The establishment of the Blair administration was not encouraging in this respect. Women seemed to be an after-thought, with 'women's issues' initially tacked on to a Minister's other duties, and then given to a Minister not paid for the work (in Scotland a man has been appointed to look after women's interests).

The problems with which I was concerned in *The Sexual Contract* are not 'women's issues', but women's standing, a matter of institutions and the *relation* between the sexes. And here is a major difficulty. The improvements have not yet been sufficient to transform attitudes and beliefs into a political culture in which (to amend slightly John Stuart Mill's comment in 1869)[1] men enjoy living and working with women who are their equals, and who share the same democratic standing as free citizens.

Among the developments of the past two decades, there has been a marked increase in public awareness of another aspect of the sexual contract: the belief that men have a right of sexual access to women's bodies. That 'right' has come under greater scrutiny and challenge than ever before; there is widespread publicity and debate about rape (inside and outside of marriage, and in war), sexual harassment, and the sex industry.

But there is still a very long way to go before women's right of bodily integrity and personal security can be taken for granted. In

Britain, for instance, the number of reported rapes is increasing, but fewer than a third get to court, and the conviction rate is now much lower than in the early 1980s. The global sex industry has expanded apace since I wrote my book. Yet the frequency of attacks upon women, and the fact that the bodies of girls and women are sold as a commodity in global markets, is still not seen as of political significance. Indeed, these issues are sometimes dismissed as merely the concern of sexual prudes and those who see women only as 'victims'. But if women's security remains peripheral to democratization, how can women enjoy freedom, and how can they take an equal place as citizens?

One of the most dramatic changes is that men can no longer take it for granted that they will find employment that will support 'dependants'. In the EU the proportion of men of working age outside the workforce rose from 8% in 1968 to 22% in 1993, and in Britain, nearly half the men between the ages of 55 and 65 are either unemployed or economically inactive. There are over 30 million unemployed in the OECD countries. High rates of unemployment have accompanied policies to cut back public provision in favour of markets and privatization, and to increase the 'flexibility' in labour markets. Such (global) structural adjustment policies have led to a substantial increase in social inequality and poverty, sections of the population exist in chronic insecurity and many people have been pushed to the margins of citizenship. 'Junk jobs' - casual, temporary and low paid, with no benefits - have proliferated.

This is the context in which many women are now breadwinners. Between 1980 and 1992, three-fifths of the increase in the labour force in the USA, and two-thirds in Europe, consisted of women workers. But women are still paid less than men, and face continued resistance to their employment and advancement. A large proportion of women work part-time; in Britain 80% of part-time workers are women. Women, that is, organize their paid work so that they can accommodate their unpaid work, their tasks of social care. Unpaid social care has increased as cuts in public spending have forced women to ensure that loved ones are not neglected. There is little evidence that men are willing to undertake what is seen as 'women's work', paid or unpaid.

Although the structural transformation of the economy has drawn the majority of women into employment, the implications for the sexual division of labour, and for marriage and women's political standing, are not yet clear. In a period of rapid change and uncertainty some people try to reinstate familiar relationships; for instance, the Promise Keepers men's movement in the USA demands that husbands become heads of families once again. However, rapidly changing circumstances, and destabilized patriarchal structures, provide an unusual opportunity to reconsider ideas and to reshape institutions - in short, an opportunity to avoid a renewal of the sexual contract and, instead, to create a more democratic society.

Creating democracy

A crucial step is to bring the political standing of women - half the citizen body - to the centre of democratization. This does not mean that pressing problems must be neglected in favour of 'women's issues'. Whether, and to what degree, there is conflict between the enhancement of women's position and policies to eradicate poverty, diminish violence, provide adequate social care, and to create the conditions in which everyone could participate in social and political life to the extent that they so wish, depends on the form of the policies and the reasons for which they are advocated. As I have been writing, articles have appeared in the British press arguing for an end to the independent taxation of wives in order to help reduce poverty. But there are other ways to meet this goal that do not revitalize coverture.

One policy proposal, for example, that could help shift the terms of debate and raise the question of women's status and the sexual division of labour, is the introduction of a basic income (if the income were set at an appropriate level). The proposal could open the way for some vital hard thinking about the meaning of 'work' and the division between, and differential evaluation of, paid and unpaid contributions. Part of such rethinking involves the issue of why employment should be so tightly woven into citizenship and democracy. Given present trends, it is an open question whether there can be jobs at a decent wage for all those who want them in the next century. This in itself provides an incentive to examine the assumptions underlying 'workfare', particularly now it is being extended to young mothers caring for small children on their own, and how these reinforce the devaluation of the tasks of social care.

If the debate were to be joined, then it must also encompass marriage and intimate relations between the sexes. Democracy can only be partial unless women's public standing is reflected in the conduct of personal relations, and, at the same time, unless wider economic, social and political changes diverge from a path in which men are the primary citizens. Exactly how women and men would allocate themselves across the spectrum of necessary work, if the meaning of 'work' and women's standing were transformed, is too far into the future to know. Nor is it clear whether the political will exists to seize the current opportunities to democratize and leave the sexual contract behind - I can only hope that the forms of subordination delineated in my book will not continue in the twenty first century.

The Best Years of My Life: Trading Sex for Security

David Phillips

Before we can start to think about a new sexual contract we need to develop a clearer understanding of the one which has been declared obsolete. Otherwise there will be little chance of reaching proper agreement. I will propose very briefly here that any such understanding must include an appreciation of the positive benefits to women of the discarded system, which have lately been overlooked.

Prevailing ideas about gender relations tend to assume that patriarchal social institutions have arisen, almost by definition, out of men's wills rather than from women's or a trade-off between the two. But I think this judgement reflects a strong bias towards the public realm, which clearly offers more to men by giving them roles outside of and on behalf of families. If however we treat the private realm of family life itself as having paramount importance for most women, then we have to see that traditional conventions have also suited or accommodated women's needs too. Patriarchal rules for mating and marriage are more consistent with the biological imperatives and reproductive programmes of women than of men. They can, and used to, be seen as embodying strategies in the sexual marketplace which enable women to maximise their long-term interests in transactions with men. Men too are controlled by patriarchy.

A complicating factor here is that the short-term sexual interests of young women are at variance with those of older. This contradiction helps to obscure the benefits of patriarchy. Any new set of conventions will have to bridge this age gap before women themselves can present a united front in relation to men.

The sexual market

The revival of interest in Darwin lately has produced several books which explore the contrasting reproductive strategies of men and women (e.g. Ridley, 1996; Wright, 1995). These suggest that lack of symmetry in the social power of men and women may not be produced by culture, through construction of 'gender', so much as we have come to suppose. Biological factors are very significant, too.

It is females who carry the great burden of reproductive labour, unless culture can find ways to get males to play a significant part. Younger females have a biological advantage of physical attraction here, which gives them direct influence over male behaviour. But this is lost quite quickly as ageing and the effects of childbearing and rearing take their toll. Then cultural factors become more important. Those patriarchal cultures which bind men into families with long-term obligations can be seen as counteracting natural sexual asymmetry, and to make men more like women, rather than magnifying difference.

Men and women meet in the sexual marketplace with very different personal needs. Men's interest in sex is much more quickly-satisfied and physical (Buss, 1994). In all cultures many men regard sex as a goal in itself, rather than as part of a relationship. Buss reports on a US study in which, when invited to participate in a date including sex, 55% of women agreed to a date, but none to sex, whereas among men 75% were interested in sex but only 50% wanted the 'date' as well. The area of overlap in interest is precariously small, and the old misogynist Philip Larkin probably spoke for more men than we like to admit when he confessed his fondness for onanism - on the grounds that it both saved you the expense of a night out and also left you afterwards with a free evening in which to do what you wanted.

For their part women rarely value sex so highly for its own sake. As mothers or prospective mothers they are concerned with other types of exchange or return as well, in the form of material and emotional supports, in most cases preferably long-term. Traditionally this is a factor which has encouraged women to play down their enjoyment of sex. Sex was something women did 'for' men, and the more openly they admitted to pleasure in it themselves, the fewer other services they could ask for in return. When they do pursue sex for its own sake, as some tried for a while in the late sixties, they find no difficulty in getting men's co-operation but then are liable to feel 'exploited' afterwards (Mooney, 1993). So the notion of 'fully equal' enjoyment has been largely dropped; and much of the feminist movement since then can be seen as an attempt to recover from this experiment, and to restore sexual exchange values in women's favour, without acknowledging sexual differences and that a mistake was made.

What most women are fundamentally looking for, not perhaps at once but sooner rather than too late, is longer-term and more secure bonding, which fits their reproductive strategy of concentrating support and care around a small number of offspring, rather than, as mother nature has programmed in men, to spread seed and risk as widely as possible (Gilder, 1973). The forms of relationships created by patriarchy are much closer to women's reproductive needs than men's, and provide strong circumstantial evidence of the central place of females in human society - just as in all other societies.

The fact that we regard admissions like those of Larkin as outrageous and even misogynistic further betrays how far social definitions of sex, and of the ground-rules governing sexual behaviour, are determined by women's preferences. As the title (and content) of Mary Batten's book (1994) shows, *Sexual strategies: how females choose their mates,* the power to contol sexual access is overwhelmingly vested in the females of a species, as the greater desire of the males for sex renders them putty in the hands of the females.

Batten herself is unfortunately led by cultural notions about patriarchy into supposing that humanity must be a partial exception from this rule. Her argument to this effect is rather confused, and probably wrong, because it seems likely that as social groupings become more complex, the control of sexual behaviour too becomes more complex and subtle. Patriarchy may in principle allocate full control to men. But in practice it does not appear to have operated like this and in many ways can be seen as giving women cultural weapons for the control of men.

Of course, not all women would be equally well placed to appreciate this, or to apply it anyway. Young women who are the object of every man's desire can be forgiven for thinking that there will always be plenty of attention and support available in a free market, so that patriarchal marriage represents a severe restriction and poor deal. A few years later on as time takes its toll, and children multiply their material and personal needs, the security which patriarchal marriage offers may take on greater importance, rendering it a good deal or investment. To understand the value of marriage to women, and probably its greater value to them than to men, we need to take account of both of these valuations.

Marriage and moral control over men

The submission by a young woman to traditional marriage has to be seen I think as a form of delayed exchange, or perhaps even a pre-emptive gift on the part of the woman, whereby men gain immediate sexual access to them in return for promising long-term economic support and companionship. The institutional phrasing of such an exchange also provides the foundation for the development of moral control over men, to bolster declining physical appeal. This is crucial.

Within patriarchal families men become attached to their children, and develop motivations to look after them, which make them more amenable both to family influences and to wider social controls. But they are still attracted to other, usually younger women, and may be tempted to draw a distinction between being good fathers and remaining faithful partners.

The nature of the traditional sexual contract creates an armoury of moral weapons which women can use to restrain them. A common theme running through this, as Dench has suggested (1994: 10), is that a young woman's initial gift of sex requires a lifetime of loyalty to repay. Her willingness, at the time when her sexual value is at its greatest, to withdraw from the market . .

> *... into an exclusive relationship is effectively a gift by a woman to a man of 'the best years of my life', and though it may not be presented as such at the time, it can be referred to later when her market value has declined, and turned into a powerful moral lever to bolster her claims on her partner for loyalty in return.*
>
> *The practice and celebration of fidelity can be a very useful investment for women, so long as it is managed in a way which steers between the twin hazards of encouraging the idea that women have themselves sacrificed pleasure (which would blow the concept of sex-as-a-gift-to-men right out of the water) and of*

challenging the convention that men are in control (which would alert them into scrutinising all of the exchange-values that they are operating with). So the 'best years' argument usually takes the form of arguing not that women would have welcomed sexual adventures for themselves, so much as that they have foregone opportunities to find a more suitable sexual partner, which is often used to imply, in a nice moral twist, more faithful.

These moral machinations used to be well understood, as part of a general appreciation that marriage did not simply represent the capture of women by men, but also contained traps for men. This understanding has been undermined by feminist accounts of women as victims of male exploitation and abuse in families. It is now much harder for older women to convince younger that traditional marriage holds any value or influence for them.

For men the underside of patriarchy has been the way in which it steers them into surrendering their freedom. The language of male volition and control means that men become identified very publicly with patriarchal rules. So if they feel that these conventions do not suit them after all many conclude that they must be deviants, or making a mistake. To voice such doubts and suggest that patriarchy does not serve men, *especially* now that it is in disgrace, is to risk being accused of sour grapes or labelled as a poor loser. Most men would rather appear good losers. So they go along with the idea that the end of patriarchy means that they have 'lost contol' of women.

In reality it may be women who are losing most control though. For when it was possible to represent social institutions and rules as the product of male will and personality, then it was far less excusable, on any level, for men to *break* the rules. If the marriage went through difficult times or failed he was almost certain to be seen as the responsible party. The man who, following patriarchal convention, declared his undying love and commitment at a marriage ceremony regarded as giving legal expression to male volition was more likely to think many times before betraying or abandoning his wife.

He was also fair game to be branded as a liar, cheat or hypocrite if he should eventually do so. And for those men who did not wholly *feel* the sentiments which they very publicly expressed, but believed that by saying them they would make a number of people they cared about happy, the marriage vow was possibly their first Big Lie. However it would not have been their last. Once uttered, the lie needs to be re-iterated for the sake of consistency, and to fend off the suspicion that in reality it occurred in the first place.

This I think sums up a common natural history of the sour, buttoned-up, irritable, poor-communicator-of-emotions manner which many patriarchs developed. It is one of feminism's manifest achievements that this type is in decline. But it may be a mixed blessing for women. It has been a fashionable sport for some years to mock the Tory MPs who uphold family values while embracing mistresses. But at least such men know that they are in the wrong, and have the decency to hang their heads in shame as their wives bravely accept them back.

Post-patriarchal man is a different animal, who may be more fun to be with but who lacks these redeeming moral features. The new style in partnerships is to say that nobody expects lifelong commitment any more. No promises: no hypocrisy. In this way Labour MPs and other reconstructed public leaders can hope to have much less fuss made about *their* private lives. This is a large part of the appeal of new values to new men.

Thus the crumbling of patriarchy is leading us towards a new pattern of sexual relationships, which is already starting to become visible, involving less fidelity and greater sexual competition and inequality. A key aspect of this is the growing number of older women who have been left in middle age to fend for themselves. The *First Wives*. We hear a lot about how divorce is initiated more often by women than men - as if this was not also the case under patriarchy, when it was seen as a mark of male responsibility and guilt. What we hear less of though is that women's chances of re-marriage, compared with those of men, are declining.

Among men there is a rather different pattern emerging whereby more men are re-marrying, or re-partnering, and re-fathering, several times over, while a growing lump of undesirables finds it ever more difficult to find a partner or mate at all. Polygyny, which occurs in some form or other more frequently outside of patriarchal systems than inside them, is on the rise in the form of serial monogamy. Some commentators like Matt Ridley (1994) believe that high-flying, professional women may find it congenial and convenient not to have a man around most of the time, and to have only a part-share in one, so that there is a potential market for concurrent polygamy as well. However, I imagine that the majority of women would not agree. There are issues here which need to be considered very carefully before we go back to the drawing-board.

Ancient truths still apply and need to be restated.

Family Roles from the Dawn to Dusk of the New Elizabethan Era[1]

Miriam E. David

In this chapter I will discuss two sets of changes over the last 45 years or so, since the beginning of what Margaret Thatcher originally called the 'New Elizabethan Era' in 1952. First, I will concentrate on the changes in the family especially in men and women's roles with respect to familial relationships, employment, childcare, children's upbringing and education; and secondly, I will interweave changing political ideologies and social movements, especially moves away from consensus politics to New Right and particularly Thatcherite critiques of the welfare state and social movements such as feminism.

I want to argue that these two processes have occurred in parallel rather than together although both are related to overarching changes in the economy. Despite the changing roles of women in economic and family life, neither New Right nor feminist ideas have been universally accepted, such that it is difficult to sustain the argument that Britain is now 'post-feminist', except in the very limited sense of individual women now having opportunities for both paid employment and public office on a scale that was unthinkable fifty years ago. These are themselves changes that can be summed up in and by one woman, Margaret Thatcher.

Both New Right and feminist ideas are part of a broad tapestry of changing political notions in relation to the changing economic, familial and social context, and they are not necessarily separable or separate from it. The title of the chapter draws on the title of an article that the then young and newly wed Mrs Thatcher wrote in 1952. I will use Margaret Thatcher's own autobiographies (1993; 1995) as evidence of these changes, as seen through her eyes and add to these with commentaries by her daughter Carol in her biography of her father, Denis Thatcher (1996). In the second

volume of her autobiography Margaret Thatcher discusses frankly
and openly her own dilemmas about her political ambitions and her
family responsibilities and roles. To quote her:

> *I had decided that what with running a home and reading for*
> *the Bar I would have to put my political ambitions on ice for*
> *some time to come. At 26 I could afford to do that and I told*
> *Conservative Central Office that such was my intention. But as*
> *a young woman candidate I still attracted occasional public*
> *attention. For example, in February 1952 an article of mine*
> *appeared in the* Sunday Graphic **on the position of women 'At**
> **the Dawn of the New Elizabethan Era'...**
> (1995: p79, my emphasis)

I will argue that the changes that have occurred over the last twenty
years or so are only partly attributable to changing political ideas,
around the New Right, and have more to do with changing
economic realities, as Margaret Thatcher would concur. There have
been myriad changes in women's economic and work roles, as well
as in their familial relationships and the changes in patterns of
marriage, divorce, separation, cohabitation and reconstituted
families. At the same time, and in part in response to these changes
over the last twenty years, there have been changing expectations
associated with the kinds of help and support given for children's
upbringing and education or schooling.

However, these changing expectations take little account of the
realities of the changes in women's family roles and relationships.
They may have more to do with attempts by the New Right to
reverse the socio-economic and familial processes at work, such as
the breakdown in family life and the growth in lone parent families
through divorce, separation, cohabitation and women's apparent
desire for economic independence rather than dependence upon a
man.

Thus these myriad changes taking place in Britain, amongst other
nations, have often been dubbed late or high modernity or post-
modernity. In the last fifty years we have witnessed massive social
and economic changes in Britain, from changes in family life and
family structures, to forms of employment and the sexual division
of labour, and social and political life broadly. Accompanying these
socio-economic changes have been major ideological and political

shifts, but the changes have been too complex to ascribe any forms of causality. Methods of analysing these changes have been equally varied from traditional empirical social sciences, to newer, more reflexive (drawing on academic feminist) approaches to post-modernism and post-structuralism, which eschew analysis in traditional social scientific terms of causality. Although these changes are extremely complicated and to some extent contradictory, they do clearly have an impact upon women's lives both within the family and the workplace and they also influence the ways in which successive generations of women, especially as mothers, understand and appreciate them.

Background to the changing context

Since the Second World War there has been a secular trend towards socio-economic growth together with a party (or bi-partisan) political consensus on state intervention to ensure such economic growth (Mishra, 1976). Thus, at the end of the Second World War, both Conservative and Labour governments were committed to the creation of the welfare state and to government regulation of the economy. Both of these commitments were to some extent implemented and gave rise to improvements in employment and educational opportunities. There was a gradual shift in the sexual division of labour, with new opportunities for female employment particularly associated with the implementation of the welfare state. Women's employment within the welfare state, as nurses, teachers and social workers, and as administrative and secretarial support, gradually gained ground.

However, in contradictory fashion, the welfare state was based on the 'traditional' nuclear family, through all of its provisions for education, including early childhood, health and social services (now known as social care), housing, income maintenance and social security. In line with Beveridge's recommendations, women, on marriage, were afforded 'other duties' than men, responsible for the care of family - husband and dependent children - rather than economic independence (Land *et al*, 1976).

Thus there was an inbuilt contradiction in the origins and nature of the welfare state such that the five major services or forms of income support were provided to families which were socially dependent upon the housewife/mother, whilst the providers of such services were themselves often women, mainly married women. This 'system' gradually expanded but there have been few changes in the ideological underpinnings, with women remaining the mainstay of families.

By the 1960s the party political consensus on economic growth and the welfare state was beginning to break down, with the Labour party committed to stronger forms of equality of opportunity than the Conservatives. There were specific instances of conflict particularly over education and childcare. In the first place this took the form of political conflict on the grounds of *class* rather than *gender*, with Labour arguing, in the words of Anthony Crosland, one of its key theoreticians, for a strong rather than weak definition of equality of educational opportunity. By this was meant equal access, through educational outcomes, to employment opportunities rather than to initial forms of education, such as access to nursery, primary or secondary education. Moreover, Crosland (1956) had intended that educational opportunities should be provided to reduce social class differences defined in terms of family or parental socio-economic circumstances.

Invariably this came to be operationalised, in both official and research documents, as *fathers' occupation* and/or income, and sometimes reclassified as a twofold definition only - manual or non-manual occupations - with the former the operational definition of working class and the latter middle class. Indeed, this definition remains conventional both officially and in much social scientific research around questions such as these (David, 1993).

The second wave of feminism began to develop in the late 1960s, influenced by social and political movements in France and the USA. In the first stages the women's liberation movement in Britain developed a sustained critique of state social policies, arguing for five policy changes, with respect to education, family planning, preschool childcare, employment opportunities and pay. Initially four demands on the state were formulated, covering equal educational opportunities, equal pay and equal work, 'abortion on demand' and twenty-four hour day nurseries (Coote and Campbell, 1976). Later a further three demands were added, including financial and legal independence. Two of the original 'demands' were to do with public life and employment, equal education and pay; two with issues within what had hitherto been seen as the privacy of the family, namely family planning and child care.

Although there were no major official responses or massive shifts, by the 1970s policies around equality of opportunity were beginning to take on board these critiques and become sensitive to issues of gender or sexual equality as much as social equality. Thus the Equal Pay Act of 1970 introduced a weak concept of equal pay for equal work, and the Sex Discrimination Act of 1975 also took on board the notion of eliminating forms of sexual discrimination in employment and public services, including limited forms in education.

Both these two pieces of legislation were part of the bi-partisan political consensus, although the Conservatives argued for weaker definitions of equality of opportunity in public life. However, neither the legislation nor the two main political parties took on board the idea of equality of opportunity, however defined, within the privacy of the home and family. Indeed, the legislation was confined to public bodies and relatively large organisations. Family businesses and private clubs, for instance, were excluded from the terms of the legislation.

On the other hand, the public bureaucracies created to implement these equal opportunities were becoming the butt of criticism with respect to democratic control. In addition, education was scape-goated for many of Britain's economic ills so that by 1979, when Mrs Thatcher as a Conservative came to power, she did so on a wave of criticism of such public bureaucracies and the educational system sustaining them. In particular, she aimed to reverse such changes and develop the privacy of the family, immune from state control. She also aimed to orient the educational system more clearly to that of the economy, ensuring economic growth rather than equal opportunities (David, 1980).

Thatcherism and Feminisms:
Laisser-faire conservatism in public and private

With the benefit of hindsight, it is clear that there were two contradictory tendencies within Thatcherism as a political ideology and as it affected government policies. On the one hand, there was the tendency, often described as neo-Conservativism and a wish to return to Victorian values, to regulate both family life and the economy, through measures which proscribed particular activities. On the other hand, there was also the neo-Liberal, *laisser-faire* tendency which allowed for the free play of market forces and the developments in deregulation therefore in what became known as privatization and marketization. This latter allowed for deregulation of the labour market and opportunities for women, whatever their family circumstances, to participate in the labour force. Most recently Quest and Conway (1997 forthcoming) have elevated this to an almost moral position, arguing for 'free market feminism'. Given these two tendencies, there was throughout the 10 year period of office and beyond into Major's administrations a tension between what others have called central control and market forces (Whitty, 1993).

However, this tension meant that women remained both the mainstay of families, responsible for the care of all family members and the upbringing of the children, including as the main negotiator with schools, while also increasingly drawn into the labour market to provide for family members (David, 1993; David *et al*, 1996). This is also in part because there have increasingly been major changes in family life, particularly in terms of relations between both gender and generation.

In other words, there have been dramatic changes in patterns of marriage, cohabitation, separation and divorce and therefore in patterns of parenting such that many children (and as many as the majority of dependent children under 16) may find themselves in single or lone parent households or in step-families for at least a part of their childhood. The traditional nuclear family, of 'natural' parents with dependent children, is no longer the dominant family form (if ever it was).

By 1993, lone mother families constituted virtually one fifth of all families but nevertheless four fifths of dependent children lived with both natural parents. Moreover, the lone parent families were, and are, a diverse group with less than 10% teenage mothers and the majority of lone mothers divorced or separated or living in stable cohabiting relationships, albeit out-of-wedlock. In addition, lone parenthood is often a temporary state since over a third of divorced mothers remarry or cohabit. These changing 'family worlds' have impacts upon both parents - mothers and fathers - and their children and the circumstances in which they bring up their children. Many mothers of dependent children find themselves having to take paid employment to support their family-households, whatever the circumstances (David *et al*, 1996).

Some have argued that this involvement in the labour force is more the result of feminism than of financial stringency. However, although feminism has, arguably, had a considerable influence and impact on women's lives over the last twenty to twenty five years it has not substantially affected either public policies or practices in the labour market. It is extremely difficult to argue that in the late 1990s we are in post-feminism or post-feminist Britain since the goals of feminism have not yet been won. Thus we need to ask what the goals of feminism are or were. Of course, as with other political ideologies or campaigns there are many variants and versions of feminism, such that Margaret Thatcher has, in the past, described herself as a feminist, despite the fact that many of her main female detractors would consider themselves feminists (see, for example, Bea Campbell's *Iron Ladies*). To simplify, on the one hand there are those like Mrs Thatcher; liberal feminists who are for changes in individual women's rights and, on the other, 'socialist' feminists who argue for broader changes in women's social and economic positions (Banks, 1985; Acker, 1995).

These latter feminists argue for changes in women's family roles as well as for changes in public life and in equal rights in employment, education and politics. However, liberal feminists are only concerned with equal rights and changes in the public and not the private sphere where they maintain a commitment to traditional family values (for an interesting discussion see for example Eisenstein, 1983).

The tension between the espousal of traditional family values and modern women's practices is no more clearly illustrated than in the story of Lady Thatcher and how she became the first woman Prime Minister. She herself represents both the possibilities and potentialities for women to play major parts within the public, especially political, sphere and, at the same time, she espouses traditional values about women's role within the private family. Curiously however it is precisely because of her particular conservative views that she can come to hold what are apparently contradictory values.

Her belief in *liberal* or *laissez-faire* conservatism, or the importance of limited government in the context of the free market, is what could lead her and her own personal life in that direction. Government is a limited public sphere and one in which only some men, with a particular individual and personal commitment to public duty, play their part. In other words, it is its individualism and liberalism, of an economic kind, that could lead her to a kind of 'liberal, individualistic feminism' or a notion of *laisser-faire* as applied both to politics and family life. Much of this contradiction about women's roles between the public and private spheres can be summed up by Carol Thatcher's final paragraph about her father:

> *It's ironic that if he hadn't been married to the first woman Prime Minister, he would probably have been very lukewarm about voting for one. He's certainly still obdurate on the possibility of women one day being allowed to blow the whistle at his beloved Twickenham. When the London Society of Rugby Football Union Referees was discussing the issue of female rugby referees, Denis rolled his eyes, pursed his lips, shook his head and said to the President, "Sir, I don't understand what they are talking about. There's no such bloody thing. It's barmy".* (1996: p290)

It seems to me that the Thatchers reconstructed, implicitly and without discussion, the Victorian values of two separate spheres for men and women in their own lives in order for them both to pursue their own interests, and in particular for Mrs Thatcher to become Prime Minister of a Conservative government, whilst married to a deeply conservative man. In fact, perhaps it is also a living example of 'liberal' *laisser-faire* Conservative philosophy in action; that the philosophy of such conservatism was limited government and that although the preserve of men it was not necessarily the pinnacle of a man's career to be in politics. Rather, a successful businessman was just as important or perhaps more so than a conservative politician. Again it is as Carol Thatcher said of Denis, on the eve of Margaret Thatcher becoming Prime Minister:

> *...my father wasn't interested in **the equality debate**; nor did he listen to the sociological waffle about the resentment of the subordinate male. Matthew Arnold's description of someone*

'Who saw life steadily, and saw it whole' applied to Denis. The thought of playing second fiddle to his wife didn't even occur to him. After all, he was a businessman, not a political consort - at least for a few more months. (1996: p104, my emphasis)

Mrs Thatcher had, even before she was introduced to Denis, decided on a career in politics. Thatcher was committed to a particular notion of separate spheres of life for men and women but, although a Conservative, politics was not a career he was particularly keen to pursue.

He was far more interested in sport and business. He became an intensely loyal and devoted husband, yet maintained this separateness throughout their marriage and Mrs Thatcher's career, first as leader of the opposition and second as Prime Minister. Again Carol's summary is apposite:

*...It might seem strange that **Denis, pillar of male chauvinism at Twickenham**, could happily walk two paces behind his wife for the rest of the year. He managed it and probably won over a whole political constituency who wouldn't normally have voted in a woman as prime minister. They admired Denis and this made it acceptable to vote for Margaret...* (1996: p165, my emphasis)

He never sought to intrude or to have his opinions divulged in the public arena; only occasionally was it known that he proffered advice, more on business/economic and finance matters than on political questions. In fact, the picture that Carol paints of her father is of a rather lonely and certainly very typical uncommunicative, if not unemotional, man, especially as consort to his wife as Prime Minister. Again it is perhaps best expressed by Carol:

But in this era of high profile co-partner consorts, Denis prefers to describe his walk-on part as 'always present, never there'. He went on:...love and loyalty...[those] two things have guided my efforts...I suppose it sounds terribly pompous but I really do believe it. For forty wonderful years I have been married to one of the greatest women the world has ever produced. All I could produce - small as it may be - was love and loyalty...
(1996: p290)

In order to appreciate these specific tensions in a traditional approach to family roles and responsibilities and *laisser-faire* Conservatism it is necessary to explore, in some more depth, Margaret Thatcher's own perspective on her marriage, child-bearing and child-rearing. This illustrates both the contradictions and legacy of these views for the late twentieth century.

A young woman in the early post-war 'man's world': the dawn of the New Elizabethan Era

After graduating from Oxford in 1947, Margaret Thatcher continued to pursue her political involvements, despite recognising the difficulties of the path that she had chosen, given that she was a woman. Indeed she is very explicit and clear-eyed about all of this:

> *I found myself shortlisted, and was asked to go to Dartford...on Monday 31 January 1949...It was the questions which were...likely to cause me trouble. There was a good deal of* **suspicion of women candidates**, *particularly in what was regarded as a tough industrial seat like Dartford. This was quite definitely* **a man's world** *into which not just angels feared to tread. There was, of course, little hope of winning it for the Conservatives...Why not take the risk of adopting the young Margaret Roberts? There was not much to lose, and some good publicity for the party.* (1995: p64, my emphasis)

But she also had a traditional approach to marriage and relationships. Carol Thatcher's view confirms that of her mother:

> *If marriage is either a takeover or a merger, then my parents enjoyed the latter. There was a great deal of common ground and a tacit laisser-faire agreement that they would get on with their own interests and activities. There was no possessiveness, nor any expectation that one partner's career should take precedence. Denis's life changed very little.* (1996: p66)

Margaret's life changed more, for on marriage she was able to give up her employment:

> *Pleasant though married life was in London, I still had time enough after housework to pursue a long-standing intellectual*

*interest in the law...Now with Denis's support I could afford to
concentrate on legal studies without taking up new employment.
There was a great deal to read, and I also attended courses at
the Council of Legal Education.* (1995: p79)

She also comments upon the gradual social and economic
transformations in this immediate post-war period and how she
responded to it:

*To be a young married woman in comfortable circumstances
must always be a delight if the marriage is a happy one, as mine
was. But to be a young married woman in those circumstances
in the 1950s was very heaven. I am always astonished when
people refer to that period as a time of repression, dullness or
conformity - the Age of Anxiety, etc. The 1950s were, in a
thousand different ways, the reawakening of normal happy life
after the trials of wartime and the petty indignities of post-war
austerity...It was the age of affluence, and with affluence came
a relaxation of all the restrictions that had marked English life
since wartime and, even beforehand, the Grantham of my
youth...The Angry Young Men and kitchen-sink drama also
appeared to challenge the West End. Again, I assumed that this
too would disappear in short order and, besides, I had had too
much of **kitchen sinks in real life** to want to visit them on my
night out...* (1995: p77, my emphasis)

Again this version is confirmed by Carol's account:

*Meanwhile, Margaret had become a young married woman of
comfortable means. Any thoughts of a political career were put
on hold, although she still accepted occasional invitations to
speak at Conservative party functions. Instead she decided to
read for the Bar. Denis supported her decision: 'Do what you
like, love,' he told her, and it became his standard response.
Fortunately, a barrister's **life is also highly compatible with
motherhood**, an event pencilled in to begin on 29 Sept 1953.*
(1996: p68, my emphasis)

Her 'kitchen sinks in real life' began to loom large shortly after she
has told of the 'jolly' times she was having reading law and pursuing
a political career. The following quote is very important with respect

to her personal family and public political involvements and values:

*The question which John Hare had raised with me about how I would **combine my home life with politics** was soon to become even more sensitive. For in August 1953 the twins, Mark and Carol, put in an appearance... [but] had to wait a little before they saw their father. For Denis, imagining that all was progressing smoothly, had very sensibly gone to the Oval to watch the Test Match and it proved quite impossible to contact him. On that day he received two pieces of good but equally surprising news. England won the Ashes, and he found himself the proud father of twins...Oddly enough, the very depth of the relief and happiness at having brought Mark and Carol into the world made me uneasy. **The pull of a mother towards her children is perhaps the strongest and most instinctive emotion we have. I was never one of those people who regarded being 'just' a mother or indeed 'just' a housewife as second best.** Indeed, whenever I heard such implicit assumptions made both before and after I became PM it would make me very angry indeed. Of course, to be a mother and housewife is a vocation of a very high kind. But I simply felt that it was not the whole of my vocation. **I knew that I also wanted a career.** A phrase that Irene Ward, MP for Tynemouth, and I often used was that 'while the home must always be the centre of one's life, it should not be the boundary of one's ambitions'. Indeed, I needed a career because, quite simply, that was the sort of person I was. And not just any career. I wanted one which would keep me mentally active and prepare me for the political future for which I believed I was well suited.*

*So it was that at the end of my first week in hospital I came to a decision. I had the application form for my Bar finals in December sent to me. I filled it in and sent off the money for the exam, knowing that this **little psychological trick** I was playing on myself would ensure that I was plunged into legal studies on my return to Swan Court with the twins, and that I would have to **organise our lives so as to allow me to be both a mother and a professional woman**...Usually, however, it was the nanny, Barbara, who took Mark and Carol to the park, except at weekends when I took over...* (1995: p80, my emphasis)

She also addresses the issue of women's changing social positions
and the relations between marriage, motherhood and a career:

*The fifties marked the start of a major change in the role of
women. Until then they tended to be well into middle age when
the last child of an often large family fled the nest; work within
the house, without the benefit of labour saving devices, took
much longer; and home was also more of a social place, visited
throughout the day by a wide range of tradesmen, from the
milkman to the window cleaner, each perhaps stopping off for a
chat or cup of tea. Consequently fewer women had the
opportunity or felt the need to go out to work. The fifties
marked the beginning of the end of this world, and by the
eighties it had changed out of all recognition. Women were
younger when the children left home because families were
smaller; domestic work was lighter owing to new home
appliances; and home deliveries were replaced by a weekly visit
to the mall or supermarket. And the 1980s saw yet another twist:
the trend whereby women started to remain at work in the early
years of marriage, but to leave the workforce to have children
for a time in their thirties...*

*Of course, these general arguments were not ones which
affected my own decisions as a young mother. I was especially
fortunate in being able to rely on Denis's income to hire a nanny
to look after the children in my absences. I could combine being
a good mother with being an effective professional woman, as
long as I organised everything intelligently down to the last
detail. It was not enough to have someone to mind the children;
I had to arrange my own time to ensure that I could spend a
good deal of it with them. As regards being a barrister after I
had become qualified, I would have a certain amount of latitude
in the cases I took on, so I could to some extent adjust my
workload in line with the demands of family. As regards politics,
we lived in London, my husband worked in the London area,
Parliament was in London - clearly, I must seek a constituency
which was also in or near London. It was only this unusual
combination of circumstances which enabled me to consider
becoming an MP while I had young children... But I wrote to
John Hare saying: Having unexpectedly produced twins...I think*

I had better not consider a candidature for at least six months...
(1995: p83, my emphasis)

Carol Thatcher also addressed these issues with some frankness:

"He was very good at remembering to wave up at the nursery
window as he left for work, whereas Mrs Thatcher, whose mind
was already on her job, would forget" (Nanny Barbara on Denis
Thatcher) I came into the world with two extraordinary people
as parents, but that didn't necessarily make them extraordinary
parents...So he took to parenthood with enthusiasm. Margaret,
who had felt unwell during much of her pregnancy, was relieved
that we had arrived safely. As she now had one of each sex, that
was the end of it as far as she was concerned - she didn't need
to repeat the process.   (1996: p69)

She continued:

In December 1954, when we were 16 months old Margaret
unsuccessfully bid for the Conservative candidature in
Orpington. It was never going to be easy because female
candidates - particularly mothers of young children - were still
regarded with suspicion. After all, they could hardly devote
themselves full-time to the task; if they did, they were likely to be
accused of neglecting their families. (1996: p72-3)

With all the benefit of hindsight, reflection and clarity about these
social changes, Mrs Thatcher has told us how her own unique blend
of fortunate circumstances led her to relatively unusual ideas for a
woman in the early 1950s. Indeed all the usual social comment is
of this period being the heyday of Bowlbyism (Riley, 1983; New
and David, 1985) and the inculcation of the idea that even middle
class mothers should 'return' home and look after their children.
Relying on domestic help let alone nannies in this period of the
1950s was becoming somewhat contentious amongst such women,
and, with the rise of the women's movement in the late 1960s,
became a major bone of contention and debate.

But Mrs Thatcher does not entertain such agonising or even
maternal 'guilt'. She presents her decisions in a cool and even
calculating fashion without regard either to her own mother's views
(which are never mentioned) or those of the growing 'psychological

and psycho-therapeutic' lobbies.

However, it was another three years - rather than six months - before she renegotiated embarking upon her parliamentary career, which then proceeded relatively smoothly:

> *In ... 1956 I went to see ...Kaberry...There was no problem in my being put back on the list of candidates...I was less fortunate in the reception I received from Selection committees...[4 rejections on these grounds]* **With my family commitments, would I have time enough for the constituency? Did I realise how much being a Member of Parliament would keep me away from home?...And sometimes more bluntly still: did I really think that I could fulfil my duties as a mother with young children to look after and as an MP?** *I felt that Selection Committees had every right to ask me these questions. I explained our family circumstances and that I already had the help of a first class nanny. I also used to describe how I had found it possible to be a professional woman and a mother by organising my time properly.* **What I resented, however, was that beneath some of the criticism I detected a feeling that the House of Commons was not really the right place for a woman anyway. Perhaps some of the men at Selection committees entertained the prejudice, but I found then and later that it was the women who came nearest to expressing it openly. Not for the first time the simplistic left-wing concept of 'sex discrimination' had got it all wrong.** *I was hurt and disappointed by these experiences. They were, after all, an attack on me not just as a candidate but as a wife and mother. But I refused to be put off by them. I was confident that I had something to offer in politics...And most important of all, Denis never had any doubts. He was always there to comfort and support me.* (1995: p93-4, my emphasis)

It is important to note that in this extract she chooses to build upon the benefits of hindsight and to contribute the well-known idea - at least in psychotherapeutic literature - of women's rivalries, which she then attributes erroneously to the women's movement (see for example Eichenbaum and Orbach, 1990). Nevertheless, as her comment about 'hurt' indicates, she is very aware of the painfulness of 'gender politics' even if she misattributes its causes and consequences. She continues in this vein:

As I had expected (at the Finchley selection committee), it was at questions that the trouble began. Could a mother with young children really effectively represent Finchley? What about the strains on my family life? I gave my usual answers, and as usual too a section of the audience was determinedly unconvinced. And doubtless it was easier for them because poor Denis at that moment was absent...I wished he were with me... (1995: p96)

Despite the difficulties of the questioning around these issues of family life and 'conventional motherhood' she was selected for the Parliamentary seat of Finchley and subsequently won the seat in the 1959 general election:

Mark and Carol were 6 when I became an MP, old enough to get into plenty of trouble if not firmly handled. Nor was Denis at home as much as he would have liked, since his job took him abroad a good deal. Because my parliamentary duties meant that I was not always back before the children went to bed, I insisted on full family attendance at breakfast....I had learned from my mother the importance of making every house a home. In particular, I insisted on a warm kitchen, large enough to eat in, as its heart. Although I like somewhere to be clean and tidy, I have no taste for austerity for its own sake. (1995: p103)

She also paints a detailed picture here of some aspects of maternal guilt and her desire to run a relatively conventional household, despite her professional political involvements:

My childhood experiences in Grantham had convinced me that the best way to make a cheerful home is to ensure that it is busy and active...We had a daily help in to do most of the regular housework, but there were some things which I insisted on doing myself. Whatever time the House rose...I would drive back to Farnborough so as to be ready to prepare breakfast for Denis and the family...I would then take one or both of the twins and sometimes another local child off to their schools - we had a team of mothers who shared out the duties between us ...I wanted the twins to be at home when they were young, though I was reconciled to their going to boarding school later...The house seemed empty without them. (1995: p104-6)

Carol Thatcher's story also echoes this:

In July 1958 (sic) Margaret's search for a safe Conservative seat ended successfully...Not only was it a highly desirable seat; it was geographically feasible for a working mother. "I had a young family and I could never have done what I did unless everything had bounced right for me," says Margaret. "I just couldn't have had a constituency a long way away. I was very lucky...In these days of feminism I am the first to say that had I got a seat in Yorkshire or Lancashire I could not have gone for it." (1996: p78-9)

Somehow she conjured up the energy to race between the Dormers, the House of Commons and Finchley, making it seem remarkably easy. "There are 24 hours in a day and if you fill them with activity, your mind is always active and you're not thinking of yourself," she says, "You're just getting on with whatever you have to do next." She explained her daily routine to the Evening News *on 25 February 1960....* (1996: p85)

Carol also showed how deeply committed to her professional career her mother became:

...I saw more of Margaret than I did of Denis in those early years. She never missed one of my Saturday leaves from [boarding] school...She had the most impenetrable tunnel vision. When the mother of a friend of mine was discussing arrangements for getting her daughter and me together during the holidays, Margaret declared that a particular date was unsuitable because she'd be "in the House". "Oh, so shall I," replied the other mother, thinking it tremendously odd to state the obvious. Margaret of course missed it. No other house registered with her except the House of Commons. (1996: p86)

Thatcherism and Feminism in politics:
at the dusk of the New Elizabethan Era:

The issues of equal opportunities for women in politics versus the politics of family life shift in balance during the course of the forty odd years covered by Margaret Thatcher's autobiography. The first volume is about her time as Prime Minister and is taken up with politics and liberal policies. There is virtually no discussion of equal opportunities questions. The second volume is about her early life and career up to being leader of the opposition but towards the end of the volume there is a discussion of the current issues in relation to politics where she returns to discuss social and familial changes and how to reassert traditional family values. I will discuss this shifting balance with reference to her own views and in her own words.

Interestingly, the theme of equality of opportunity on grounds of sex in public life is threaded through her account of her early political career. She also draws attention to it in her discussions and contrasts the House of Commons with industry:

> *Masculinity, I soon found, however, did not degenerate into male prejudice. In different ways I had on occasion been made to feel small because I was a woman in industry, at the Bar and indeed in Tory constituency politics. **But in the House of Commons we were all equals**; and woe betide ministers who suggest by their demeanour or behaviour that they consider themselves more equal than the rest....*   (1995: p108)

However, it is left to Carol to illustrate the continuing dilemma when Margaret became leader of the opposition in 1975:

> *... After the excitement of victory - and the novelty of having a female leader - had worn off, sections of the press and the Conservative Party began promulgating the idea that Margaret's grip on the leadership was both tenuous and temporary. **She was a misfit: a woman in a man's world, a political curiosity and - worse - a feminist experiment**. How long could she survive before the Conservative party regained its senses and dumped her for a man?*   (1996: p103-4 my emphasis)

Increasingly, however, the autobiography takes on a more party political hue as Mrs Thatcher begins to discuss her roles as leader of the opposition and then Prime Minister. There is less direct comment about women's rights, politics and her own position within politics.

Policies, and policy differences with the Labour party, dominate subsequent discussion, illustrating her particular brand of 'liberal' individualistic conservatism. By this stage her own gender had become rather less important, and certainly subordinate to the task of first, in opposition, and second, as leader, recreating a *laisser-faire* conservatism in the public sphere, covering both education and family policies.

She does, however, address the question of her commitment to what she called *Victorian virtues* which may well have grown out of this period of reflection whilst in opposition between 1974 and 1979. Her previous conservative values were rather more equivocal. She discusses her Victorian values in her autobiography of her years as Prime Minister:

> *I had a great regard for the Victorians...I never felt uneasy about praising* **'Victorian values'** *or the phrase I originally used* **Victorian virtues***...they distinguished between the 'deserving' and the 'undeserving poor'. Both groups should be given help but it must be of very different kinds if public spending is not to reinforce the dependency culture... the purpose of help must not be to allow people merely to live a half-life, but to restore their self-discipline and through that their self-esteem...* (1993: p627, my emphasis)

However, this discussion comes out of her defence of her much quoted comment that there was 'no such thing as society' for she argues that she went on to say:

> *There are individual men and women, and there are families. And no government can do anything except through people, and people must look to themselves first. It's our duty to look after ourselves and then to look after our neighbour. My meaning, clear at the time but subsequently distorted beyond recognition, was that society was not an abstraction, separate from the men and women who composed it but a living structure of individuals, families, neighbours and voluntary associations. I expected great things from society in this sense...The error to which I was objecting was the confusion of society with the state as helper of first resort...Society for me was not an excuse, it was a source of obligation. I was an individualist in the sense that I believed that individuals are ultimately accountable for their actions and must behave like it. But I always accepted that there was some kind of conflict between this kind of*

individualism and social responsibility. I was reinforced ..by the writings..on the growth of an 'underclass' and the development of a dependency culture... (1993: p626)

In her second volume she also devotes a whole chapter to what she calls *'Virtue's Rewards: policies to strengthen the family, curb welfare dependency and reduce crime'* (1995: p538-564), looking both at theories and 'evidence' about crime and welfare dependency, including differences in families. She argues:

> *The family is clearly in some sort of crisis: the question is what... Most public attention to changes in demographic structure has, however, focused on the case of the teenage single parent. Understandably so, for this 'lifestyle' is an exceptionally irresponsible one...imposes severe disadvantages on children ...without a father's guidance...moreover, it is a problem that is getting worse. The number of one-parent families with dependent children as a proportion of all families with dependent children in Britain has approximately doubled since 1976...to over-simplify greatly... That said, the number of single parents, though growing, actually understates the problem. Very often single mothers are concentrated either in a particular area or a particular ethnic minority... Not only...do children grow up without the guidance of a father: there are no involved, responsible men around to protect those who are vulnerable, exercise informal social control or provide examples of responsible fatherhood.... Of the 1.3 mn single parents in Britain nearly 1 mn depend on benefits, costing the taxpayer 36.6bn a year...* (1995: p549)

> *...the increase in divorce is also a clear threat to the family.. It would be difficult to reverse the reforms of the 1960s which...made divorce easier...but... if we are serious about the family as the fundamental unit of society, that has implications for economic policy too. It should for example be reflected in the tax system...To encourage the traditional family means more tax relief not less.* (1995: p564)

However, she acknowledges that whilst in office as prime minister it was not simple to develop policies to reflect Victorian values and her own position which was somewhat at odds:

> *The question of how best...to support families with children was a vexed one...I believed that it was possible - **as I had - to bring up a family while working**, as long as one was willing to make a great effort to organise one's time properly and with some extra help. But I did not believe that it was fair to mothers who chose to stay at home and bring up their families on one income, to give tax reliefs to those who went out to work and had two incomes. *It always seemed odd to me that the feminists - so keenly sensitive to being patronised by men but without any such sensitivity to the patronage of the state - could not grasp that. More generally there was the question of how to treat children within the tax...I would have liked to return to a system including child tax allowances...All that family policy can do is to create a framework in which families are encouraged to stay together and provide properly for their children. The wider influences of the media, schools and above all the churches are more powerful than anything government can do. But so much hung on what happened to the structure of the nation's families that only the most myopic libertarian would regard it as outside the purview of the state...*
> [*her footnote: *I was though content to make one minor adjustment. This was to provide tax relief for workplace nurseries.*]   (1993: p631 our emphasis)

Thus increasingly she contrasts her own position as advocating equal rights for women in public life, particularly politics, with that of those she calls 'feminists'. Thus it could be argued that by the 'Dusk of the New Elizabethan Era' Margaret Thatcher might consider herself a 'post-feminist' and public life and politics to be 'post-feminist', to contrast with the early period in which equal rights for women as politicians were, by her own admission, not available. However, this is not a discussion in which she engages in either volume of her autobiography. Neither does Carol Thatcher discuss this since her account is largely focused upon her father, and there are only occasional glimpses of her mother and her politics.

Nevertheless, both Margaret Thatcher and other New Right commentators such as the American social commentator Charles

Murray, on whom she tends to rely, concur with the evidence of both more dispassionate social researchers and the new Labour government about the numerous changes in family roles and relationships. It is the interpretation of these changes and the political implications that are made around which there is so much disagreement. Charles Murray (1993) in particular asserts a fundamentally moral position with respect to the changes, by dubbing people in 'traditional families' who live in middle class, Conservative supporting constituencies in England as 'the new Victorians', whilst those who live in Labour supporting constituencies, with purportedly high rates of marital break down and lone parent families, are called the 'new Rabble' or the 'underclass'. His policy aim, which Margaret Thatcher endorses, is to remove state support for such families in order to ensure that single mothers do not depend upon state support but are forced to rely on men and marriage, even though he also demonstrates that areas with high rates of 'out-of-wedlock parenthood' also have high rates of 'working aged unemployment' amongst men and high rates of male juvenile delinquency.

Thus both Margaret Thatcher and Charles Murray argue against state support for women as lone or single mothers with children to bring up; they rail against 'the nanny state' as much as against female economic independence, hoping for a return to Victorian values and the traditional patriarchal family. Their desire is for traditional male headed households in which women as wives and mothers look after the family, using nannies at home alone where appropriate. However, their *laisser-faire* approach does allow them to argue for equality in the labour market which, as Quest and Conway (1997) also argue, can be achieved without public policies, if women have the same abilities as men. Regulating the workplace, in their view, fetters both men and women's employment opportunities; the labour market left to its own devices will allow for equal opportunities. Moreover, there is also no need for measures for public child care or financial support which hinder men and women's freedom.

These approaches to equal opportunities strain at the traditional definition of equal opportunities and feminism. Traditional feminism has argued that the free play of market forces has not accomplished equality of opportunity but has confined men and women's roles and responsibilities to separate spheres. Without policies to constrain the labour market and to remove discrimination against women there is little chance of achieving even equality of opportunity in public life. The New Labour government also have recently recognised the problems of the rapid growth of lone parenthood, especially amongst women with young children. They too have proposed policies to 'get women off welfare and into work' but are also concerned about the issues of childcare and how to support such women with their family responsibilities, especially for childrearing.

Conclusions: women, the family and Feminisms throughout the New Elizabethan Era

Margaret Thatcher was indeed far sighted in her article written forty five years ago about the changing roles and responsibilities of women in the 'New Elizabethan Era'. During the course of this era, which is now drawing to a close, women's roles and responsibilities have changed dramatically, both in terms of employment and family life. However, the question of how to deal with these changes has been fraught and not easily resolved by any of the political approaches adopted. On the whole those arguments which have held sway in the party political arena have been relatively traditional and have not taken cognizance of women's own views and perspectives on these changes. Feminism has not been taken up greatly in the party political arena, except for a very 'weak' version, to use Crosland's notions with respect to equality of educational opportunity.

In some respects it can be argued therefore that there is now a liberal feminist variant of change but that hardly allows the title of 'post-feminist'. Feminist changes would require a major trans-formation not only of public life but also approaches to the family and private life, most of which are a long way from being achieved. We may be in a post-Victorian era but we are not yet in a post-New Elizabethan Era, with all that that entails in terms of post-feminism.

Nearing Full Circle in the Sexual Revolution

Geoff Dench

It is generally accepted that a revolution has taken place in sexual relationships over the last twenty to thirty years, and that the conventions previously governing how these should be organised, and what personal exchanges they entail, are no longer tenable. But I believe that both the nature of this revolution and where it may be leading us are widely misunderstood.

The orthodox interpretation emphasises that medical, demographic and economic changes in the West have come together in recent decades to liberate individuals - especially women - from societal regulations which are no longer needed or wanted. In a world of smaller and later families, people can negotiate with each other to live how they like, without church or state telling them what to do.

I believe that this is only part of the story. What has been largely forgotten in public accounts is the extent to which the former regulation of relationships was rooted in the give and take occurring inside family life. The ground rules which have been discarded were not *imposed* on families from the public realm. They were formulated within them and were then *endorsed* by wider social institutions and authorities. Their removal was not really a defeat for public control, but a victory for regulation over 'private' families from the centre.

Clearly there are crucial political dimensions to this, and I suspect that contemporary libertarian orthodoxy may itself embody the ideology of a new regime. We are still too close to events to see the links between different aspects of change in proper historical perspective. But the rise of new meritocratic elites in the West, who regarded family life as a restriction on personal freedom, must have greatly complicated the processes of adjustment by families to the new demographic possibilities. Political modernisers since the middle of the century have allied themselves with the desire of youth - all youth that is, not just the ambitious - to escape from the tiresome controls of family elders. They have also chosen lately to represent this revolution as conducted mainly by and for women. All this has been a powerful influence on directions of change.

My own recent researches (e.g. 1996b) indicate that this more critical view of 'progress', although given little space by the media, is shared by large segments of the population. The majority of ordinary people, certainly by the time they reach their mid-thirties, *regret* the loss of institutionalised state support for conventional family life. Many see the new state libertarianism which has replaced it not as a withdrawal of interference in private lives so much as the exercise of a new set of rules privileging a powerful interest group. This perceived new elite, which has definite 'meritocratic' features, consists of professional 'two-career' couples, who are better off when taxed as independent workers, plus a growing entourage of fellow-travelling adult 'singles' whose relative affluence is similarly promoted by fiscal policies treating 'family life' as an individual lifestyle choice. Far from allowing people to choose what is best for themselves, current state policies minimising community restraints on this group may ignore the wishes of the majority concerning the type of collective supports they would like to see provided, thereby making it harder for them to run their own families as they want.

I further suspect that the political mobilisation of anti-family sentiments over the last generation has probably delayed the adaptation of sexual divisions of labour to changing demographic circumstances. What could have been a process of pragmatic and incremental adjustment has been turned into a lengthy and conflictual sexual revolution. We will still get there, but only now that harmful consequences of the revolutionary deregulation of family life are at last being recognised. This is happening partly because such effects of change take their time to work through. But it is more the result of movement by the rebellious youth of the nineteen-sixties and seventies into grandparenthood, and adoption themselves of elder status and a managerial perspective towards family life.

At the same time, and reinforcing this, the first generation of meritocrats have taken their place within the establishment and no longer need to tear up the social fabric to create space. Indeed, among *their* children there is now a widespread return to tradition, with a revival of domestic service occupations and class consciousness to match the social divisions which meritocracy has itself produced, and to help them sidestep sexual labour demarcation disputes within their own households. So there is now no need to continue a social revolution which never has had a genuinely popular basis. As we move into the new millennium we can expect a steady return to normalcy in family and sexual relations.

Sexual revolution and youth culture

There are many questions raised by the argument I am putting forward, only a few of which can be dealt with here. What I want to focus on mainly is how a revolt which was originally directed against parents, then probably encouraged by a rising elite, appears to have turned into a conflict between women and men, and what the implications of this may have been.

A major misconception in the orthodox interpretation of the sexual revolution, and an important key to its ideological role, lies in its portrayal of 'traditional' social structures as serving the interests of men. Virtually all societies, and certainly all of any complexity, are 'patriarchal' in the sense of attaching greater formal rights and responsibilities to men. But as I have argued in detail elsewhere (1996a) this does not mean that these systems *serve* men. In most cultures it has, on the contrary, been seen as implying that the social position of men is more *problematic*. Men have a much greater tendency to be marginal to community life, so that in order to develop orderly motivations and have any chance of approaching the level of socialisation achieved by women they *need* to have their obligations and rewards spelt out and made public. Without these cultural roles, human societies would be much closer to those of other species, which revolve openly around females. Patriarchal rules and roles are instruments for mobilising men.

The notion that patriarchy and traditional society can be equated with male domination seems to be a political tool, and to become most salient during periods of intense social revolution when, I suspect, it provides a useful device for engendering support among women for the dismantling of existing institutions and undermining incumbent elites. Historically the likes of Engels and Robespierre have turned the idea of patriarchy to their own purposes, and I think that it has similarly been a key factor in the postwar attack on hereditary class structures by statist meritocracies.

The importance of having female support for a social revolution hinges on, and I think also helps to indicate, the very *central* position of women in society. It is women who perform the great bulk of essential work, whose relationships of mutual support form the basis of community life, and who know best how society works. They are accordingly the main guardians and transmitters of culture, with a considerable stake in existing practices and institutions. Men largely take their moral leads from women, and tend to see male activities as instrumental, executing goals defined by women. A movement which does not have some women on its side, approving its ends, will lack legitimacy and will not get very far.

Among women it is always likely to be the younger who become allies of revolutionary ideas. They are often strongly controlled by the older, and in those societies we currently regard as most patriarchal it is older people generally, *not least* women, who are seen explicitly by younger people as the holders of real power. Young women usually accept this authority. They need the help of older women during the long years of childcare, respect their knowledge and experience, are attached to them by family ties, and recognise their own stake in the system as future family managers. But there are tensions involved too, which can be played on by advocates of social change. If a young woman can be persuaded that the wider community will provide her with the opportunities and personal care and resources to enable her to raise her children *without* submission to the will and whims of a mother or mother-in-law, then she may well be prepared to endorse a programme of social transformation and impart her female licence to its cause. By weaning young women away from solidarity with older, and weakening families, revolutionaries can gain legitimacy for their centralised regimes - in which people are controlled by rewards and punishments issuing from the state - while reducing the competing authority and decentralising social influence of older people.

Such attacks on the private realm of family life are by their nature also liable to set women against men. Families run closer to women's hearts than men's, and discreetly empower women in relation to men. The devaluing of families by political revolutionaries may appeal at an intellectual level to young women. But by alienating them from family values and placing private life under greater control of the public realm in which men are visibly dominant, it sooner or later leads women to develop a sense of subordination to men, and general victimhood, which far fewer of them experience in more settled times when society and the state are according due respect to family life and motherhood.

What happened in the West during the sixties and early seventies can be seen as a classic case of the co-option of young, idealistic women as handmaidens for somebody else's social revolution. We tend to think of the sixties phenomenon as a movement by women against male oppression. But this aspect was taken on later as it became politicised. In essence the original sixties thing was a generation revolt against parents and the established 'society' they stood for. Young women were especially prominent in it from the outset. The combination of the postwar expansion of education and career opportunities with improving contraception meant that they were suddenly less dependent on families and older people, and freer to behave more like young men did. Their participation helped to make the movement socially significant and amenable to exploitation by political modernisers. But in the early years at least it was from elders and stuffy tradition that women felt liberated, *not* from men, who were seen as allies in the new-found freedom. It was a generalised youth culture, not feminism, which characterised the spirit of the era.

Meritocracy's female face

It was not long however before youthful revolution became overlaid with the imagery of a sex war. At first this was mainly tactical, through use of young women as symbols of modernity. But as tactics came to govern strategy, and young women started to believe in their own revolutionary destiny, eventually it became a sex war in substance as well.

The major driving force in these developments has I believe been the rising meritocracy, generated by the pace of technological changes and educational expansion, which was represented in

Britain mainly in the modernising wing of the Labour Party since Harold Wilson's first administration. Wilson came to power on a wave of revulsion against Conservative cynicism and corruption, epitomised by the Profumo affair. The party was starting to lose its traditional working-class base, after opposing immigration controls, and Wilson's governing plan, which some at the time believed might keep the party in power for the rest of the century, lay in developing a new constituency among the ballooning class of upwardly-mobile technocrats.

Wilson had no problem appealing directly to women in this reconstruction of Britain, and in using them in turn as images of the future. Opening up opportunities 'to all talents' had special and genuine relevance to girls, because women were the largest untapped pool of labour. Modernising the economy was portrayed in terms of replacing sweaty old factories powered by coal and muscle with clean new science-based industries using brainpower. A New Jerusalem fit for bright young women would be built on the social ruins bequeathed by Mac's dirty old men. The old regime took on a male aspect. When coming into disagreement with their mothers many girls used this - perhaps conveniently reducing tension a bit in the process - by defining them not as the real villains but simply as 'friends of the enemy' (Mooney,1993).

This identification of progress with womankind came to have particular importance when the social foundations for the new order were laid. Wilson's young supporters wanted to be freed from the family obligations which tied them down. Nothing is quite so irksome to a meritocrat as endless demands from relatives, and the party came under increasing pressure from younger members to promote personal freedom of choice. Certain reforms, for example those liberalising divorce and abortion, required specific legislation. Here the obvious fact that a majority of young women supported change was used to justify new laws even though the measures were widely unpopular in the country. Young women, after all, were the future. Their opinions had an over-riding legitimacy.

Other measures indirectly promoting freedom from family ties were developed under cover of executive action and Finance Bills. Wilson and then Callaghan both expanded state social services very rapidly, enabling many people to pass responsibility for the care of troublesome or burdensome relatives onto the state with a clearer conscience, and providing direct support to citizens in their own right rather than as members of families. Reforms in the structure of taxation which whittled away the financial interdependence of partners and incentives for marriage soon followed.

All this shunted a great deal of caring activity out from the private realm of family, where it hindered women's careers and had required them to be supported by male 'family wages', into the public realm where they created more congenial paid work for qualified women. Here again *legitimacy* had to be conjured up for this transfer. Many older women were not happy about it, but the visibly female character and staffing of the new social service professions neutralised their reservations.

These developments were profoundly altering the balance of power between female generations and their respective capacities to influence public definitions of family life and values.

Undermining older women and the private realm

Most older, traditional women were accustomed to exercising *personal* authority over younger members of their families. They also tended to contribute to public debate mainly through men, and considered this to be good for family life, as the resulting role for men as family spokesmen helped both to make them more responsible, and to give them a direct interest in family affairs. This double act between women and their sons and partners was to be seriously undermined by the growing participation of younger women in the public realm. For these now expected to speak for themselves, and their combination of moral legitimacy as women and eagerness to 'communicate' gave them tremendous promotional advantages over older women and men alike. Soon they started to assume that they were speaking for women as a whole, and set about redefining personal and sexual relations on terms which better suited themselves, but went outside of, or beyond, what most women desired.

Thus a transition was set in motion, some time around the middle of the seventies, whereby activist women moved from being female voices for meritocracy and began to articulate the interests of women against men. The handmaidens of revolution decided to do things *for themselves*. Commenting last year on Tessa Jowell's announcement of Labour plans for a Ministry for Women, the *Telegraph* leader-writer noted acidly that '*Assuming that women did object to being represented by male politicians, it is difficult to think of a woman less typical than one who has become a Labour MP'.*[1] But during the seventies it was precisely this type of woman who was springing up as spokesperson for the future. The femocrat was evolving. Such women were highly committed to careers and to collectivist political activity, and scornful of conventional family life. They believed that personal power via the labour market was the only sort worth having. Many were very disappointed that men, former allies in revolution, were not themselves spontaneously opting for an 'egalitarian' sharing of roles across home and work, and saw confrontation in the public realm as offering the best way of putting pressure on them.

They did not believe that traditional ways of dealing with men, within families, were relevant or effective, and had little reason to respect the life experience of older women, or even listen to them at all. So the views of older women, which could no longer be expressed usefully via men because of the growing identification of men with reaction and the oppression of women, were losing public force and value. As dissenting voices were stilled, a pattern of gender division and conflict took shape around policies seeking strict public equality of men and women.

These have enjoyed a long monopoly of legitimacy. Only as their full implications have started to unfold have sceptical voices been listened to again.

The family strikes back

In Michael Young's satirical novel (1958) the meritocracy falls to a popular revolt, led by an alliance of communitarian young women and older male socialists. In real life nothing so colourful has happened yet, and today's Girton women seem to be the embodiment of progressive zeal rather than the counter-revolutionaries prophesied.[2]

However, there are signs that much more importance is now - or perhaps it is *still* - attached to the private realm than modernisers are willing to appreciate, and also that more people are starting to expect the state to help families on ordinary families' own terms.[3]

Class differences may help to obscure this. People in elite positions can find personal fulfilment and satisfaction in the public realm. For most people though this sense of value comes through close personal ties with others, where family life is central.

Thus most mothers do not want to be so involved in the labour market that they cannot play a major part in bringing up their children, especially when they are young. They do not want to be herded into full-time work while their children attend full-time nurseries. Parenting is not for them just a job like any other, where all that matters is 'skill' measured according to some universalist criteria. It is a personal relationship, located very clearly within the private rather than public domain, and a key to life-long moral exchanges between generations. Above all it constitutes a major source of personal meaning and autonomy. For many women in ordinary jobs, full-time work is alienating. The best assistance that the state can provide for them as mothers lies in ensuring decent 'family wages' for men, enabling women to receive enough financial support from male partners during the child-rearing years.

This judgement may seen odd; even archaic. But it is I believe true for many women. If we think otherwise then this may be because it is not the sort of interpretation which finds favour in the public realm, and so does not get widely disseminated. Popular attitudes on these matters are *not* reported fully and honestly, and this is in large part because media people and academic researchers are mainly modernisers, who see themselves moreover as having a missionary role. Even when very clear evidence of public indifference or hostility to radical restructuring of family lifestyles turns up, it is liable to become less convincing in their hands.

To take just one example here, it is interesting to look at how the latest report arising out of the National Child Development Study deals with its findings (in Ferri & Smith, 1996). This is a piece of 'longitudinal' research using periodic re-interviewing to chart the lives of a panel of children born during a week in 1958. The latest volume deals with panel members and their partners in 1991, at the age of 33. The main thrust of the report, which articles in the press covering the publication reflected, is that the quality of family life of respondents is dependent on the level of involvement of men. Male work, especially the time spent at it, is revealed as the enemy of happy families. The broad conclusion drawn is the sexually egalitarian one that work and family life should be shared more between men and women. Surprise, surprise.

There is of course some basis for this interpretation. Tables in the report show definite links between the amount of time spent by men at work, the general happiness of female partners, and the latters' assessment of the extent to which their men shared in family chores. However, some of data is not very 'hard'. Thus the measures of male partners' levels of sharing in family work are rather subjective, and distinguish in a very rule-of-thumbish way between high and low involvement. It seems possible to me that women who are happy with their lives and partners will be more likely to report them as doing a decent share of housework, than will those who are not, so that the variable presented as dependent, 'happiness', may in fact have a considerable influence on the other.[4] As a result many of the correlations are circular and self-serving. But on balance a case is made for the relevance of male work in family relations.

What is *wrong* with the report though is that it fails to give at the same time an adequate indication of the popularity of traditional gender roles among participants in the study. Some other tabulations in the report show the connections between the level of happiness of respondents and the type of sexual division of labour in their household. The measures of sex roles used in these are technically *stronger* than those subjectively distinguishing between high and low male involvement. They are not based on off-the-cuff assessments, but are determined by the objective employment status of household members. So the fact that these findings are given very little prominence in the report, and are absent from press coverage, is very telling. It suggests that there is not deemed to be an audience for what they have to show.

What they do show, quite unambiguously, is that those respondents recording the highest levels of general satisfaction with life were those living in 'traditional' households. The pattern of responses on this is remarkably consistent. The highest levels of happiness, and lowest levels of unhappiness, among both men *and* women, are found in households where the wife is a housewife and the husband the sole earner. Similarly, the lowest levels of happiness, and highest levels of unhappiness, for men and women, are found in role reversal households where the wife works and the husband stays at home. Those with some type of 'dual career ' pattern, or no earner, came in between.[5]

Levels of contentment are thus directly associated with mutual dependence around thoroughly conventional, sexually-specific roles. This is not explored in any detail in the report, and where further details *are* given these conflict fundamentally with the report's main argument. For example, the single earner fathers are the category most likely to work long hours, which is in general terms presented as being hostile to family life. But this does not appear to stop their wives being the happiest group of female respondents! Similarly this group of households is not well placed economically, by comparison with dual earners. Thus "The fact that as many as one in three families with only the father in employment were in the bottom income quartile underlines the importance of two earned incomes for a satisfactory standard of living." (*op. cit.,* p16) But clearly this does not seem to *matter* to this category of respondents! The conclusions of the report, which focus mainly around the need for state intervention to promote more involved fathers - such as through paternity leave regulations - do not arise at all clearly out of the data collected, and seem unconcerned with its subjects' own values and perceptions.

What makes this particular study significant is that we are *not* dealing here with a generation of entrenched older people refusing to accept that the world is changing. The respondents were in their early thirties when interviewed. They were children during the late sixties and early seventies when new lifestyles were being pioneered. The fact that they are now choosing sexually-defined lives means that our present-day mix of lifestyle prescriptions cannot seriously be portrayed as a transitional stage on the road to strict equality. This, perhaps, is the simple truth which is too unpalatable to be spelt out.

This example also indicates the insidious consequences of allowing our ideas about family life to be controlled within the public realm, where professionals and modernisers occupy most powerful positions. Those young people found to be happy in their traditional lives are not getting any feed-back endorsing their lifestyle choices. In fact the main public messages arising out of the study they participated in could well suggest to them that they are deviants, or part of a dwindling and doomed minority. No wonder that young people are said to be confused.

I suspect that many people's personal experiences, especially women's, are in conflict with what they read about family life in the press. But the longer that they *live* their own experiences, and come to trust their own feelings, the more chance they have of developing a healthy scepticism towards orthodox accounts. So it is among older women, not the girls of Girton, that opposition to sexual revolution attacking conventional families, and an explicit rediscovery of the importance of the private realm, has been gradually building up. My own research findings (1996b) show that as they grow older, moving through the life-cycle and seeing the consequences of sexual revolution from different perspectives, many women become seriously concerned about the future of families in Britain under current social policies. They worry about idle and feckless adult sons who seem to have no stake in society, about daughters who cannot find reliable and committed partners to help raise their children, and about grandchildren denied the security of a stable home-life and from whom they may even be alienated by relationship problems or breakdown in the parental generation. And many blame 'alternative' family conventions for spawning all of these problems.

The women who resisted parental pressures and threw off convention in the sixties and seventies have moved into authoritative positions, as grandmothers, in the private realm. Few might want to restore the patterns of family life of the fifties in their entirety. But most now believe in broadly conventional sexual partnerships - entailing long-term mutual commitment and some sexual differentiation of roles - as the basis for successful rearing of children. They are a force to be respected. Having stood against their parents in the sixties and seventies, this generation of women is not going to put up with younger women, or governments citing only them, telling them what to do. The counter-revolutionaries are the original rebels themselves, grown older and wiser.

Repairing the damage of revolution

The wheel of sexual revolution is turning, and we are collectively rediscovering that conventional families and roles may offer after all the surest basis for community life, and above all for rearing children. Whereas in the eighties and early nineties almost the only popular articles about family life, outside the Daily Mail, were phrased in terms of the importance of defending (women's) *choice*, there is now a fuller diet of views available in most papers on what may be happening to family life and on possible links between changes in sexual partnerships and wider developments in society like the gap between work-rich and work-poor classes. The concerns of the private realm are breaking through into the public.

But that does not mean we can just go back to how things used to be, even if we wanted to. The world has moved on and objective technological and demographic changes mean that a revitalised family will have to reflect new realities. This certainly means a larger direct role for women, freed from much domestic drudgery, in the public realm. It may also, to a lesser extent, mean a larger domestic role for men. I am not greatly impressed by many of the claims that men are already doing more, as these are too often based on the notion that historically they did nothing. Here again the NCD Study has some fascinating but under-publicised findings. For example, the fathers of panel-members in the early nineteen-sixties survey, before these issues had become politicised, seem to have done marginally *more* childcare and housework than reported for their sons in 1992, when there were large prizes of moral virtue to be earned in the public realm by declaring it (Ferri & Smith, pp 30/31). So things may have changed less than we think, or in different ways. By the same token, altering people's behaviour, that is men's, may be achieved more easily by operating within the context of traditional sex-specific roles, than through divisive public sex war.

Where the sexual revolution may actually have the most lasting consequences seems likely to be where it started - that is in *generation* terms. Development of young adult lifestyles which do not revolve around the care of children has effectively created a new life stage of liberated adulthood, which can be enjoyed *before* responsible parenthood for most people or, for those adults who choose not to have children at all, offer an *alternative* to conventional family life. This new or enlarged stage in the life cycle can accommodate a variety of new lifestyles in which very different forms of sexual contract, or even no contract at all, can apply. We now have a burgeoning singles culture, which has evolved out of sixties innovation and experimentation and caters for many adults, including homosexuals, who want to opt out of family life altogether. It has transformed city centres and people's lifestyle options, and there is every reason to believe that with longer life-spans these choices will continue to evolve and multiply.

It is one thing to welcome a flowering of adult lifestyle choices. It is quite another to regard these as providing appropriate settings for bringing up children; and something which does emerge very clearly from my own research is that *most people with experience of childrearing* believe that conventional family patterns are best in households with children, and that they need support and encouragement in the community which they do not at present get. As the example of many non-European cultures shows, it is fine to have 'free' states for adults who are just looking after themselves. But once they have children dependent on them then it is better to live in conventional family systems, where people have consistent and compatible expectations of mutual care and support.

Where we have perhaps made a mistake in Britain over the last twenty to thirty years, or rather our political masters have on our behalf, is in seeing alternatives to conventional families as morally equal to them. Families built around agreed mutual expectations are fundamental to social and community life in ways that these alternatives are not. They provide a stable environment for rearing the next generation. They set a framework of key personal relationships, with people of all sex and age categories, which endure when other ties may fade, and which provide the context for practising give and take and learning about fundamental social behaviour and values. They give us a place in what would otherwise be an anomic universe. Without a menu of lifestyle options we could survive. Without family life communities would soon disintegrate.

The lesson we must re-learn is that a sound polity has to be built around respect for the autonomy and priority of the private realm. What this means in practice is the state restoring a privileged position to families rather than taxing them as a form of individual consumption. And it also means restoring power to parents against the experts and professionals in the public realm, like teachers and social workers, who have increasingly seen it as their public duty to interfere in family life and tell or advise parents what to do. Most parents do not want to be taught what to do - increasingly, it has to be said, by people with academic qualifications but no personal experience of parenting themselves - but want simply to be allowed to get on with it. Very many people cannot understand how and why this is no longer the case.

This is arguably the single most important factor behind current alienation of ordinary people from politicians, and there is an interesting test ahead for the Labour Party, which still appears to be programmed to pursue strict gender symmetry rather than the needs of whole families. Ironic as it may seem in the light of Labour Party performance and its closeness to the modernising movement, many older women appear to have voted Labour in 1997 in despair at the continuing failure of the Conservatives to come up with measures to match their pro-family rhetoric. The Children Act addressed some obvious problems, and the CSA looked to have the right objectives. But little had been done to revive tax incentives for marriage, or to back up the rights of parents against intrusive professionals, or tackle the roots of family poverty.

Although the signs so far are not encouraging, New Labour may do better than this. By getting so many women into parliament it has in an important sense already dealt with the symbolic business of gender parity. Now it can turn to matters of substance. When it does so it will discover what ordinary women really want, and might respond to this because of the electoral consequences.

Older women are a large and growing sector of the electorate. In 1992 they kept the Conservatives in power against pollsters' predictions. Most are by inclination more in tune with Tory world-views, and this more than anything probably accounts for Labour's long exile in the wilderness. If Labour is to have any hope of keeping their vote at the next election it will need to re-examine its attitude in government towards the private realm. This is perhaps the most potent reason for believing that this cycle of revolution is nearly complete.

THE STATE WE ARE IN

Sex in the Commodity Culture

Roger Scruton

Erotic feelings notoriously by-pass moral judgement, fixing themselves on the most bizarre or tawdry objects, and dragging down their victims, as Des Grieux is dragged down by Manon or Swann by Odette. At the same time, erotic *love* idealizes its object, strives to vindicate its vast investment by believing that the cause is worthwhile. The tension between desire and love has traditionally been resolved in marriage. The married couple are bound by an eternal vow, rather than a temporary contract, and the bond between them necessarily outlasts, therefore, their erotic desire, which becomes a 'stage on the way' - the means but not the end of their relationship.

Connotations of contract

In modern democracies love, marriage and friendship are increasingly marginalised and even disapproved. For they are sources of privilege, and therefore potentially offensive to those whom they exclude. In a democratic society what you are is less important than what you have agreed. Contract replaces status as the source of rights and powers. Gifts, which threaten the egalitarian order, are looked on askance, as are all forms of privilege which derive from family and friends. Relations based on contract replace the old relations based in loyalty. The very idea of a 'sexual contract' - conceived in the narrow sense of 'contract', as an agreement for mutual services - indicates the extent to which perceptions of sexuality have changed, so that physical desire, rather than erotic love, is now given the primary place in our sexual adventures. Contracts are not eternal but finite: there is a point at which they have been fulfilled, and therefore brought to an end.

(That is why love requires a vow and not a contract, and why marriage, which is the expression of a vow, is a vanishing phenomenon. Vows are eternal, and make sense only if the Eternal is present to sanctify them.)

Secondly, contracts define a relationship of reciprocal rights. Friends do not, as friends, have rights against each other, and the duties of friendship, such as they are, remain open-ended and enquiring. Thirdly, contracts are undertaken and discarded by agreement, and need nothing *but* agreement for their validity. Although marriage, for example, is a kind of choice, it is also a choice to be bound by something other than choice.

Fourthly, contracts involve an exchange of goods or services. Nothing is given absolutely, and all the benefits of contract are conditional on the other party's behaviour. Hence the matter of a contract is always defined independently of the contract: there cannot be a contract simply to be bound by a contract. The subject-matter of a marriage, however, is itself. It is marriage that is offered and received.

Democracy can be seen as a kind of universal contract - an extension of the contractual principle to society as a whole. As in any contract, there is formal equality between the participants, and the democratic order is one in which every person is open to a deal with every other. Democracy therefore promotes universal friendliness, an eagerness for good relations of the kind that we witness in a market-place. This friendliness is not a sign of friendship, in the higher sense praised by Aristotle - the relation founded in the mutual recognition of virtue. If there is friendship here, it is of the lower kind exemplified by business partnerships and day-to-day companionship. Friends in a democratic society tend to be either workmates, or 'family friends' whose significance does not reside in any special personal relation, but merely in an enhanced form of neighbour-love.

This does not alter the fact that people in a democratic society retain their admiration for the higher forms of human relation, and sustain themselves in their ever-increasing hours of leisure with fantasies of love. Such fantasies are both gratifying, since they lift us above the routine of calculation, and also troubling, since they cast judgement on our lives. Various stratagems have therefore evolved, with which to deal with the trouble caused by love and friendship, and to neutralize the privileges which they threaten to reintroduce. These stratagems are extremely interesting from the anthropological point of view.

Stratagems for dealing with emotion

The first stratagem is the sentimentalisation of the moral life. Sentimentality is not unique to democratic societies; nevertheless, it has assumed an importance in modern times that has no clear parallel among older and more aristocratic cultures. The most salient feature of a sentimental emotion is the prominence accorded to the subject, rather than the object, of the feeling. It is not the beloved who attracts the most intimate attentions of the sentimental lover, but the lover, who is the hero of a drama scripted by himself. The beloved has become the means to the lover's exaltation, the excuse for his high emotion, and the proof of his noble soul. In short, the beloved is not the true object of emotion, but a mere occasion of it, in danger of dropping out of consideration altogether, as the subject bathes in his warm self-regard. (Hence sentimentality in literature is, as Leavis pointed out, characterised by vagueness and a lack of any concrete invocation of the object. The object of emotion has been veiled by the subject: the object is not truly *observed*, and, by the same token, the emotion is not truly felt.)

Sentimentalisation can be seen and heard in popular culture, and plays an important role in confining the individual within the sphere of his own interests, by persuading him that he is enjoying the higher forms of love, when he is in fact enjoying only a simplified and sanitised picture of them. By this means love, friendship and dignity become commodities, that can be bought and sold in the market. They are reduced to doll-like simulacra which can be possessed without any other cost than the price of purchase.

The second stratagem consists in the adoption of friendliness in place of courtesy. (Courtesy is a form of deference, and implies social hierarchy and unequal worth.) Each person in a democratic society stands on display in his invadable space. As little as possible is held in reserve, and anyone who knows the first name of the occupant can enter his space and examine the goods contained in it. Moral and social distinctions are discounted, and those things which must be held in reserve if they are to exist at all - love and friendship, for example - are replaced by more saleable plastic versions, which are as passionless and undemanding as dolls. The person who defends his territory, and who requires some moral or social qualification from those who seek to enter it, is condemned as 'judgemental'. He is the enemy of the democratic order, and his space must be invaded by force if need be, so as to ensure that he is concealing nothing dangerous within it. As for the rest of us, our primary social duty is to put as much of ourselves on offer as possible, and to reassure our friendly visitors that whatever lies in the store behind the shop, is of the same kind and quality as the matter on display.

The third stratagem is directed specifically against erotic love, the traditional consequences of which - vows, unbreakable loyalties, families, and the consequent network of privilege, power and inheritance - threaten the egalitarian order from within. The stratagem is to replace erotic love with 'sex', construed as a commodity available to anyone and from anyone, regardless of the relation between them. Sex education and pornography have the function of removing from the democratic order any sense that sex is to be held in reserve, or treated as a gift, in which one person offers himself to another without terms and eternally. Sex must be deprived of its sacred quality, its personal intentionality, and its aura of moral tabu. The shamelessness of modern sex education is a necessary part of its function, which is to abolish shame, and to ensure that no child matures to the point where the sexual urge might flower into true erotic feeling.

By teaching children to 'have sex', rather than 'make love', and by insisting that there is no real moral question concerning who or whom, sex education helps to neutralise one of the greatest of anti-democratic forces, one of the greatest sources of privilege and inequality, and the greatest temptation to depart from the contractual norm in our relations with our kind. In order to be effective, sex education must not merely marginalise the old practices of marriage and erotic love, but emphasize those forms of sexual activity - 'gay sex', for instance - in which the sexual act has no relation to anything outside the two contracting partners, and in which the body becomes an instrument of localised and merchandisable pleasures.

Sex education is not the only device in this stratagem. Equally important, as I have suggested, is pornography, to the manufacture and defence of which most of the culture industry is now dedicated. Important too is pop music, the social function of which is to 'lyricize' the new conception of sex.

The fourth stratagem is perhaps less often noticed. This is to make the higher life of love and friendship into a purely *philosophical* pursuit, as Plato did in democratic Athens, and Allan Bloom in democratic Chicago. If we see the higher moral life as the privilege of bookish people, formed, fulfilled and also corrupted by a literary diet, then we remove friendship and love from the democratic market-place, render them immune to egalitarian subversion, and preserve them as pure icons, accessible through study, but remote from the empirical world. We resurrect the aristocratic idea, by placing a new and *intellectual* barrier before those who would aspire to membership. Not that this stratagem resurrects the old experiences of love: on the contrary, it replaces them, by exchanging heroic passion for a tissue of sophisticated gossip, and the human heart for a frozen monument.

One of the important components in this fourth stratagem is the loud denunciation of the rival stratagems, and the invocation of a world that is all but lost, thanks to the decline in education, the universal failure to read the Great Books, and the scorning of Western culture by the new barbarians (who, however, are usually themselves educated people, competing for their own position in the forum of philosophical debate, and aspiring to their own form of moral 'tenure'). As everyone knows, however, the old experiences of love never depended upon education, still less on the Great Books which recorded them. The stratagem is not to restore the world of love and friendship, but to help us to live without it, by imagining it in purely literary form.

A choice of futures

The result of these stratagems is a new form of human happiness (although whether 'happiness' is exactly the word for it is a deep question which I must here pass over). People learn to put themselves on display, to live comfortably in their invadable space, and to feel free to engage in any act or relation, subject to the consent of the other parties. An academic industry is devoted to the theology of this new moral order - excreting theories of justice in the manner of Rawls, of law in the manner of Dworkin, and of culture in the manner of the deconstructionists. The agenda of such writers is to persuade us that all people and all cultures are of equal value - a result which follows logically, once it is established that no person and no culture is really worth anything at all. In the new world that these theories aim to justify you are absolutely safe, however second-rate you might be, so long as you deal openly and honestly in the market of desires. Jealousy, possession, grief and despair have been abolished, since their precondition was love, and love is only a sentimental memory.

On the other hand, a new kind of policing is required by the egalitarian order, especially in sexual matters. The separation of sex from *eros* is an elaborate artefact. It needs constant reinforcement if it is to persist. A continuous process of retraining and counselling is necessary if people are to live in the way required by the egalitarian culture. They may think they have managed it, only to be unexpectedly thrown from their dreaming orbit into another world, where love and shame are still realities. Then comes the desire for revenge against the person who betrayed them. New crimes are invented with which to punish the miscreant: 'date rape', 'sexual harassment', and so on. These crimes are necessary, in order to warn people against encounters in which the world of real emotion may erupt from the cupboard.

With the help of careful policing, many of our gurus believe, an equilibrium will be achieved. After a few decades, people will enter a peaceful world of thin attachments and purely contractual ties. In that world there will be eccentrics, whose space is filled with books and scores and liturgies. But they too will enjoy the friendly hilarity of neighbour-love, provided that they permit their space to be invaded, and scrupulously refrain from enacting what they read. Such is the vision of the future that has been encrypted in the sacred texts of the new academy - in such old testament prophets as Rawls and Habermas, as well as in new testament iconoclasts like Foucault and Derrida.

On the other hand, suppose we gave up the attempts at policing the new order. Suppose we ceased to indoctrinate children through sex education, ceased to allow pornography to be freely available, abolished the new crimes against the a-moral order, and allowed shame once again to grow at the heart of social experience. Suppose we encouraged young people to take love and loyalty seriously, to suffer from their absence, and to look with contempt on those who try to avoid them. Would human nature survive this act of collective violence? The evidence of history suggests that it would, since it did. And there is no evidence from history to suggest that our brave new world of disposable attachments has the ability to reproduce itself. On the contrary, however much we police it, this sentimental dream will surely fade into nothingness.

Was Feminism Wrong about the Family?

Ros Coward[1]

A cross-section of British newspapers in September 1997 revealed the usual spread of 'state-of-the-sexes' stories. The Daily Telegraph serialised Nicola Horlick's book *You Can have It All*, a position hotly disputed by columnists in other newspapers. All the tabloids covered the court case of James Whyte who successfully sued his former employers for unfair dismissal after he had refused to do any more travelling for the firm because he would 'miss seeing his baby girl grow up'. The Daily Mail, however, found evidence that these involved dads were not always welcome, quoting findings at the British Psychological Society Conference to the effect that, 'Caring, sharing *New men* who get too involved in their partners pregnancies can give mothers the baby blues'. What was clear from the open-ended questions and the level of dispute between protagonists is that question of the most appropriate sex roles and ways of behaving in the family, the best way of being a parent, are still unrsolved; we are still living in the after-shock of the feminist revolution.

This uncertainty is at first glance surprising. These articles were written in the aftermath of Princess Diana's funeral and elsewhere the newspapers were confidently claiming that this event was conclusive proof that British society was now 'feminised'. Many commentators linked Diana's funeral with evidence of new Britain. Like Tony Blair's election victory the previous May, it signified that the British had finally embraced 'modernity' with all that implied for sexual relations. When the hundred new women MPs crowded round Tony Blair for their photo on the steps of the Houses of Parliament, this was meant to symbolise the end to the old male hierarchies in politics. The open emotion shown on the streets for Diana's funeral similarly indicated the end to emotional repression, the behavioral manifestation of the social structure of the British patriarchal family. But while there's no doubt that both these phenomena were eruptions through the surface of something which had been growing under the soil for some time, they do not represent the end of the story. There have been many more complex shifts and changes between the sexes, not all presenting the same happy egalitarian picture, not all making the contribution of feminism feel like the enriching movement that its most committed exponents wish us to believe. There have been more complex changes affecting the sexes, changes which feminism kick-started but now does not always know how to respond to, let alone assess. The spread of articles found at this time bear witness to the unevenness of these changes, experienced often by the sexes in different ways. They show that while many changes feel like progress, some bring confusion. Others, like Nicola Horlick's female triumphalism, also bring resentment.

Decline of the patriarchal family

Society has changed almost out of all recognition from the male-dominated society in which feminism first formulated its demands. Then, the assumption that women would find exclusive fulfilment in the home and in her children led to discrimination against women in the labour market as well as frequent abuse of rights within the home. Feminism's fight was against this unearned power of men - at work and within the family - and few dispute its moral justice or the advantages of equality and openness which it has brought. When society first began to change in response to feminism in the seventies, the changes were steady and gradual responses to calls for equality in economic, legal and financial matters as well as improvements in women's status within the family. Feminists grumbled that changes were not fast enough and not radical enough; men still earned more on average, and women still bore the main burden of domesticity. Late seventies feminism defined its main problem as how to shake up masculinity and change men's attitudes to work and family.

But in the eighties everything changed. The combination of recession and the development of the global market destroyed the old gender patterns of employment; the economy suddenly delivered many of the changes which feminism had always hoped for but not necessarily in the form they had wanted. Men were hit particularly hard by the needs of the global market for job flexibility. 'Contracting out', 'down-sizing' and 'delayering' meant the end to steady career paths. For many this meant periods of unemployment. For others, it was 'self-employment', part of a shift to personal autonomy in the labour market in which 'career ladders' are giving way to 'portfolio careers'. The idea of the unilinear career had been the basis of masculine identity. It involved sacrifices, either of the body to physical labour or of the soul to the company, to provide for the family.

Not only did women benefit from the growth in part-time work but they were simply better prepared for new employment patterns. Women are used to interrupted employment. They have learnt to market their diverse skills and are even praised for balancing home and work. During the eighties it became clear that women as a group were benefitting from these economic changes, while men were in trouble. Instead of the coming of an egalitarian nirvana, economic changes were putting gender relations on a different axis and changing the meaning of gender in society. Whatever disadvantages women continued to have, they were also experiencing many positive changes. For men however it was the opposite story. By the early nineties there was the growing evidence that males were in crisis - more prone to failure at school, at the sharp end of escalating unemployment, and more prone to suicidal depression. For women, on the work and public front things looked very different. Feminism had given women confidence to move into masculine areas, combining work and motherhood, and even seeing new opportunities in new work patterns. Men on the other hand were experiencing their work changes, the so-called feminisation of labour, more like a smack in the eye.

Left-wing research units and think tanks are given to representing these changes as the slow march of progress or a levelling out of a previously tilted playing field. Painful maybe but necessary. And perhaps it would have been easy to share such interpretations had these changes not also raised anxieties among men about how fully they were needed within the family. For this was the point when the consequence of legal, social and financial changes, all enabling women and children's autonomy from men, became visible in the dramatically increasing number of single parents.

In better times, this would have been the moment many feminists had been waiting for, the time when men renegotiated their relationship within the family, no longer able to exercise an unearned authority and dominance over humans who were born their equals. But these were not good times. Such has been the speed of creating a fiction of a new Britain that it is easy to forget just how recently the dark days of Conservative Britain were with us. And in the darkest days of the nineteen nineties, at the fag end of John Major's government, crisis after crisis seemed to suggest that instead of a nirvana of sexual equality in a society of non-coercive, non-hierarchical family alliances, we were in deep trouble.

The spectre of unfettered masculinity

Concern about escalating violence and anti-social behaviour reached new levels with the murder of little Jamie Bulger by two ten year old boys; the tragedy suggested that the disintegration of traditional communities and the father-dominated families on which they were based had simply spawned a generation of lawless, amoral and, worse, deeply unhappy children. When the Rosemary West trial followed not long after, a shadow too was cast over the whole history of sexual libertarianism. Who could have read Duncan Campbell's evocative account in the Guardian of the Forest of Dean in the sixties without feeling a twinge of distress that the philosophy of personal sexual fulfilment had been used for such ends? The same question hung over revelations about the extent of child abuse in Britain or the paedophile rings in Belgium. Was there after all a terrible cost to losing the constraints which might previously have prevented disturbed individuals from exploring their darkest fantasies? Was it possible that in denying the authoritarianism of the patriarchal family, we had let loose an irresponsible, undervalued and unfettered masculinity which was ultimately more dangerous?

Surprisingly, the answer given to these questions was remarkably similar from both the Right and from some feminists. In the early nineties British conservatives turned to the American sociologist Charles Murray to offer an explanation (1993) for this perceived moral disorder. He diagnosed the 'new rabble' or underclass. This sector had been caused partly by the increase in unemployment but mainly by the increase in single mothers, in his view a tragic legacy of the sixties and feminism. What was being created were dynasties where none of the generations had jobs, where daughters of single mothers became single mothers themselves and where young men, increasingly alienated from the mainstream life of society or the family, were sinking deeper and deeper into criminality and violence.

These views chimed in with interpretations by British conservatives. Starting with general anti-social behaviour, taking in the increasing incidence of uncontrollable children in school and on the streets, right through to criminal and murderous acts, the cause was always assumed to lie not in the problems of poverty, marginalisation and ravished communities. Instead it lay with selfish individuals - the fickle parents and the me-first generation who had destroyed the stable family with demands for working mothers, easy divorce, welfare for single parents. Strangely enough, some feminists came up with their own version of this. In Bea Campbell's *Goliath,* Murray's vision was turned on its head. The single mothers became the abandoned but heroic 'active' citizens. Men on the other hand, without the civilising influence of women and family life, had floated free to form their own communities where expressions of machismo made up for the lost pride of male work or patriarchal power in the family. Elsewhere Sue Slipman, then chair of the National Council for One Parent Families, responded to the woman-blaming of Murray's analysis, with a comment to the effect that no-one can explain why any self-respecting women would want to take a member of this rabble into her home.

Such views give a taste of just how difficult it is to sort out what has really been happening in the family and to sex roles. To do so involves cutting through right wing panic about the family and masculinity, and feminist romanticism about women. In these views masculinity reverts towards barbarism without women's edifying and civilising influence. Yet any knowledge of the poor and impoverished communities described by such theories involves understanding that expectations about masculinity and femininity are closely intertwined, that women's expectations of men often encourage many of the acts of violence and bravado, and much of the crime too.

The one advantage of these theories is that they do at least take seriously issues of behaviour and morality and what this feels like to ordinary people. This is an advance on liberalism which, on detecting any undercurrent of nostalgia for the old authority of the patriarchal family, simply cries 'moral panic'. Liberalism explains away anti-social behaviour, violence or 'horrendous' incidents at the centre of moral concern; they could have happened at any point in history had the chemistry been right between the individuals concerned. At least in Murray's and Campbell's work there is a recognition of popular discomfort at how changes in family relations are being lived.

Understanding family needs

But we have to look elsewhere to find an understanding which is not prejudiced by nostalgia for patriarchal family values, nor insensitive to the difficulties which might be arising from shifts in family values. The clearest understanding comes not from the politicians or social analysts but from people involved closely with children - the care workers and teachers. Amongst these child care professionals, all agree that they meet more disruptive children, more in conflict with the simple authority of schools and society, lashing out and causing misery not only to others but themselves. Significantly they do not confine these observations to poor or disadvantaged communities but recognise it is a phenomenon crossing all sectors of society. In other words, what has been happening in family and sex roles is as important as economic and social conditions.

Most of the professionals working with difficult or disruptive children would distance themselves from the moralistic nostalgia for patriarchal authority in the family. They would recognise that the cost was simply too high - to women and to children whose fundamental human rights were often violated by such family forms, and whose emotional structures were not without their own terrible consequences. Yet it has been surprising to hear the word 'authority' cropping up so much in recent years, even from those who would vigorously oppose the punitive mentality based on the old patriarchal model.

The word 'authority' also features amongst those who believe that the disruptive child is not a devil but often a disturbed and distressed, vulnerable child. Such children are being turned around by programmes which use a combination of consistent attention, behaviourist techniques and, crucially, restoring the parents' confidence in controlling their children. Early intervention through these programmes have convinced the Audit Commission that they are more cost effective than authoritarian punishment. They are currently being adopted in a number of American states to deal with that most difficult group, adolescents in care, and also by a number of specialist behaviour units in England.

The theory behind these programmes is that children behave badly and become anti-social because they are frightened; they feel out of control because no-one will control them. This creates aggression and constant testing of the limits. So the central terms are consistency, firmness, building self-esteem and most importantly encouraging the parents to gently reassume control. There is no suggestion in this programme that the parents are any different from most families across the country. Many will recognise a familiar spiral - trying to negotiate gently with a child, who pushes the limits, which then provokes inconsistent attempts to control by the parents and often ends with escalating negatives and sometimes in violence.

What is key here is not loss of patriarchal authority or unfettered masculinity but loss of parental authority. It is a symptom that we are living through a period of a profound change and uncertainly about the roles of men and women in the family, not that these changes are wrong. The old authoritarianism of the father has died, and with it the structures which mirrored it: the patriarchal church and the authoritarian school. The 'moralistic response' mourns the passing of this patriarchal order but the majority, whatever their party political views, are probably not sorry to see it go. The power of the patriarch was unearned. It often abused human rights, was violent and dictatorial, and terrifying for those in its power. And if the pay off was relatively controllable children, the price was almost certainly the gross subordination of women.

But at the same time, these changes have created a power vacuum within the family. With women demanding more status and both men and women reluctant to allow men their old authority, each family has been left to negotiate its own moral and disciplinary order in their families. Deprived of the authoritarian father and the support of external institutions built on its model, families now have to make the rules up as they go along. This is no collapse of a moral order but the difficult birth of a new morality that tries to avoid the old authoritarianism and instill morality without fear.

With increasing frequency the responsibility for discipline and authority has fallen on women, not least because of increasing numbers of single mothers who literally have to cope on their own with the children. Yet evolving a liberal morality requires both good structures of outside support and strong, confident people who can invent the rules, stick to them consistently, and do so without becoming violent and authoritarian. And women face particular problems left in that position.

Women's self esteem has not necessarily matched the structural changes. Most women are not that confident in their authority, nor are there many places to turn to for relief and backup. It is hard not to feel bitterly disappointed in self and child when what started as an attempt to be a child's friend spirals towards endless negativity. These problems are much greater for families under the stress of low pay, unemployment, poor quality of life when it becomes quite simply impossible to deal with children who have not been subdued by other external forms of authority. A single mother who has to face this literally on her own has the added disadvantage; she is at the centre of the storm without even the life-raft of a companion to share her concern at the outcome.

Feminism's mixed balance sheet

Some of feminism's responses to these changing family roles and situations have been unhelpful. Fearing to support patriarchy, many feminists have poured scorn on the role of the father altogether. Fearing to blame women for the increase in single mothers, they have encouraged women to get on without men. Fearing to give back men authority which they didn't earn and didn't exercise well, many women have claimed women can do it all and do it better. It has led to a have-it-all, do-it-all triumphalism which is quite simply unhelpful in difficult and changing times. When the image of Nicola Horlick hangs over contemporary discussion of sex roles - an image of megalomaniac exclusion of men from any significance in the home - it is easy to see why many commentators feel that feminism has exchanged triumphalism for egalitarianism.

But if we return to the funeral of Princess Diana, where this chapter started, we can see a very different picture. Aside from the welter of commentary on the feminisation of British society, it is worth remembering that for many women, the unhappiness of her life had come to symbolise the damage which old fashioned patriarchy can still actually inflict.

Evaluating the Effects on Children of Mothers' Employment

Patricia Morgan

It is a truism about child development that parental attention is good for children. But efforts to abolish the sexual division of labour and encourage women to participate in the labour market have reduced our willingness to recognise publicly the value of motherhood, and the problems which may occur as a result of mothers' work commitments. After looking at some of the pressures on women to work, I will examine evidence relating to the impact which their withdrawal from childcare may be having on their effectiveness as mothers and on parents' ability to enjoy their children.

Pressures on mothers to work

Mothers who make an effort to provide adequate care are represented as clearly 'pulling down overall female wages; sabotaging the achievement of overall parity in outcomes in pay and position between men and women throughout the life cycle'. Complaints that women 'still earn only 80 per cent of men's wages' are to be read in the light of this goal, not as suggestions that employers are breaking the law on a mass scale by paying unequal wages. Actually, childless married women, single men and women earn much the same, on average (Ferri, 1993), with indications that full-time female employees earn more than single men.[1] What is constantly reiterated as a matter of scandal and concern is how the mother of two spends 15.9 less full-time equivalent years in employment and foregoes 57 per cent of her childless counterpart's gross earnings.

If children put women 'at a great disadvantage in competing with men in the labour market' (Moss, 1988: p27), this is attributed to the way that 'only 1 child in 9 under the age of eight has a place in a nursery, with a registered child minder or in an out-of-school scheme', so that 'Unsurprisingly... 45 per cent of women work part-time', as 'mothers have to find time to be at home to look after their children'.[2] This is presented as nothing to do with choice but as the result of the absence and/or cost of childcare. Indeed, part time work is apparently 'not often desired' as well as having 'negative consequences for a possible career' (Klein, 1995).

As well as the way to equal, or superior, labour market outcomes for women: 'Full-time employment is the route by which women achieve financial independence from their partner' (Ward *et al* 1996: p229; Lister, 1992). From the standpoint that 'pooled income is wrong', mutual support or 'income dependency within couples has been identified as a chronic problem, where three-quarters of wives 'receive income flows from their partner because they do not match or exceed their husbands' earnings' (Joshi *et al* 1995). However, over a half of childless women are 'independent' in terms of 'the balance of economic power', compared to only 17 per cent of mothers.

As well as preserving the earnings and independence of women, continuous, full time maternal employment is also seen to enable 'the economy to utilise and conserve the stock of human capital embodied in women who become parents'.[3]

Such claims that the economy must be operating below capacity if women are caring for children neglect, however, the fact that those children are the generators of future wealth, whose productivity depends to no small extent upon the investment made by parents in their upbringing. Moreover, whereas an adult can retrain or revitalise their vocational skills, there may be no second chances where children's development is concerned.

Even should time given to the care and welfare of husbands and children detract from a woman's personal accumulation of income and 'human capital', it does not follow that domestic work makes no contribution to the performance or productivity of other present and future wage-earners. A mother's conscious investment in the husband's marketability in the child-rearing years is undertaken, not least, to increase her home contribution, and the benefit she perceives this brings to the children. If this has become something demonstrably worthless or wasteful to be discouraged and disadvantaged, then it marks the decisive shift of emphasis away from protecting the family's overall economic security and ability to meet the needs of a new generation, in favour of economic power for women.

Devaluing parental care

However, there is no conflict of interests if it is true - as Save the Children claims - there are 'benefits for children of greater personal and economic independence of women'.[4] Indeed, daycare is presented as so beneficial to children that, as predicted in the plans drawn up for Barnardos, there will be 'far reaching social gains and the possibility of savings in other services (such as special education and crime prevention), at the same time as the economy gains the work experience and skills of mother's' (Holterman, 1995). Parental care seems neglectful in comparison as, from all directions, the message is how:

> ... *children reap benefits they would not have if she [mother] stayed at home. ...going to a daycare centre does the children good, helping them to relate well to each other and to their parents. There are enormous benefits in terms of getting children as young as possible used to an educational environment. But, most important, every child would have the advantage of individual attention, early learning of social skills and the joy of mixing with other children.* (Kon, 1992)

Daycare children are 'if anything more creative, confident and assertive' than those without such experiences (EOC, 1990). Daycare can 'teach your infant or toddler lessons about co-operation, independence, self-sufficiency and even friendship he wouldn't learn were he at home with you' (Sanger & Kelly, 1988). In turn, the advantages that accrue to the children of working mothers include an higher I.Q., better social adjustment and educational progress, progressive sex-role ideology, greater self-esteem and confidence, more positive views of women, more vocational options and a potential for greater economic independence.

Childcare certainly affects children, and employment affects parenting. Child outcomes are dependent on parental attitudes, parental behaviour, family structure and other aspects of the home environment, including work patterns, as well as upon the nature of the child and the care provided while parents are away.

Most obviously, where we have dual income households or fully employed parents, there are time constraints. Almost two-thirds of respondents to a *Parents at Work* survey of their membership (overwhelmingly mothers in white collar jobs) routinely worked longer than their contract hours: 42 per cent might work over 50 hours a week and 27 per cent of the full-time workers worked over 60 hours when busy (Burns, 1995).

The more hours mothers are employed, the less time they can give to 'primary care activities', such as playing or talking with the children, or helping with homework if they are older. On average, the American employed mother puts in half the average hours per week of undivided childcare of her nonemployed counterpart, or 6.6 compared to 12.9 (Robinson & Godbey, 1995). Even if the husband increases his share of household chores (and total workload), each parent must put in more hours to meet basic responsibilities. Having to attend to domestic tasks in the short period that remains after both have put in their time at work and commuting competes with children for attention.

Effects of mothers' work on family relationships

Fitting attention into a 'happy hour' or 'quality time' may not be very relevant to small children, for whom it is 'impossible it is to schedule togetherness times' (Belsky, 1988b). How do you 'persuade a one-year-old who wanted you to play with him this morning to take his one and only chance and play right now' (Leach, 1994: 79)? Moreover, if the mother monopolises the child's attention during her short time at home, this may displace the father, by taking over the time he would otherwise have with the child (Belsky, 1988a). While, in one study, the daily separation of mother and child led to enhanced mother-initiated physical contact upon reunion (Stith & Davis, 1984), others report that parents in dual-wage families provide their babies with less stimulation, and attribute it to the 'overload experience' of these couples (Zaslow *et al*, 1985). What, anyway, is 'quality time'? 'Does family dinner count if the TV is on? Very softly? All we reliably know is that whenever time with kids is in short supply, calling it "quality time" makes parents feel better' (Shapiro, 1997).

However, what parents may most want after a weary day is for the child to sleep well until it is time to get up for the centre or minder again. Yet, if a child's sleeplessness is a common complaint of working parents, so night times are the only chance children may have to get the parental attention they have missed all day. A recent national survey of parenting problems found the lowest incidence of behavioural and family problems reported by couple families where only one parent works, whether compared to couple families with two working or nonemployed parents, or working or non working lone parents (Roberts & Cronin, 1995).

In the *Parents at Work Survey*, 72 per cent of the mothers claimed to be exhausted by the end of the day, and the incidence of insomnia, depression and other stress related symptoms was high (Burns, 1995). This is underlined in Pamela Daniels and Kathy Weingarten study (1982) of American couples, where the price of holding down two demanding occupations, one at home and the other away, was 'constant fatigue and overloaded circuits': in no other situation was so much conflict so consistently reported. A similar British study (Lewis & Cooper, 1987) also conveys this sense of being constantly rushed. For all the dual-earners, the problems of combining parenting with employment led to immense pressures and conflict, as well as shortage of time in which to accomplish anything. Mothers had lower levels of job satisfaction than all other groups, with many regretting that they could neither enjoy their children nor their careers.

Parents who have low occupational status, work commitment and aspirations and take the child to non-home based care arrangements feel the greatest stress.[5] The widely publicised dual-career couple, who are highly committed to high status, high paid, careers and can afford child-care and other help at home 'may be relatively protected from the negative impact of work-family pressure' (Lewis & Cooper, *op cit*). The chairman of a company who has 'a nanny and a couple at home to cook dinner' is in a different world from the woman who takes a child to the minder or nursery at 6.30 a.m. before going into the cornflake factory (Garner, 1988).

Diane Hughes and Ellen Galinsky's study (1988) underlines how, if balancing job and family responsibilities is extremely difficult for most parents, the period before children enter school is the hardest of all, with 'one out of two male employees and two out of three female employees...having a hard time managing'. With the demands of work and childrearing at their most incompatible, it is 'the time when stress, anxiety, and perhaps defensive withdrawal from the child are most likely to occur'. Even with older children: 'approximately two out of every five employees, male and female, were feeling conflicted and torn by all they had to do' (Owen & Cox, 1988). Mothers with children under 18 had the highest stress levels, more psychosomatic symptoms and significant work-family interference.

A long sequence of well conducted studies show how infants from all classes and family backgrounds are significantly more likely to have insecure and disturbed relationships with their parents where there is extensive non-maternal care.[6] One of many, a longitudinal study of young families, showed how twice as many infants were securely attached (67 per cent) as insecurely attached when their mothers were not employed, while twice as many infants were insecurely attached as securely attached (33 per cent) when their mothers were employed full-time (Owen & Cox, 1988). Difficult behaviour was associated with maternal employment at any time in the first year of life and grew with the number of hours the mother worked.

Another study of middle-class infants showed that when mothers worked for more than 25 hours a week before their babies were eight months of age, barely a half were securely attached, compared with 81 per cent securely in the non-employed group, with security levels improving where mothers returned to work later in their children's development. This was despite the fact that early employed mothers had more years of education, and bigger family incomes (Weinraub & Jaeger, 1991). Overall, boys tend to be more adversely affected than girls. Where the father-child as well as the mother-child relationship has been investigated, it is apparent that sons of fully employed mothers are also more likely to be insecurely attached to their fathers compared to other boys.[7] Because infant boys 'are already developmentally delayed compared to girls, their abilities to regulate their attention and emotion and find order in the world are particularly in need of help from a sensitive healthy caregiver' (Sharp *et al*, 1985).

Such evidence has been hotly contested. However, when a foremost critic attempted to set the record straight with her own review of 16 studies in this area, she conceded that this still showed how 'infants whose mothers work full-time during their first year are consistently and statistically significantly more likely than infants of mothers who work part-time or not at all to be classified as insecurely attached...'(Clark-Stewart, 1988) and other sceptics have come to similar conclusions (Lamb *et al*, 1992). Indeed, an overall or meta-analysis of worldwide childcare investigations by C. Violato and C. Russell (1994) estimated that regular non-parental care increased the risk of children developing insecure bonds by 66 per cent. (They noted that if this was a matter of disease due to environmental factors, it would be considered extremely serious and result in public health initiatives.)

A sensitive, responsive caregiver is important to the development of a secure attachment in early life - promoted as this is by prompt attention to distress, appropriate stimulation, general warmth and the parent's synchronisation of their responses with those of the infant. This is 'intuitive parenting', but it is easily disrupted if relaxed time is not available in which to learn the baby's particular signals, and repeated separations make it difficult to maintain a relationship. Whether infants are insecurely attached because '40 hours of care is hard on infants' or because '40 hours of work is hard on mothers' (Clarke-Stewart, 1989), later attachment can be predicted from the quality of early contact and the mother's time with the baby (Cox *et al*, 1992). Both are independently linked to security of attachment and, inescapedly, work is the main reason for mothers having less time for their infants.

Of course, attachment may be discouraged as inconvenient, inappropriate and painful - 'I don't want her to get used to having me around'. If a child is going to be spending much of its waking life with strangers and a parent has so many others calls on her time, the notion of an 'independent' baby is attractive. Investigating problems with childcare which keep lone parents out of the labour market, Reuben Ford (1996) identifies the primary determinant of the use of childcare as the willingness of parent and child to spend time apart. An assumption here seems to be that, were there less or no attachment to parents and the child were indifferent to parental care, there would be no problems of separation and no hesitation about using daycare.

Sensitivity to a child's distress was also found to be a barrier to mothers working, when:

> *Everywhere I left him he was just upset all the time* (Ford, p118).

> *He was six months old and it was heart rending... He turned out to be a very well balanced child, but I saw other kids the same age as him who started at day nurseries same situation - because we had no choice but to go out to work - and they turned out to be very insecure little children* (*ibid.* p114).

> *Go into this woman's house: she had no toys. I used to leave him standing at the window just sort of standing there and when I got back in the evening, he'd still be standing there. ...and that was awful because you knew that she didn't give a damn what he did and what happened* (*ibid.* p131).

Yet, the question is seen as one of 'how coercive parents are prepared to be, since some mothers persisted with childcare unpopular with the child and saw the child's reaction diminish with time' (p119). Moreover, as apprehensiveness about the standards of alternative care has an adverse effect on mothers' willingness to work, where this means a deterioration in the care their children receive, it is seen as 'hopeful' that those in work also identify problems - as, in one case, a baby going unfed all day - but it 'rarely meant lone parents gave up work' (p136). As it is 'much more difficult to justify a decision which brings about deleterious consequences than it is to justify continuance of the status quo', so 'parents in work may be better able to continue to use care of a quality which deters potential new work entrants' (p137).

New yardsticks for children's behaviour

Such, not uncommon, accounts betray an astounding ignorance of human development and callousness towards children who, it seems, can be subjected to virtually anything as long as their mothers are got to work. For all the talk of daycare being beneficial for children, *it is clear that we are being asked to accept lower standards of childcare, and harsher parenting.* What have hitherto been seen as deficiencies and difficulties with child development become positive attributes. Not only disturbed attachments, but the bad behaviour and conduct disorders repeatedly reported in studies from all over the world for children who have spent long hours over a long period in group care (Morgan, 1996), are seen as something to celebrate.

> *What this pattern of behaviour may suggest... is ... that children who have been in daycare beginning in infancy or later...think for themselves and that they want their own way. They are not willing to comply with adults' arbitrary rules... Children who have spent time in daycare, then, may be more demanding and independent, more disobedient and aggressive, more bossy and bratty than children who stay at home.* (Clarke-Stewart, 1989)

But are aggressiveness, disobedience and hyperactivity virtues in children? Moreover, how helpful is it to be 'independent' as early as possible? After all, studies of the life course suggest that it is the people who were the most 'dependent' in early life who often turned out to be the best balanced and assured adults (Leach, 1994: p92). In turn, there are many accounts of disturbed and violent people who, for various reasons, failed to have their dependency needs met in childhood.

The emotional bond with parents is a central and critical element in human development: it is the gateway, not the barrier, to the social world. The unattached child is not some kind of autonomous, superior person. The very least of the consequences of early insecure parent/child attachments, is that the child is more susceptible to the effects of stressful events encountered later.[8] It is children with secure attachment histories who tend to be more socially competent;[9] less withdrawn, more self-confident and tolerant of frustration, better at using adult support in ways that promote intellectual and social development, and more sympathetic to the distress of others. They are less likely to be judged as having serious behavioural problems in the school years,[10] where early insecure attachment is particularly associated with negative outcomes for boys (Belsky, 1990: p890-1).

The role of maternal 'guilt'

The investigations of Margaret J. Owen and Martha J. Cox clearly connect early resumption of employment with low investment in parenthood (Owen & Cox, 1988). This, together with the long hours worked by early returners badly affected the security of mother-infant attachments, and lowered the quality of parenting generally. Interestingly, while high commitment to work vis-a-vis parenting may mean less strain for mothers (O'Neil & Green Berger, 1994), this will not necessarily be in the children's interests. Middle class women with low commitment to work, experience less strain when their jobs are not professional or managerial in nature. Work that is less scrutinized by others and less demanding may generate less pressure. It is the women with a high commitment to work but low commitment to parenting who have less role stress in higher status jobs. Thus, if work is important to personal identity, employment that involves high esteem may mean less stress, and less sensitive parenting.

We frequently hear that the only real problem with maternal employment is 'guilt'. As a product of antiquated social attitudes about mother's role and children's needs, this makes mothers feel torn in different directions and unable to take proper advantage of employment opportunities. This 'guilt' would be even more maladaptive if it really is true that putting occupational fulfilment first benefits children. However, while women who feel less 'guilt' or anxiety about leaving their children, and few if any misgivings about putting their work first, may make their own lives easier, evidence is that they do not make better parents. This is demonstrated where children whose mothers were reluctant to put them into daycare had better development, or were more co-operative, compliant, persistent and socially constructive, than the children of mothers who did not hesitate (Everson *et al*, 1984). The higher levels of conflict in the families of securely attached infants, had much to do with the mothers difficulties or misgivings about putting them into daycare. Similarly, infants exposed to long hours of parental separation are not only more likely to be insecurely attached if they are boys, fussy or difficult, have mothers who are limited in their interpersonal sensitivity, or unhappy in their marriages, but if their mothers have strong career reasons for working (Belsky & Rovine, 1988).

The effects as children grow up

Like the associations between long hours of non-maternal care and poorer parent-child attachment, or increased aggression and early group care, the finding that sons of fully employed mothers score lower on intellectual measures has also occurred frequently enough to warrant very serious consideration. Some while ago now, a series of Canadian studies showed how the 10 year old sons of middle class employed mothers obtained lower scores on mathematics and language achievement tests, and a comparable group of English speaking (but not French speaking) four-year-old sons also had consistently lower I.Q. scores than either daughters of employed mothers, who showed only a very slight drop, or children of non-employed mothers.[11]

Results from the *British National Child Development Study* also suggested that the five-year-old children of mothers working outside the home had poorer social adjustment at school than children of mothers who were not employed. While employment in the pre-school years had ceased to have a measurable effect on adjustment at seven (Osborne *et al*, 1984), those whose mothers had worked full-time had poorer reading and arithmetic scores at this age than children of mothers who had not been employed or who had part-time jobs. The highest scores on vocabulary tests were achieved by children of at-home mothers and the lowest by children of mothers in full-time manual work, followed by children of mothers in part-time manual work. Even children of mothers in non-manual employment or working from home had slightly lower scores than those of housewives.

Similarly, research on 500 American four-year-olds revealed how boys from high income families with working mothers had lower scores for cognitive development. Furthermore, those whose mothers worked in the first year had the poorest levels of cognitive ability (Desai *et al*, 1989). As boys are more vulnerable, such negative effects may be because of their experience of unstable care arrangements or less attentive care at home in infancy. Some girls in the study did a bit better in terms of cognitive ability when a very particular comparison was made between those whose mothers returned to work in their second year and those whose mothers did not return to work at all. This may reflect a general tendency in recent studies, for part-time work to have the same or better outcomes than no maternal work. As mothers have entered the labour market in increasing numbers, samples of completely non-earning mothers tend to be the more heavily weighed with women with disabilities and other physical or mental health problems, as well as the least educated and qualified.

More has been made of the way in which, in the Canadian series and elsewhere, the daughters of working mothers are more career-minded and have less stereotyped sex role attitudes. It is, of course, regarded as most important for girls to have the approved outlook on work, or that both sons and daughters should have 'a role model of a competent woman... for their later lives' (Scarr *et al*, 1993). Boys development tends to be a secondary consideration to 'respect' for 'women's rights and achievements [where] how better can they learn that women can be as accomplished as men than by living with an accomplished mother?' (*ibid*).

However, some studies show *adverse effects on the attainments of both sexes.* In the U. S. the *High School and Beyond Study*, involving a random sample of 15,579 children from primary age to 16, maternal employment was consistently linked to lower maths and reading scores for white children from two-parent families (Milne *et al*, 1986). The more the mother worked, the stronger the effects. The negative effects of working full-time over the child's lifetime were greater than the negative effects of working part-time or full time at some stage.

A similar picture emerges from the analysis of the intellectual development and behaviour of American three- and four-year-old white children from the *National Longitudinal Survey of Youth* (NLSY-- Bayler & Brooks-Gunn, 1991). Maternal employment in the first year had detrimental effects on both measures, regardless of sex or poverty, with the effect falling dramatically if employment was postponed to the third year. Just as white and black four- to six-year-olds from the same study were significantly more non-compliant when their mothers had begun full-time employment in the first two years of life (Belsky & Eggebeen, 1991). Under ten hours a week was least detrimental, but there was a slightly larger effect in this study when mothers worked 10-19 hours compared to where they worked over 20. (Children in the middle range may have had more experience of *ad hoc* and unstable care arrangements.)

In turn, children of mothers in full-time manual or non-manual employment, and those who had recently left employment, had higher anti-social behaviour. Those of mothers who worked part-time, manual or non-manual, had only slightly higher scores than children of non-employed mothers.

Where we consider the children *of working mothers* only, the research suggests that those who have the most favourable development and environment have mothers who not only have high occupational status, but seem to manage to square the circle by having little stress from dual responsibilities and are available to their children. In turn, employed mothers may tend, on average, to have higher educational aspirations and put a greater emphasis upon qualifications than those who keep entirely out of the workforce. But, as work hours increase, even positive educational attitudes and high occupational status may fail to counter-balance the increase in anxiety and lack of time in which to attend to the children. As Adelle E. Gottfried and her colleagues found, once the number of hours that mothers of five-, six- and seven-year-olds work start to rise beyond 30 or so a week, the negative relationships to development emerge: lower achievement scores on intelligence tests, lower ratings for reading and lower educational stimulation at home (Gottfried *et al*, 1988).

Whether the worrying findings on older children are attributable to events in the pre-school years, or are maintained and even engendered by the two full-time jobs pattern in the school years, is unclear.

The maternal investment issue

Certainly, one of the crucial functions of parents of teenagers is monitoring, whether this means tracking their movements, overseeing their homework, surveying their friends, or generally keeping an eye on how and where they spend their time. The role of mothers in nurturing and supporting their children's education has been particularly well documented in working class families. In Margaret O'Brien's and Deborah Jones's study of 600 Dagenham and Barking teenagers and their families (1997), factors like aspirations and income did not alone ensure examination success. This was also dependent upon parental time, involvement and supervision, where 'maternal investment through emotional capital and daily family practices appeared vital. Mothers were the first port of call for children's worries including concerns about school progress and homework.' A result was that children whose mothers worked full-time were twice as likely to fail their GCSE examinations as those who worked part time - independently of the mother's own occupational and educational status.

When these results were used on a *Panorama* program (3rd February 1997), they met with furious denial, as 'deeply politically incorrect in an era when most mothers work'. Not least, the subjects were denounced as untypical: 'How can you extrapolate the experiences of these [working class and lower middle class] families and apply them to, say, affluent families with access to the best nurseries, nannies, or indeed, a boarding school like Eton?' (Toynbee, 1997). Nobody *had*.

On this as well as other occasions, professionals insisting how daycare children had higher intelligence and better school performance, cited the results of 'showpiece' educational projects for highly disadvantaged children at severe risk of every form of failure and institutionalisation.[12] Such intensive learning programs with their specialist staff and curricula, and home visits to improve parenting, have little resemblance to the daycare that working mothers use. The outcomes are irrelevant to ordinary middle and working class children. However, the project which is invariably cited, is Perry pre-school (Schweinhart *et al*, 1993), which was alone among American experimental programs in achieving long term improvements in the social and educational performance of the 58 children it taught over 25 years ago.

Evidence which is far more relevant to the daycare and working mothers debate - like the only large scale study of the children of full-time working mothers attending workplace and private nurseries for the Thomas Coram Research Unit - tends to go unpublicised.[13] Perhaps this is because these predominantly middle class children were significantly slower in language and cognitive development at age six, compared to children who had stayed at home - despite their high status, highly qualified and high income mothers.

This is, again, not an infrequent, but increasingly typical finding of daycare studies. As with an analysis of impact of daycare participation in the first three years of life on the cognitive functioning of school age children from the U.S. NLSY, only children from impoverished home environments had higher reading and mathematics scores if they attended childcare centres (O'Brien

Caughy, 1994). In contrast, middle class children did worse on both accounts. As it is a matter of the interaction between the pattern of daycare and the quality of the home environment, even children from the very worse homes may do better to remain with their unresponsive mothers than to attend some of the poorer quality of care which is available. As said:

> *This evidence linking quality of infant care to infant development has stark implications for policymakers and families, given the poor quality of much of the infant care observed in this study and other studies ... These results suggest that infants' cognitive and communication skills may be jeopardized .. by their childcare experiences, and that this is equally true for children from poor and middle-class families.* (Burchinal et al, 1996)

Having fully employed parents in later childhood, like being reared largely out of the home in the early years, means a fulling quality of care for many children. For daycare to foster development, it would have to match or exceed the quality of maternal care which would be provided by the child's own family. In most cases it does not. Overall, the daycare available to most working mothers is inferior to their own care, and nobody has shown that 'self-care' is actually good for older youngsters. These are especially likely to make inroads into the 'advantages' often ascribed to a middle class upbringing.

It is disconcerting that the widely advocated pattern of early, full time work, should be the one overwhelmingly associated with adverse reports. In contrast, the disapproved pattern - where one parent provides the whole or bulk of care for pre-school children, and then incrementally increases their labour force participation on a part time basis as children go to school, is often associated with the least problems. It is also, of course, the preferred pattern for the vast majority of women - of whatever educational or occupational background.

Facing up to the issues

There is a basic conflict between parenting and the demands for equality of achievement in the workplace at each point in the life cycle. As recognised by establishment feminists, the latter will be undermined by women themselves so long as they put more value on their family and reduce strain by taking less responsible work.

The choice is between less investment in children and more investment in work, or more investment in the family and less in work. However, this choice is bound to be reflected in the developmental outcomes for children. This should lead to a re-assessment of claims, as by Hoffman (1989) that employment necessarily makes a woman a 'better mother to her child' because it must 'enhance a woman's life, providing stimulation, self-esteem, adult contacts, escape from ... housework and childcare, and a buffer against stress from family roles'.

The Fragility of Fatherhood

Sebastian Kraemer

When they are just born human males and females differ less than at any other time in their lives, but as time passes the gap widens. How much of this is inevitable? As a boy becomes a man he is subject to powerful biological and social forces that seem hard to disentangle. Yet the bodily changes are fairly obvious, while the social pressures are almost invisible, as if they had always been there like the air we breathe. Everywhere you look in history there are men and fathers, emperors, popes, kings, gods, conquerors, heroes.

Until as recently as my own childhood democracy was still defined in the now very odd phrase 'one man one vote'. My mother was amongst the first generation of women in Britain to have the vote on an equal basis with men, but the idea that women counted as citizens still took another generation to sink in. Something quite monumental has taken place in the past few decades, which was barely questioned before. Talking about boys and men creates states of mind that are drenched in centuries of culture, and until the recent past few people questioned the order of things between men and women.

Origins of male power

Why is the male generally seen to be more powerful than the female? The obvious answer is that he has stronger muscles. This is true except of course for the most powerful muscle of all, which a man does not even possess - the uterus. This can do what no biceps can, which is push a baby out of a tiny confined space into the open air. Yet male superiority has been unquestioned in most societies for most of human history. If it only depended on muscle power, we might well ask why it lasted so long. There are males in other species, such as the gorilla, that are even bigger in comparison to the female, and there are the majestic lions with their flowing manes to reinforce fantasies of our masculine heritage. These are thrilling beasts, but it is worth noting that they do not necessarily have the kind of power that we assume they have. Male primates, for example, have impressive ways of showing their might over other males, but they can be surprisingly meek when confronted with females. We might think that males that are so much bigger than females would easily be able to do what they want with them, but they can't. For example, in non-human primates, rape is virtually unknown in the wild (Silk, 1993).

Before we can make sense of gender differences in the present there is something peculiar about the evolution of human maleness that needs explaining. The crucial factor is consciousness. However sophisticated, apes and other higher primates do not speculate about the nature of things the way humans do. Modern ethologists show just how delicate the social lives of chimpanzees can be (De Waal, 1991; Dunbar, 1996), but they do not have the same preoccupation with meaning that we have. As humanity evolved there was an enormous increase in the size of the brain, and a corresponding explosion of ingenuity and thoughtfulness.

One of the most important discoveries was the facts of life themselves, as we quaintly call them, which would have had a dramatic effect on the perception of gender. It is almost impossible to imagine what life might have been like for people before they knew how babies were made. They would have been unlikely to know how anything else was made either. The breeding of domestic animals, for example, was only started at around the time when people discovered how to grow plants from seed. Before that, food was gathered, and sometimes stored. If it was animal food, of course it had to be caught first, and it is one of the most persistent myths about humanity that the only food prehistoric people would eat was meat. The truth is far more likely to have been that most food was gathered or caught by hand - roots, fruits, insects and other small creatures - and that this could be done just as easily by women as by men. No doubt prehistoric men played their part in human social life, but they did not necessarily assume any superior role in it (Cucchiari, 1981) .

Although all we have to go on is archaeological remains, there is some very good evidence to show that while in prehistoric times people worshipped female gods, within a thousand years of the discovery of agriculture and the development of cities and of writing, males had taken over, and the gods that we now think of as eternal were invented (Baring & Cashford, 1991).

Men began to think about themselves in a self conscious way and realised that, apart from the genitals, all they really had in comparison with women was greater muscle power and deeper voices. Women on the other had actually produced the babies, a feat which men could only marvel at, and in many places spent more time bringing them up too. This meant that they would have had to learn many more things about the needs of children, about how to protect them from danger - how, for example, to give them food that did not poison them but instead helped them to grow. All this was important knowledge which, if men had it too, they probably learnt from women.

Men's fear of women

This does not sound very familiar, and of course it may be another myth. But there are surviving hunter gatherer societies (Hewlett, 1987) where men and women do not behave in such unequal ways as they have through most of our history, and it is at least possible that our ancestors were like that also. I use this narrative to help us to think about the particular problem of the human male, with all his brains and brawn and an ambition to be just as good as the female. As they say, the rest is history. There is a strong streak of envy and rivalry in the makeup of historic man (Kraemer, 1991).

The promotion of male gods went in parallel with the promotion of male leaders in society - kings and emperors were not the same as big gorillas, they were political rulers who dominated everyone, men, women and children, and animals. Big apes only dominate other males, leaving the females and infants to look after themselves. Furthermore big apes do not own anything. Big men owned people and property (Service, 1975); the archetypal father is not so much a parent as a boss.

Once human civilisation got going men found that they were really in awe of women and had to do something to stop themselves from feeling so inferior. One way of doing this, which seems to be very familiar even today, is to put women down - to say that they are the inferior ones and that we are better than them. But the result of this is that what is projected into them has to be kept at bay with fierce energy, in case it comes to haunt you. Thus there developed a real terror of feminine power in many societies, which has survived right up to the present. This is a brief extract from an anthropological text of how in some traditional societies, men keep women at a distance:

> *Many ethnographic accounts describe how men spend much of their daily lives in their communal houses or sweathouses, gossiping about the evils of women, purifying themselves from female pollution, and guarding sacred objects that they believe their wives are trying to steal from them... The Mundurucu believe that the sex that controls the sacred musical instruments also controls the society and that originally women controlled the instruments. Although men eventually wrested control from women, women are constantly attempting to retrieve it and resume their once dominant social position. The instruments, then, are strictly guarded from women, who are permitted neither to see them nor to hear them played. Mundurucu husbands say that if a woman were to see the instruments she would be dragged into the bush and forced to submit to gang-rape.* (Paige & Paige, 1981)

The highland people of Papua New Guinea are even fiercer. The male initiation cult involves learning how to dominate women.

> *Inside the cult house, which no woman may enter, the Nama men store their sacred flutes whose sounds terrorize the women and children. Only male initiates learn that it is their fathers and brothers who make the sounds and not carnivorous supernatural birds. They swear to kill any woman or child who learns the secret even by accident...*
>
> *..After being secluded in the cult house the initiates emerge into adulthood. They are given a bride whom they promptly shoot in the right thigh with an arrow to demonstrate unyielding power over her. Women work in the gardens, raise pigs, and do all the dirty work while men stand around gossiping, making speeches,*

and decorating themselves with paint, feathers and shells.
(Harris, 1993, p65)

Manhood and fatherhood

How do boys become fathers? The short answer is that many do
with very little effort. For a boy who has not yet done so the idea
of having sex with a woman may seem like an impossible task, but
it turns out not to be so difficult, eventually. Nor is it difficult for
most couples to conceive. It may be that the alarm over falling
sperm counts will make a difference to future men, but it is too
early to tell.

Although, as we have seen, manhood and fatherhood are social
definitions, there are obvious biological differences between men
and women which make a difference to their experiences of
parenthood. A male needs only a few minutes at most to impregnate
a female. Unless she has an abortion, she then has no choice but to
look after the baby until it is born. Men have the choice of staying
or leaving at every stage from conception onwards. Parenthood is
entirely voluntary for a man. You could argue that this is also the
case for the woman, but only after the baby is born. The difference
is that she has usually had nine months of pregnancy during most
of which she will have known about the impending arrival. During
this time also the process of attachment will have begun - getting
ready for a baby, a cot, some clothes, maybe a room, thinking about
names and so on.

It is very hard for women to avoid thinking about a new baby,
but it is quite easy for men to do so.[1] By the time of birth, if it is
their first child, most women have begun to feel like mothers, even
if they are terrified and ill-prepared, whereas most men haven't a
clue. And, as we know from clinical and social work experience, it
is relatively rare for women to abandon their babies. Attachment,
even when it is anxious and insecure, is a very powerful magnet.

The male parent does seem to be at quite a disadvantage. He is
probably less attached to his newborn infant, and socially
unprepared for the role. In good enough circumstances a young
woman will have the help of her own mother in starting to care for
a new baby, but what support is there for a young man? Does his
father come along and show him how fathering can be done? And

what would this actually mean? One can imagine very easily the newly promoted paternal grandfather finding every reason not be too involved with his son. Maybe he has a busy job that he cannot leave - and what would his employers say if he asked for grandpaternal leave?

This is a very familiar model of fatherhood, which many men in the grandfatherly generation know well enough - absence. Absence from the birth itself, absence from the nursery, and later from the school, and so on. It is only in the last twenty years or so that it has seemed right to question such a role. After all, the father has to make money for his family, especially when the baby is new and there are lots of things to buy. It is a very expensive time, and someone has to pay the bills. This has all changed enormously, and very quickly, in the past few years. Now half the labour force is made up of women, and many expect to return to work fairly soon, even within a few weeks, after the baby is born. So the breadwinner is not necessarily the man in the house.

The other change, of course, is that there are many more women who find themselves bringing up children without a man at all. He is not only absent during the day but also at night. He may be nearby and may visit and provide some money, but he is not part of the household. At the last count over one in five children were living in a one-parent family in Great Britain; 2.3 million children, over three times the total in 1961. Just under a tenth of these live with lone fathers but the rest, still over 2 million, are with mothers, single (36%), divorced (32%), separated (18%) and widowed (5%). The vast majority of these families are relatively poor (National Council for One Parent Families, 1996).

Are fathers needed?

Faced with facts like these what is a boy to think? He can see around him women making do without men, and may think that he is not really needed as a parent. This is the first of several threats to his esteem. The second is the lack of job opportunities. He can see that there are many men who do not have jobs. Although unemployment has gone down a bit since 1991 there are still well over three million unemployed people in the UK, and far fewer unskilled jobs available than in the past. The only growth is in professional and managerial work, beyond the reach of many poorly educated boys.

And that is the third threat. On average girls do significantly better than boys at school, are less likely to fool around in class and more realistic about what they can do when they grow up. They are the ones who will get the new jobs in service industries as managers, receptionists and trainers. Some boys still imagine that they can do the kind of work their fathers did, even though the evidence is there: while the top jobs in industry and government are still held by men, ordinary unskilled jobs for men have all but gone.

The paradox is that while in daily life it is clear that women are gaining ground, in the political stratosphere the old patriarchal world carries on just as before. The heads of government, of multinational companies and so on are almost all men, and they seem to have got to these positions by demonstrating a very impressive sort of power, the kind that pushes aside anyone who gets in their way. So up there are some unattainable but fascinating heroes, in a world from which women are still excluded, just like in the old days.

Down here the balance is very different. The only two things that boys do better than girls are committing crimes (Utting, 1996)[2] and committing suicide (Hawton, 1992). Both have shown disturbing increases over the past few years. Maybe there will be more jobs for men in future, but we cannot count on it. One thing is certain, and that is that people will go on having babies. It is true that more women are now deciding not to have children, but they are a small minority. For the rest life goes on essentially as it always has. Couples get together and the woman gets pregnant. Is there a role for men?

One answer to this must be some kind of job description for fatherhood. As we have seen it has changed quite a lot in just one generation. In the past fathers were defined by how different they were from mothers - they tended to have an outside role, while mothers were inside. Now the difference has narrowed, a source of anxiety for many boys. This is the fourth threat - the fear of femininity. Almost any boy, however liberally brought up, will resist doing things that he thinks are only for girls.

There is a sort of panic that can overwhelm a boy when faced with femininity. In parallel with the historical and prehistorical development of gender difference mentioned at the beginning there is a similar psychological process at work. Because all of us come from inside the bodies of women we have a very powerful sense of having been enclosed by something feminine. For girls this is an issue too, but it is not the same one as it is for boys. They have to establish an identity that is distinct from the mother yet one that is still of the same gender - a subtle and complex task.

In contrast, boys as they grow up are bound to feel that their gender is different from their mother's, because it is. But the way this is discovered and understood is crucial. It is quite easy, especially in a world where the only effective men seem to be powerful political and industrial leaders who get their way by bullying, to think that this is the path to follow; that to become a male it is necessary to abandon all identification with the accommodating female. No doubt something quite profound has to happen but it does not have to be so drastic, like the Mundurucu or Nama men who barricade themselves away from women in holy terror of them. And of course it is nonsense to say that looking after children is necessarily a feminine role; it is just that women have been doing it for a long time.

The old model of fatherhood was closer to this patriarchal image than the new one. That is not to say that fathers in the past were just bullies or that they did not love their children, but there was no pressure on them to adopt what would have been regarded as maternal modes. You were not expected to attend the birth and the showing of affection was not encouraged, even when it was felt. Here is a man, now in his eighties, talking about his second son, who was born in 1949.

It wasn't that they shouldn't ever cry. I think it was rather that having seen what a rough, tough world it was, they should be able to face it. Life doesn't owe you a living, you've got to get out there and get stuck in and make your own way. I don't think that either of them were cry babies. I remember an occasion, John used to walk about a lot with bare feet and he used to go into my workshop where I often had odd things in there and he picked up a very heavy condenser, about six inches long. He dropped it on his little toe and the howl of agony that went up went straight to my heart, a cry of despair. I picked him up and hugged him. I did my best to see that they were not mollycoddled

and grew up as tough youngsters and I think they are.
(Humphries and Gordon, 1996)

No one would say that this father did not love his children, yet he is clearly afraid that there is a danger in being too affectionate in case they become too dependent on him, or perhaps even not manly enough. Manliness on this view means a kind of self reliance. Even though some fathers have changed since those days the model of manliness that he implies is still very clear, and compulsively interesting to everyone. This is the cool pose of the teenage boy trying not to seem anxious. He is like Clint Eastwood, 'the man with no name' in his most famous screen role; he says little and looks after himself. He has no need for anybody. The defining quality of this type of male is that he is ashamed of being ashamed (Krugman, 1995), so he cuts himself off from a whole range of feelings, especially tender ones. But these are precisely the kind that he needs if he is to become a successful modern father.

A further threat, the fifth, is the fear of sexual attraction towards children, even one's own. This is real enough, but as long as it remains a taboo it appears more dangerous than it is. Parker and Parker (1986) did a controlled study of fathers who had committed incest against their daughters. These men had far less intimate involvement with the girls during infancy - they rarely changed nappies, bathed, or fed the children. This suggests that committed and involved care from the very beginning can help to prevent later intimacy from turning into sexual abuse. (Of course a determined paedophile can still get himself into a partnership with a woman with the express aim of having children that he can later abuse, but these will be a tiny minority.) But even when sexual abuse is not an issue there are in any case differences between the erotic experiences that men and women might have when in contact with children. There is a difference between an erect nipple and an erect penis, for example, which is one of the obstacles to fathering that is rarely mentioned.

New models in fathering

In spite of the bodily differences between men and women, the new model of fatherhood is not so very different from mothering. The trouble is that not many boys, or girls for that matter, know this. Nobody wants to talk about it. Kyle Pruett, an American psychiatrist who has written very sensitively about fatherhood, says: 'Unlike women, men tend not to talk about their children's caretaking needs in social groups; rather they "own" their experience privately, as if they had discovered a wonderful secret that can be preserved only by not calling attention to it' (Pruett, 1993). This could just as well apply to the father just quoted, in that he somehow felt he was not meant to hug his child, and probably never talked about this incident until interviewed for a TV programme in the 1990s.

The difference now is that not only is the old model of fathering seriously under threat, but the new one is very fragile and hardly established. It is important to make clear what I mean by the new kind of fathering. This is not the new man so beloved of advertisers. He is, as everyone now knows, a bit of a myth; he looks good and says all the right things, but does no more childcare or housework than the old man.

The new kind of father is something far less glamorous. He has probably been around for years but only recently has there been any discussion at all about his experiences and tasks. Essentially he is a father who takes a reasonable share of childcare and discovers that it can be both rewarding and maddening, just as mothers have always known. These are men who have discovered something very simple. Children want their fathers in just the same sorts of ways as they want their mothers. Sometimes the desire is not so intense as for mother, but sometimes it is even stronger. This is not to say that they want the same from each parent all the time. On the contrary; it is the difference that is so interesting, but it does not have to be forced. That is what fathers have to learn, which is not easy after all these years. Even if he does not feel like it, a young man is often under pressure to show off his masculinity (Gilmore, 1990), yet this obligation does not help him learn to look after, nor even to think about, small dependent creatures like children. If the father is more involved, and takes more responsibility, this will change. What cannot change is that the child has never been inside the father, who in that sense must always represent something 'outside'. If he plays an active part, this outside person is more present than absent (Kraemer, 1995).

Though children no doubt enjoy exciting moments with either

parent, what they want from the father is not some wonderful patriarch, or adventurer, or breadwinner or bully, or even playmate, but a parent who can look after you and think about you, even when you are not there. This simple discovery is deeply disturbing to the collective male, which is why it has had little press. It does not seem to be very newsworthy in any case.

What is so special about men who look after their children in an ordinary good enough way? Nothing, except that it is probably happening in more and more families, as mothers go out to work and become more aware that childcare does not always have to be done by women. Any man who gets admired for this - 'isn't he wonderful!' - might well find an angry woman at his side saying 'what is so wonderful about this. We have been doing just this for centuries, and nobody admired us!'

From the point of view of the children themselves, there is no doubt that having fathers look after them alongside mothers is good for them (Lamb & Oppenheim, 1989; Russell & Radejovic, 1992; Burgess, 1997). The research consistently shows that collaborative parents who do not make a major distinction between their roles produce confident and thoughtful children who are also less tied to the old fashioned gender distinctions.

Of course this is not an easy arrangement. It is probably simpler to follow the traditional pattern, since that effectively leaves the mother in charge of the children and the father bringing home the money. That way they do not get in each others' way. But, except in increasingly rare instances, the old model is no longer possible. What is most interesting about this quiet revolution is that it is almost certainly what the children want, and would always have wanted if they had been asked. Of course it is nice to have a Daddy who comes home from far away places with presents and so forth, but it is even nicer to have him around in an ordinary daily way.

The noise of divorce and family breakup has obscured these changes in families over the past few years. Even in families that subsequently break up these may persist. Although there are few families in which men take an equal share of parenting, many others now think it is their duty to take part. A generation or two ago this simply was not an issue. Men were visitors in the nursery. You were considered a strange bloke if you wanted to change your baby's nappies or carry the child around with you, and of course there were none of the baby slings that now make it so easy to do that. Here is an account (from the same BBC programme) of how it was for one father whose daughter was born in 1953.

I used to do all the nappies, nursing, feeding, whatever was necessary, I did it. Take her out for long walks in the pram, give the wife time to kind of get the housework done or what she needed and I used to enjoy that. I used to walk for miles round here, pushing the old pram, "she's mine". You know. People in the neighbourhood, you'd walk out and you'd see them. "Huh, look at him, pushing a kid". But it never used to worry me, that. They used to look and say "What's up with Joan, is she ill?" I'd say, "No, she's just doing something, ironing, I'm taking the kid." "Oh, you wouldn't get me doing that." You know that was the general attitude, and I used to think, "Well, what the hell is it? She's my daughter, she's my flesh and blood, what's wrong with pushing her around in her pram?" I just couldn't weigh it up. I used to think, "If they say anything I'll flatten 'em." I used to think it was the right thing to do. These are your children, and why not?'

(Humphries & Gordon 1996, 198-200)

Supporting equality and choice

It is important for children to be looked after by women and men. Little children see women being effective both as parents and workers. Unless fathers are included in childcare, how are the children going to see what men are really like, and how can men find out what children are really like? The non-domestic world may still seem to be dominated by male values, but the fact is that men are increasingly marginalized. Without the opportunity to be useful parents, men will slide further into meaninglessness. Even now there is a problem for men as fathers. Behind closed doors it is fine to get on with it, but in public many men are a bit reserved about being seen to be too maternal. A visible sign of this is how men tend to drive a baby push chair with only one hand, as if to say 'this isn't really my job - I'm just standing in for the wife'.

There is no serious social encouragement for men to share parenting. In Sweden it took 50 years to break the mould of centuries, yet in Britain we have yet to see government action on paternity leave (Moss, 1995) - that is leave from work when the baby is born - let alone on parental leave,[3] which is the right to take time off work when a child up to 8 years old is ill or has to be looked after at home for some reason, such as on teacher training days. What happens is that mothers usually have to organise to take over, by phoning work to say that they are themselves ill, because they are not allowed to take time off for children's illnesses.

Few families can expect to care for their children without help. Even in these times of disintegrated families, many grandparents still help out, but most parents also rely on extra help, which is usually paid for, either in cash or in kind. The underprovision and minimal regulation of such caregiving is shameful. It does not have to be like that. With a political will the lives of children, and hence the lives of the next generation of adults, could be greatly improved (Kraemer, 1997).

With properly trained (and properly paid) staff to look after them, children will thrive in non-family day care, but they also need to be looked after by their mothers and fathers, especially in the morning and early evening. Britain has the highest proportion of men working overtime in the EU, and the pressures on those in work to overdo it will continue, because jobs, and to some extent partnerships too, are insecure. Either partner may find themselves without work, or indeed without the other partner. So-called 'family friendly' policies in employment are rare. Even if many men cannot afford to work shorter hours, they could work them more flexibly.

Men and women will always differ, as they must. Equality of opportunity in the workplace and at home does not imply that people will carry out their tasks in precisely the same way. Equality is about difference; it promotes greater richness and variety. No society can prescribe how the sexes should behave, but a civilised modern state cannot restrict the range of opportunity afforded to either. It must allow the greatest freedom to choose, from the traditional arrangement where men earn and women care for children, through equal sharing of earning and childcare, to a total reversal of tradition, in which men stay at home and women go out to work, and of course it must expect a proportion of parents to be separate, even from the beginning.

If it was clear that the choices couples made would be backed up by benefits and leave arrangements then there would be much less of a crisis in family life than there appears to be now. Such a trend would not necessarily halt or reduce the rates of parental separation and divorce, but if men are able to be involved in their children's lives from the beginning, it is a fair bet that they would be more likely to stay in touch with them even if they did have to leave home later on. And if boys were prepared for parenthood at school, for example, they would not be so incompetent when the day came for them to take responsibility for their own children. They might even find that it is a job worth doing.

Conclusion

As we come to understand the primary tasks of parenthood it is clear that the differences between maternal and paternal roles are fewer than the similarities. The promotion of secure attachments is, after all, dependent primarily on attentiveness and consistent firmness, tasks which either parent can perform. Yet the differences are all the more important for that. Children need both parents precisely because they are of different (we still say 'opposite') sexes. Boys can become fathers if they are encouraged to do so, but it is a political as well as a private matter. There is nothing in the biological makeup of the male that prevents him from being a competent parent. This does not mean that men have to be like women to be ordinary good enough fathers, only that they have to deal with their fear of femininity in doing so. In order to be a father a man does not have to try to be different from a mother. He already is. That is the whole point of the exercise.

There are signs of hope. The way boys are brought up is not so separate from girls as it was forty years ago. Most education, for example, is co-educational, and both boys and girls can see for themselves, if they are allowed to look, that women and men do not have to lead segregated lives. Yet there is a real pressure, including from some of the contributors to this book, to reverse this fragile progress to protect the now so vulnerable male. This is mistaken. While women have begun to be liberated from their traditional roles, men are predominantly still trapped in theirs. A just rewriting of the sexual contract will not be achieved by reversing the advances that have already been made, even if that were possible.

Fathers as Mothers:
Lone Parenting for Men

John Griffiths

For the past thirty years women have, with some justification, been tearing up the old inequitable sexual contract. Today three out of every four divorces are initiated by them, and the old rules are dead. But if a new contract between men and women is to be written with any hope of sticking then the current termination clauses will need to be drastically revised. Men resent these because they are so heavily weighted against them, and do not reflect the needs of children. If revisions are not made, then not only will many men suffer injustice, but their children will be further damaged.

The late twentieth century has been the age of serial monogamy rather than of life-long partnerships, and it follows that the early part of the twenty first will be an age of sequential or parallel parenthood. However, little account has yet been taken by social forecasters, yet alone politicians, of the consequences for children who are no longer being brought up from birth to maturity by the same two parents, one of either sex. Certainly little thought has been given to the who and how of these children's rearing. Present practice embodies an ill-considered acceptance of a family pattern - of paternal provider and maternal home maker - which is itself becoming obsolete. How else can we characterise a situation where, despite almost two adult women in three now going out to work, the father is bringing up his children in only eight out of every hundred separated couples?

Such disparity could only be justified if there were some innate quality in women, lacking in most men, which made them naturally and significantly superior as child rearers. A combination of social convention and misapplied maternal bonding theories still lead many mistakenly to consider that there is. However, were this true, since death and divorce are quite arbitrary in their selection of which fathers are left to bring up their children, such children should turn out less happy, less academically and economically successful, and less healthy than those reared by single mothers. They do not. Indeed, there is now a substantial body of research (e.g. Phillips & Anzalone, 1982; Lamb, 1987) which demonstrates that there is no difference, as far as the outcome for children over the age of two at the time of separation is concerned, whether they are brought up by a lone father or a lone mother. Other studies have shown that while it is important for a child's development that it form a close bond with an adult, or better still adults, this need not be with a female nor even with a natural parent (Rutter, 1972). Men do not have to be dependent on women any more to care for their children for them. They can do it by themselves.

The resident father

My interest in this is not just academic, as I have been through it myself. I did not want my marriage to end, and when my wife left me and our daughter for her lover I was in a state of shock for a time. A couple of weeks *before* she left, the business I had founded collapsed as a result of withdrawal by its majority shareholder, and shortly afterwards my first wife had died. So for a while I was in danger of wallowing in self-pity. But this ended quite quickly after my five-and-a-half year old daughter, Emily, found me crying. She took my hand and said 'cheer up Daddy, I'll tell you some jokes'.

As she stood in front of me solemnly reciting the riddles of her infant class I did indeed smile, dry my eyes and in pitying her loss began the long process of ceasing to pity myself for mine and to appreciate my good fortune. The very circumstances that had conspired to knock me down now coincided to pick me up again. My daughter needed me. Moreover, needed me as a supportive, loving, practical parent to solace her in her bewildered unhappiness, not as a self-absorbed wreck. Because I no longer had a job I was in a position to provide that support and because I loved her I was determined to do it.

Looking back, after seven years, I do not honestly know how much my attitude was governed by my own need to keep with me at a time of so much loss the daughter I so loved of the woman I still loved, and how much by my firm and genuine belief that Emily would be better off with me than with her mother. I believe that the decision has turned out to have been the right one, but whether for the right or the wrong reasons I shall never really know. Much of the credit for any success is due to the co-operation of Emily's mother Carole. Although there have been deep disagreements, and fierce quarrels over what was the best thing for our daughter at different times, we always thought and spoke of her as our daughter not my daughter or your daughter.

Now disagreements are rare and rational, and Carole and I are good friends who turn to each other for advice and help. The guardian of this peace is Emily, who will never allow either to say an ill word about the other. So few men have the joy and privilege of bringing up their children, of exploring and strengthening the daily bond which is many women's richest reward. As more and more come to realise what they are missing, so more separating fathers will want to secure that reward for themselves.

Obstacles to paternal care

Nevertheless, men who seek residence of their children have first to erase in the minds of judges and (predominantly female) social workers several notions instilled by an outdated feminism. These are that men are violent, feckless, irresponsible, emotionally repressed whingers incapable of forming a close relationship with another adult let alone with their children. This image ignores many salient facts. That men are no more likely than women to abuse their children, that absent fathers are four times more likely than absent mothers to contribute to their children's maintenance and will contribute three times as much as their female counterparts, that men are more likely to continue to love their exes than women and more likely to encourage contact between child and absent parent, are all inconvenient facts to be ignored when judges and social workers are deciding who shall be the resident parent when a family splits up.

In the face of such prejudice it is not surprising that in only one divorce case in ten does the father dispute the award of residence of his children to their mother nor that, in Britain at least, only three in a hundred of those that do seek residence in the face of the mother's opposition are likely to win. This is in marked contrast to the less hidebound Australians, who award a third of such cases to the father and half to the mother - with the remainder a joint legal responsibility.

If the father is not married to his children's mother his prospects of seeing them, let alone of bringing them up, are even worse. When she puts her name to their birth certificate she is staking an irrefutable claim to the right to determine the shape of their pre-adult lives. When their father inscribes his alongside hers he is writing a blank cheque of financial liability for the next eighteen years, without any automatic claim to any say in their future if he and their mother part or she dies, let alone any claim to be the resident parent. Indeed, unless he has taken out a prior Parental Rights and Responsibilities Order - not something most men think of doing in the throes of love and amidst the first joys of early parenthood - he has no more claim than the milkman and possibly less if the milkman happens to be his ex's latest cohabiter.

On the whole, children brought up by the same two parents from birth to maturity, so long as the relationship between their parents is relatively harmonious, turn out better for themselves and for society than those reared in step families or by single parents of either sex. However, this is a declining pattern. On present trends, within a decade or so children of life-long (or even child-long) relationships will be in a minority. So the questions which need to be addressed in rewriting the sexual contract are whether or not quasi-nuclear families can be reconstructed in some child-benefiting way by social engineering; and if they cannot, how should the upbringing of children can be apportioned between mothers and fathers so as to minimise the damage to the offspring of 'broken' families.

Keeping the absent parent in touch

Perhaps we should make more progress if we thought of these children as being in divided or separated families, rather than broken ones - with all the connotations of irreparability the latter word implies. But that redefinition presupposes that the absent parent will continue to play a major part in their child's life. Sadly, over half of absent fathers will not see or communicate with their offspring at all within two years of parting from the children's mother. In the great majority of cases this is not because they do not love their children or do not wish to sustain a relationship, but simply because it becomes impossible for them to do so. In forty per cent of such cases in one major research project this was due to their being always or sometimes deliberately denied access by a vengeful partner (Parke, 1981). My own research suggests that those who have residence rights seem to take a more constructive attitude towards absent mothers - perhaps because so many of the men still love their exes. In my own recent study all of the mothers who had been separated for less than two years were still seeing their children, albeit infrequently and irregularly in a quarter of the cases (Griffiths, 1997: app. 2, table 7).

The average father in my survey is a forty year-old with two children of about ten whose mother, in two thirds of the cases, is still seeing her children, but in a third of them less than once a week. Almost half the sets of parents were in complete agreement about access, and a quarter were in total disagreement. It is obviously not a subject for easy compromise - but *opinions* about access did not seem to significantly influence either its extent or the outcome for the children. In practice the most important cause of contact breakdown was the obvious, if seldom cited, one of practicality. A journey time in excess of forty minutes marked a very distinct watershed beyond which contact fell off sharply. The same cause is likely to explain loss of contact by absent fathers.

A much more intriguing possibility to emerge from my survey was that the standard court access order of one weekend a fortnight plus occasional holidays might be the worst of all solutions for the children. Those who rated highest in terms of health, happiness, behaviour and school progress were either those who saw their absent parent three or four times a week or more - the majority of whom lived within a few minutes journey - or those who did not see them at all. This suggests to me that *certainty* is the most important factor in the relationship with an absent parent. Perhaps the child who has no contact can at least construct an ideal, if imaginary, parent to fill the gap.

Coping with isolation and poverty

For the majority of single parents of both sexes the most difficult feeling to cope with, once loss and anger have diminished, is the sense of isolation from 'normal' society. The lack of money, and also of anyone to relieve the resident parent of child minding for a while, greatly reduces the opportunity for many of them to socialise - let alone to find and court a new mate. This seems generally to bear harder on lone fathers, for several main reasons.

Firstly, men do not usually have the social networking skills which women seem to develop from childhood. Related to this, girls are now, rightly, educated to have jobs or careers as well as to run homes and rear children, but boys are still prepared in most schools and homes only to be providers not carers. Men thus fail to develop the necessary skills, and therefore the self confidence, to fight for lone parenthood.

Secondly, the chances are that all or nearly all men's acquaintances in the same lone parent predicament will be single mothers. Many of these have been made hostile to men by their own experiences, and some of them even regard child-rearing by a man as unnatural. While men may sometimes win surprised admiration for taking on lone parent responsibility they also often incur suspicion and disapproval, sometimes even downright violence, from women for usurping 'woman's mothering role'.

Finally men tend to define themselves by what they do, and what they earn. So those who have been employed find themselves transferred from an objective-orientated *team* ethos to a person-focused *solo* role. A third of the fathers in my survey spontaneously mentioned this sense of isolation as the aspect of lone parenthood which they found hardest to bear. Rather surprisingly, although all but two were worse off than they had been and half of them lived near the bread line in both relative and absolute terms, far fewer cited poverty as their greatest handicap. Fifty two per cent had incomes of less than £7000 a year. On the other hand, unlike the great majority of their female counterparts, thirty one per cent still earned over £12,000 a year. However the drop in income for all was substantial. Before separation thirty nine per cent earned more than £20,000 a year and only eleven per cent less than £6000. *After* separation only fourteen per cent earned over £20,000 and thirty nine per cent earned less than £6000. For some the blow to pride and pocket was particularly dramatic. One man's income fell from £68,000 to £9,800, another's from £50,000 to £6,450.

Intriguingly almost all these impoverished fathers said that they *felt* better off - largely because they were now in sole control of family expenditure, which had sometimes been subject to the irresponsible whims of their exes. Nor did poverty appear to be a major direct determinant of the outcome for the children - though it may have influenced the happiness or otherwise of the fathers, which was. On the whole the children of the poorer parents were doing better than those of the wealthier - perhaps because the latter had been unable completely to shed the pre-separation habit of putting career and self esteem before family. Many of the poorer either were or had been unemployed and thus already had some experience of parenting and domestic management and of undertaking them successfully.

The way forward

I have suggested in my recent book (*op cit*, 1997) that there is no good reason why we have such a relatively small proportion of children living with single fathers in Britain. There is ample evidence that, certainly for children over the age of two, those brought up by single fathers are as happy, healthy, successful at school and well behaved as those brought up by single mothers. So it cannot be to the benefit of the children of divided families in general that only eight per cent of them are brought up by their fathers. About a third would seem a fairer and more child-centred proportion.

Child-rearing is certainly exhausting, exasperating, distracting and all the other negative things parents complain about, but it is also immensely rewarding in so many ways. That being so, why should men not have an equal opportunity with women to choose child care as a way of life as women now rightly expect equal opportunity and reward in other fields? While some inequalities may still be suffered by women in economic and public life they are much smaller than they were a decade ago. The same cannot be said of the inequalities suffered by men in the private life of the family and in the right to equal care of their children when their parental partnerships end. Nor, I suggest, can this disparity meet the even more important right of children to the equal care of *both* their parents.

We need, I believe, to pursue three major social changes, which together go to the heart of the sexual contract. We need changes in the *law* to put unmarried fathers and widowers as well as divorced men on a genuinely equal footing with women in all aspects of their children's upbringing. We need changes in *social attitudes*, which will make it as acceptable for a man as for a woman to be the lone resident parent after separation or divorce. And we need changes in the way men are *educated and trained*, so that they have not only the necessary skills and confidence with which to bring up their children on their own, but an attitude of mind which will enable them to embrace that responsibility enthusiastically and successfully should they want and win the right to undertake it.

Families after Separation: Equal Careers and Equal Parenting

John Baker

What happens to roles *after* a parental couple has split? What policy - personal and public - is needed there? Such a policy is vital unless there is to be a rapid end to family break-up, and that seems highly unlikely. And since gender roles and the parental relationships of children after a break-up are influenced by what happened before, what stance by 'intact' families best protects the children of divorce and separation?

The end of sexual interdependence

Although challenges to it are emerging, the convergence of gender roles is likely to be with us for a long time. It has enormous political pressure behind it and seems to correspond to external social, medical and economic facts. The 'traditional' difference corresponded to an economy where the greater brute physical strength of men was needed for many tasks, and the phase in women' s adult lives before their first pregnancy was short, and they often died before their last child was independent. The economy now requires skills which neither sex has any major advantage in supplying, and the dependency of pregnant women and the need for childcarers is now a short phase in the life cycle.

A belief system which sees male and female roles as very different is no longer buttressed from outside. It may still correspond to some essential psychological difference between men and women, but the precise nature of any such differences - apart from a major overlap - is controversial and unclear. Increasingly it seems that believers in distinct gender roles are making value judgements. These could of course spread, even become socially dominant once more. There might be desirable results. But whereas once they went with the tide of economic and social need, now they go against it.

For the foreseeable future, one has to look at how to organise child rearing in the context of a situation of men and women having increasingly similar economic roles. This is sometimes seen as a cause of the increasing breakdown of intimate relationships. There could be a link, although the common reason given is illogical. Previously, neither men nor women could manage in a socially approved way without a mate. This is seen as having fostered stability. But since it did not matter much who their partner was, provided they performed the relevant duties, there was no particular reason why they should stay with one. What we have seen in the last 30 years has not been a rejection of the idea of living in a partnership. The pressure and yearning for that remains intense. It has been a greater readiness to change partners.

If men and women have distinct social and family roles, it is important that appropriate models are present in the lives of children. Hence the often greater concern with the stability of the traditional two parent family in 'conservative' circles in which the father often had little to do with children. But if mothers and fathers are not so distinct in their social roles it matters less if the children don't have both models. This was perhaps the reason for the lesser concern with children being 'paternally deprived' in circles which defined themselves as 'progressive'. But there is an asymmetry. The convergence of roles means that while fathers may not be seen as so necessary they should also be seen as adequate *substitutes* for mothers. This has not happened and in fact 'equality' has meant that women can compete with men in traditionally male spheres, but the barriers remain against men entering female areas. 'Fathering' in any broader sense than insemination is seen as less necessary than it was, and insemination itself no longer requires even a fleeting relationship. A gendered 'mothering' is, however, seen as being important as before.

This asymmetry raises questions about the interpretation of 'traditional' gender roles as exploitation and subordination of women by men. Some of the most assertive advocates of women's rights in economic and 'public' life are among the most vigorous defenders of mothers' rights to retain control of children. Few individual women seem willing, when challenged by their ex-partners, to share or surrender their dominance in the lives of children despite the literature which portrays childcare as an unvalued and even oppressive activity. No woman (except in rare circumstances) now has to have children against her will, and many 'career women' (whom one would suppose are making informed choices as to which lifestyle they prefer) ultimately opt for motherhood despite the so-called 'sacrifices' involved.

Perhaps after all child-rearing is the emotionally richest part of life, which informed people with a choice prefer over other options. It has a downside, but overall it may have more to offer than even 'stimulating' careers. If this applies to professional people, how much more strongly it must do to people who drive fork lift trucks or check forms or do any of the other tedious or 'dead-end' jobs that many men and women endure in order to fund family life? Instead of male subordination of women in the family perhaps one should talk of ending male exclusion from an area of life offering far deeper rewards than those conventionally available to them.

Reassessing domestic work

It is often commented that feminism in its late 20th century form remains primarily a middle or even, to use a improperly underused term, upper class concern. Perhaps some of its supporters should be regarded as the heirs of the ladies who once had nurses, nannies and governesses. They enjoyed the status of 'mother' and the right to control and to select what involvement with their children they wanted, while imposing on social inferiors the aspects of childcare and housework that were less stimulating than social, voluntary and intellectual activity. Such women now have a choice posed on different terms. They wish to remain 'mothers'. But to do the most attractive parts of that they have to do things they regard as beneath them as well as, or sometimes instead of, more interesting activities. While the recreational aspect of childcare is surely, to all but a tiny group, more pleasurable, interesting and rewarding than *almost any* employment, the cooking, cleaning and washing is probably less stimulating (and certainly more socially isolating) than much work in the professions. *However it must still compare rather well with a lot of normal paid work.*

The early alliance of some feminists with Marxism is surely ironical. From a Marxist perspective housework and childcare is part of 'social reproduction' and essential to the maintenance of labour power for a capitalist class. But the work itself is surely not *directly* exploitative or oppressive. In the jargon it is not 'alienated'. The worker consumes what they produce - in hygiene, cleanliness, diet, appearance. It is under the control of the worker. They decide what to do, how to do it, in what order, at what pace. There is variety in it, perhaps of a limited sort compared with middle class jobs, but considerable compared with much factory or office work. Housework must compare well with much low-grade employment in terms of health risks, dirt, noise and so on. Nor is there necessarily a lot of it.

A person in sole charge of young children is always at least 'on call', and serious exhaustion is a possibility, at least until babies have regular and near-normal sleep patterns, and before they start school opportunities to do anything other than respond to their needs are extremely limited. A person in sole or primary charge of babies can easily find themselves personally isolated, unable to participate in anything else and all too commonly depressed.

Happily such situations are minority ones and temporary. In other cases the needs of housework and childcare can be exaggerated. Claims are based not on what is essential, but on the time people *decide* to spend on it. Houseworkers with modern labour saving equipment have mostly made a choice to enjoy higher standards rather than reduce hours. This choice is at least partly their own, or a least the result of pressure within a group of peers, and not - as a rule - the result of any sexist oppression. There seems to be general agreement that men are usually content with lower domestic standards than their female partners. Some domestic conflict follows men's failure to conform to the rules and expectations that their partners wish to impose on them. The tendency of men to do very little housework is unfair, but a by-product of men doing more would be to give men a greater credibility in attacking exaggerated statements about it. There once used to be a male mystique about 'breadwinning' and the demands and stresses of life in the workshop or office. This has now gone, as a result of women now having experience against which to assess it. The same needs to happen about childcare and domestic work.

What however about the needs of children? During their childhood many children will see their parents break up. Parents will in various combinations at varying intervals live on their own with or without the children of a relationship, and have other intimate relationships with or without other children being involved. How should social arrangements adjust to this?

The priority of motherhood

The adjustment that our society has made so far is clear enough. The bond with the mother has been regarded as central, and possession and control of the children is awarded to her unless there are compelling reasons to do otherwise. The children follow her in her 'family career' which may and often does include periods living in a single parent household or involve one or more 'stepfathers'. The natural father's role has been seen as economic provider but as marginal in emotional or caring terms. In public law, there are coercive arrangements to compel men to perform their traditional breadwinning role. The Child Support Agency has been instituted to compel fathers insultingly labelled as 'absent' to pay maintenance in lieu of social security. There are no legal or social institutions whose function is to impose on fathers any caring duties. In the case of divorce or separation there is private law in which the reality is that men may, if motivated enough, have some opportunities to challenge an assumption that children belong exclusively with and to their mothers. The subjective experience of many fathers of these is of a battery of arrangements to cut down the aspirations of fathers who want to be involved to the amount of contact that their ex is willing to accept. Those fathers who do not want major personal involvement are, in a sense, the lucky ones. They get what they want with little trouble or condemnation. Whether that is satisfactory for the children is something that a new sexual contract should address.

This emphasis on the father's economic contribution alone is a slight oversimplification. A father married to the children's mother - still a majority but a declining one - has permanent 'parental responsibility' for his children under the Children Act. However, this is often more symbolic than real. Schools, for example, should now treat both parents equally. In practice the non-residential parent may have to threaten the school and risk upsetting them to get treatment that is theirs by right, for instance getting reports or being invited to parents' evenings. The contact parent has the right to go to court for orders allowing the children to spend time with him, but in practice a father is in a very weak position against a mother who opposes this. And so on.

Social and political sympathy is overwhelmingly with the mother. There are widespread and usually unchallenged statements about fathers 'abandoning' children. In reality this seems less common than mothers leaving the family, often taking the children, or mothers asking their partners to go, with a complex interaction between the partners preceding the break up - in which it is not clear who is 'responsible' - being most common of all. An example of the pro-woman agenda is the stance of the National Association of Probation Officers, the professional body and trade union for Family Court Welfare Officers. FCWOs write reports for the Court on the welfare of children where the residence and contact arrangements of the children are contested between the parents. These reports are usually decisive. In 1996 NAPO issued an 'Equal Rights/Anti-sexism' document which states its 'policy objective and targets' for the Family Court System as follows:

a   To develop and promote policies and strategies which strengthen and enhance the ability of women to make and carry out choices within separating families.

b   To develop and implement policies and strategies which challenge the experience of oppression of women in separating families.

c   To support the rights of lesbians as mothers and carers.

d   To develop policies and strategies which challenge the discrimination against women in contested residence and contact decisions.....

Such statements arise out of - as well as seeking to extend - society's attitude to parenting roles. They determine the outcome of most contests and virtually all other cases, as those not formally disputed are settled in the shadow of those that are.

I believe that the children of divorce and separation are not best served by segregated gender roles. Rather, one should seek to complement the greater involvement of women in activities outside the home by the greater involvement of men with children. This would be good for mothers, whose choices would be enlarged. It would be good for fathers, who now commonly miss out on the emotionally richest part of life. Above all, it would be good for children who would have more, and more varied stimuli. The group it would be best for would be the children of separation and their parents.

The importance of shared parenting

I want to start with the statement by Penelope Leach, whose writings guided my own childcare.

> *...research studies reveal, and common sense confirms, that children thrive in any kind of family where there is consistent love and nurture, support and discipline, and in no kind of family where those qualities are missing.*(Hewitt & Leach, 1993)

The important feature of this statement is that it attempts to shift the debate away from legalistic debates about the proper nature of the family and roles within it, to the experience of the children. In the probably mythical golden age of the family the needs of children were met by a full-time mother, older siblings and a female-dominated extended family. Just as this family was probably idealised - the care of a full-time mother had to be shared across more children and with equipment-less housework - the present decline from it is exaggerated. Non-working mothers are not uncommon, and family-centred working mothers now the norm, especially where there are young children. The extended family is still important, even if does not have the immediate face-to-face availability it once had. The greater life expectancy means that we are the golden age of multi-generational families. The three generation family is not as gendered as it was when grandmothers usually did not go out to work and grandfathers worked until they died or shortly before. Both grandparents are likely to be retired and both equally free to be involved. But there is still risk of a parenting deficit compared with an ideal if not with the past.

Unless mothers are to return to domesticity, sharing childcare between the parents is an obvious place to look. Present political moves, driven by Treasury-led pressure to economise on the cost of social security and not by child welfare, are to encourage and maybe later pressurise mothers in 'one parent families' to earn. There are no compensating moves to remedy any parenting deficit, merely promises to develop institutionalised day care. Fathers - many of whom are now unemployed and able to provide care, or who may be available at relevant times because they or their ex work 'unsocial hours' - remain ignored.

An important question however is what happens to this 'consistent love and nurture, support and discipline' if the couple unit splits, to be followed often by further 'family re-organisations' of both parents - with each 're-organisation' likely to be less and less stable the more there are of them?

The need to guarantee continuity in children's relationships with their mother is not disputed, either socially or legally, by the organisation I am active in - *Families Need Fathers*. Rather the debate is about, firstly, the *exclusive* importance of that relationship, either before or after separation of the parents. Secondly, it is about what can be done by way of damage limitation, to ensure continuity during what is often, for the children, a bewildering and distressing series of changes. Unless there is an involved father the parenting deficit, possibly present before separation, is likely to become worse after. Commonly the children lose one of their parents and the other has more problems to cope with herself as well as needing to care for unsettled children.

It is becoming clearer that father substitutes - the new men in the mother's life - are best regarded as a mixed curse. They may partially alleviate economic problems, but bring new ones on the personal/parenting front. Even if there is one 'around' and as 'available' to the children as the natural father was, their position is often highly problematic emotionally. It seems that the 'social performance' of children in 'reconstituted families' (the inaccurate jargon for new partnerships) is, on average, below that in 'single parent' ones, despite the lower incidence of poverty. There may be some positive outcomes here but on balance it is clear that 'reconstitution' is not a reliable substitute for the original parent. Separation is a stressful thing for children and parents, usually combining severe practical, economic and personal stresses. Ideally these can be compensated for by as much involved parenting as possible, and should not aggravated by avoidable loss.

The basis of parental loss or retention lie in what happened before. The less involved a father was in childcare before the breakup, the less likely he is to get, or be able to cope with, shared parenting after. A previously uninvolved father may have internalised a view that his caring role was unimportant or unvalued, or that absence would do no harm to the children. At the simplest level, an uninvolved father might not miss his children. He may be in a network of family and friends which do not see him as having a right or duty to be involved. Indeed, some men are urged (sometimes even, in FNF's experience, by judges in Court) to leave their ex and their children 'to get on with their lives'. This may well be commonest when the mother has re-partnered and has a 'new' family in which the former partner is seem as unsettling. Most fathers resist their new, marginalised status. The exception to this generalisation is that some intensely involved fathers 'cut their losses' totally, often pouring their feelings into becoming devoted step-fathers. This needs researching further, but the hypothesis must be that they opt out because their natural children are allowed so little contact that their father cannot cope with it.

Divorce and separation are distressing and damaging experiences. The practical needs of the children continue; their emotional needs increase. A parent with children living with them has to go on providing for some of these. A parent who does not have to provide a home, or cooking, or clean clothes for school, may find that caring for them is something they in their distress fail to cope with. A father not deeply involved beforehand may not find that his children want his company or to continue seeing him. One with very young children, and no knowledge of their care needs, may feel simply incompetent. Fathers of adolescents heavily involved in peer groups may not feel able to set or enforce boundaries, or cope with the children manipulating his weak position.

A high proportion of the children of separation lose contact totally with one parent.[1] The reasons for this are not fully known, but it is inconceivable that three factors do not play a part - the responsibility for childcare before the split, the social expectations on fathers and mothers, and the attitudes of public authorities and especially the courts.

A father involved domestically before separation may have successfully negotiated shared parenting with his partner. This may have a knock-on effect after separation. She may be less opposed to shared parenting after, because it is nothing new and she accepts it. The reason why shared parenting happened before may still apply

- for example that it makes it easier for the mother to work or have a life not exclusively dominated by domestic and childcare needs.

If there has been shared parenting before, both parents are likely to have overcome external stereotyped gender roles. The most important thing, however, may be a father's better chance of convincing public authorities - particularly Family Court Welfare Officers and Judges - that he ought to be involved and is skilled and willing. However, this probably only improves the odds. These people may not believe his statements about his involvement, particularly if it is denied by his ex. Secondly - and this seems particularly likely to apply to senior judges - they might regard such behaviour as not appropriate for a man. (A Judge still cited as an 'authority' once wrote that against the benefits of contact had to be set 'the repeated disruption of the child's normal life'.) But at least such a father can argue with subjective confidence that he knows what is involved in caring for children and that he can do it, for he has the experience. This is better than the 'traditional' model of how to demonstrate that care will be satisfactory in the 'contact home', which is to have an alternative 'mother'.

Promoting equally shared parenting

If it is decided that shared parenting before separation is desirable for children, to protect them after, what public policy is called for?

Divorce law changes would send relevant signals to parents after, but also before, separation. These might even prevent some families dividing. At present solicitors are mostly able to advise mothers who approach them that if they separate from the children's father they may suffer economically, but that their control over the children will, if anything, be reinforced. If they had to be told that shared arrangements would be necessary, and that they could not expect to expel their ex from the lives of children, some might think harder before pursuing that course.

Thus there should be a presumption of joint childcare arrangements symbolised in a joint residence order. There used to be something of a presumption that 'mother knows best' over contact arrangements. This is still claimed, but is now more likely to be successfully challenged. It ought to be taken for granted that liberal contact is best for the children unless there are reasons otherwise.

This is the law in France where parental loss is much less common than in England and Wales.

The shift in the philosophy of the law - that the welfare of the children is the paramount consideration - should be reflected in actual attitudes and decisions. At present discussions and decisions usually try and broker between *adult* demands, and impose resulting agreement on the children. Instead, attempts should be made to get the parents to behave in ways that will further children's needs.

Contact denial should be made a crime just as its close relative, abduction, already is. Conversely, there should be some way found of penalising those few fathers who really abandon their children. In France they can lose the equivalent of parental responsibility.

Economic and housing arrangements after separation should reflect the need for shared parenting. What commonly happens now is that the father and/or the state has to provide for the needs of the children living with their mother as the first priority. The father can only accommodate and fund their life with him if enough is left. Contact loss appears to be closely related to social class, and the cost must be a factor. Under social security law there is no provision for the cost of contact for fathers on benefit. On the contrary, their income is reduced by a margin below their childless peers, to 'remind them of their responsibility'.[2]

There appears to have been no research into the cost of contact parenting, in contrast to considerable information about residential parenting. Fixed costs may be no less for contact parents than for residential ones - having a house with bedrooms for the children if there is to be 'staying contact' for example - and the common need to have duplicate sets of clothes, toys and equipment. In some cases the only economies may be in food and heat, perhaps offset by high travel costs and the need to fund activities in week-ends and holidays which are more expensive than watching TV between school and bed, which is what many children do in the week. Public provision for the cost of contact parenting - for example in social security, housing, child benefit and child support law - varies from nil to very little.

However, the law governing separation is only a modest factor. It can give the right signals, and help fathers who wish to stay involved with their children, but the barriers to shared parenting are mostly set up long before. The preservation of the family bonds of children of separation depends on removing the barriers to male involvement with children across the board. Right from birth girls are brought up - primarily by women but with the collusion of men - to be concerned about children and families, and boys not to be. This is reinforced in schooling and training, where there is no encouragement for men to do anything child-centred or woman dominated that matches the efforts to help girls shake off traditional gender roles. Cultural images of babies and children still rarely feature men, who are stereotyped as abusers vastly more frequently than the facts justify.

A crucial area is, of course, work. The most determined of parents seeking joint involvement with children will find it difficult to overcome pressures which prioritise maternal care and male earning. Children bring increased costs and increased work. A whole battery of provisions - including of course sexual discrimination in pay and promotion, the low levels of family benefits and lack of day care - induce men to specialise in working harder and longer in paid work to close the financial gap, and women to work harder and longer at home to close the childcare gap. It starts with maternity leave. Leave or pay for longer than it takes the mother to recover her strength is for *the baby* - but only *mothers* can have it. The demands of employers for workers able to work long hours and do other things which people with responsibility for children cannot provide, together with lack of job security, make it hard for a family not to offer one parent to the employer and one to the children.

In sum, the need to preserve *consistent love and nurture, support and discipline* for the children of divorced and separated parents requires *not* a return to sharply gender segregated roles, but more convergence at work and at home. This does not, of course, mean we all have to conform to some sexless, genderless stereotype. It just means that both men and women have to be competent, empowered and autonomous economically *and as parents*. In France again, for all its (modestly) greater gender equality in some respects - including parenting, but emphatically not housework - sexual differences are celebrated and pursued by both men and women with some style.

The Father from Heaven

Rt. Revd. James Jones

The fatherhood of God

If God is the source and the ground of all our being - and to believe this is certainly a matter of faith but not more so than to disbelieve it - then all social institutions and relationships merit theological reflection.

The task of the theologian is to enquire about the nature of God and how his character is or ought to be seen in the created order. The Christian understanding of God is expressed in the doctrine of the Trinity: the Father, the Son and the Holy Spirit are three persons in one community. The relationship is not hierarchal but mutual. Each person of the Trinity affirms the worth of the other. This is the model of a healthy society where members engage in mutual respect and affirmation.

The tools of Christian theology are creation (natural theology), sacred texts (Biblical theology), the person and teachings of Jesus Christ (Christology) and the doctrines of the Church (systematic theology). When it comes to offering a theological perspective on fatherhood we have recourse to all four strands. Theology offers us principles and not practice. For example, there is nothing to tell us whether a father should or should not be present at the birth of his child!

In a society such as Britain where over 750,000 children never see their fathers on a regular basis and where many children have a negative experience of their father, some wonder whether we can continue to call God 'Father' in our prayers and worship.

The most famous prayer of all, known as "The Lord's Prayer" begins with the invocation "Our Father who art in heaven." Should it be abandoned?

Significantly the prayer suggests three features of fatherhood:

1 The father as *provider*. 'Give us this day our daily bread.'

2 The father as *forgiver*. 'Forgive us our trespasses as we forgive those who trespass against us.'

3 The father as *protector*. 'Deliver us from evil.'

People of faith are encouraged in this prayer to experience God as father in these three specific ways. If the fatherhood of God is expressed as provider, forgiver and protector, then it becomes an article of faith and an example to human fathers also to relate to their offspring as provider, forgiver and protector.

Of course, women as mothers also provide for their children, forgive them and protect them. Indeed, in some households the mother may earn considerably more than the father and be the chief breadwinner. But that would be to focus it too narrowly, for parental provision extends beyond the material to embrace other dimensions including the emotional. What the model of fatherhood expressed in the Lord's Prayer is suggesting is not that the father alone delivers these things for his children's sake, but that he assumes responsibility for their provision.

Long before the Child Support Agency came along, here was a theological principle being declared in the world's most popular prayer that fathers had a calling to provide for, forgive and protect the children they had sired.

God as an example to man

We have to remember that in the biblical culture the attitude to children was more positive and the bond between parents and their offspring stronger than it is today, for the simple reason that in the absence of a welfare state, children were the parents' walking medical insurance policy and old age pension. If anything happened to the parents it was the child's responsibility to cover these. Parents had a vested interest in caring for their children.

Our culture is vastly different because social mobility, economic forces and the tax and benefit system permit the loosening of the familial bonds. This may be a relief to some. Yet recent reports from the Audit Commission and NACRO make it abundantly clear that children brought up in stable families and loving relationships adjust better and become more integrated into society.

Young men abandoned by their fathers are not only denied a role model but are often robbed of seeing at close quarters how a man might relate to a woman emotionally. Such young men become vulnerable to less socially constructive models where physicality and brutish attitudes to women become the tokens of manhood.

The theological model of fatherhood where the man provides for, forgives and protects his children appeals to intellectual, emotional and physical attributes. The father is required to think how that provision for the physical, emotional and spiritual needs of the child is to be met. This is an exercise of the intellect.

The father is called to relate emotionally to his child, to forgive (and in my case, at least, to say sorry as often); the restoring of relationships invariably operates at the level of our feelings. Only a person in touch with his own emotions can find the wherewithal to forgive and to seek forgiveness.

The father is called to protect, which engages both wit and at times physical strength. The physical energy evident in alienated young men is often directed in anger and frustration against authority and even self. It has a destructive power. The image suggested in the Lord's Prayer is of this natural masculine strength being channeled into the protection of the vulnerable child.

In and through an encounter with the person and teaching of the strong and sensitive Jesus Christ, Christians experience the fatherhood of God as embodying the three features of provider, forgiver and protector. Here we come face to face with the divine model of the Good Father, the Father of all fathers, the *Father from Heaven.*

Interestingly, the other person of the Trinity, namely the Spirit, is in the Hebrew language of the Old Testament a feminine word. But that is the subject of another article.

Patterns of Change in Gender-Role Attitudes[1]

Jacqueline Scott

Discussion about gender-role attitudes is all too often limited to the way women's roles in both family life and public life are changing, as if the roles of men are not subject to change. In part, this reflects social reality, as women's roles have been changing in a more spectacular fashion than have those of men. It is not so long ago, after all, that it was safe to predict that when a girl reached adulthood she would be a wife and mother. Her identity and her energies would be devoted to family life. A boy, on the other hand, was just as likely to become a husband and father, but his predominant role was seen as breadwinner and his identity would be closely bound to his job. Public and private sectors were separate with role specialisation along gender lines. Now however changes in employment and family life and the way they intersect at different points in the lifecourse have brought the traditional gender-role division into question.

In this chapter I will discuss the way in which changing gender-roles interlink with changes in family life and employment. I will also present evidence from attitudinal surveys concerning how changes in gender-role attitudes differ by gender and generation and how British attitudes compare with those of the United States and other Western industrial nations. Is Britain at the forefront of change, or is it dragging its heels compared with other European nations and with the United States? There are important political and institutional differences between countries in their approaches to easing the tensions between work and family life. Both Britain and the United States, in so far as they have any policy response, tend to leave individuals to work out their own solutions.

Thus the pro-family rhetoric that was part of the 1980s Reagan and Thatcher administrations did little in policy terms to promote the economic welfare of traditional families (Abbott and Wallace, 1992). This contrasts markedly with the former West Germany, where there was a quite strong tax disincentive for two-earner couples and where the implicit objective of policy is to support mothers staying home to care for young children (Alwin *et al*, 1992; Braun *et al*, 1994). In Ireland, there is very limited public provision of childcare for working parents and the rate of labour force participation for mothers is relatively low compared with Britain (Hantrais and Letablier, 1996). In the Netherlands, the labour force participation of mothers is increasing and the traditional division of labour is still prevalent, but there have been some moves in a more egalitarian direction with, for example, introduction in 1991 of parental leave of up to six months for either partner (Ditch *et al*, 1995).

I will conclude with a discussion of the way attitudes (and behaviour) might be encouraged to change in the future. Much of the gender-role debate hinges around issues of choice and equality. The right of women to participate in the labour force is widely acknowledged and concerns are focused on insuring that women have equal employment rights as compared to men. Yet perhaps emphasis on equality has been at the cost of ignoring choice. What happens if women choose to prioritise child-rearing over work and want a traditional gender-division of household labour? Are the interests of women inherently at odds with the interests of children and the family? It is often questioned whether a woman with a husband and small children can hold a full-time job and be a good home-maker at the same time. The same question is not posed for men. There is a clear double standard of parenthood.

The State can respond in different ways to this. Gender-blind policies seem doomed to fail if, in part, the objective is to tackle inequities of the status quo. The neo-conservative approach advocates policies which are moulded to the traditional roles of the sexes.

A more radical approach advocates policies designed to alter the skills preferences and expectations of men. Yet, although public opinion is clearly moving in a more egalitarian direction with respect to gender-role ideology, the evidence presented in this chapter suggests that, without some bold family policy initiatives, the pace of change is likely to be very slow.

Changing employment and family context

Over the last few decades there has been a marked increase of married women and mothers in paid employment. Changes in the domestic division of labour are minimal in comparison, so that women have been depicted as doing a 'double shift' - combining their responsibility for family care with the demands of a paid job.

The conflicts of work and family life have been given considerable media exposure and, as public attention is focused on the negative impact that women's employment may have on children, there may have been a backlash in the public's support for more egalitarian family roles. Economic recession and, in particular, rising levels of male unemployment may bolster approval for a more traditional division of gender-roles, with the man earning the money and the woman looking after the home. On the other hand recession may have made dual incomes necessary for households to maintain a reasonable standard of living, maintaining support in Britain for the two-job family. Of course many families, especially lone parent families, lack even one wage earner and new welfare-to-work policy initiatives bring debates about the compatibility of parenting and employment into sharp focus. Parenting, in this context, is rarely gender neutral - it is *women's* employment and its compatibility with motherhood that is at issue.

Women's employment activity has changed dramatically in recent decades throughout the industrial western world. Yet the pace of change and the importance of part-time work has varied considerably within different national contexts. In Britain, women's participation in full-time employment rose quite slowly over the past four decades (from about 30% of women in 1951 to 34% in 1991). In the same period part-time work quintupled (from 5% in 1951 to 26% in 1991). Part-time work can allow women to combine labour-force participation and family responsibilities, with women maintaining primary responsibility for the home and children, while at the same time contributing to the family income. Whether women choose to work part-time in order to juggle family and work roles, or whether lack of child-care alternatives leave them with no choice, is something that is far from clear. What is clear, however, is that part-time work has considerable disadvantages for women in terms of poor rates of pay and loss of promotion prospects (see Dex,

1988). The prevalence of women in part-time work also exacerbates the ongoing gender segregation of the work-force. To understand the significance of changes in labour-force participation for women's role in the family, women's employment patterns must be placed in the context of the family life-cycle. Prior to World War Two, a woman's labour-force career tended to end at marriage. Since the war, women's employment more usually continues through to the birth of the first child, and then the gap in women's employment is often only temporary. Mothers are returning to work sooner, and an increasing proportion of mothers of pre-school age children are taking on the dual burdens of child-rearing and paid work.

Women's employment behaviour has changed markedly, but have attitudes kept in line with these behavioural changes? Clearly attitudes and behaviour are linked, although it is almost never possible to determine to what extent one might be the cause of the other. Certainly, to the extent that women's employment is a matter for choice, it is reasonable to assume that attitudes will influence labour-force participation. At the same time, employment experience may well change people's beliefs about the compatibility of employment and family life. More important, perhaps, is that people's own attitudes and the attitudes of their immediate family members help determine whether work and family goals are viewed as compatible. If people feel that employment is incompatible with being a 'good mother', then mothers who work are likely to feel considerable role-conflict and strain (Scott and Duncombe, 1992). Moreover the general climate of public opinion provides a standard against which the acceptability of changing gender-role behaviour is judged. Shifts in public attitudes can undoubtedly facilitate as well as reflect social change.

Changing ideas about work and family life

In this section I use evidence from nationally representative surveys to answer four questions:

1   To what extent have gender-role attitudes changed over recent periods? Has there been a backlash against more egalitarian gender-roles?
2   Has the change been uniform, or have gender-role attitudes changed in some areas, but not others?

3 How far do men and women have different gender-role attitudes?

4 Have changes been consistent across national contexts, where the social conditions for combining work and family life are very different?

Three types of gender related beliefs and attitudes can be distinguished: First, beliefs about *gender ideology,* or attitudes towards traditional gender-roles; second, beliefs about the *consequences of women's employment* to the family and children; and third beliefs about the importance or *economic necessity of women working.*

Attitude changes in Great Britain, 1983-1994

In the British Social Attitudes survey, questions about gender-role ideology have been posed since the early 1980s. As can be seen from Table 1, the belief that a "husband's job is to earn the money, while a wife's job is to look after the home and family" is increasingly rejected. For women, but not for men, the attitudes are traced back to 1980 when the same item was carried in the Women and Employment survey. Women are more rejecting of the traditional gender-role ideology than men, which is hardly surprising given the relative economic and psychological advantages men and women reap from the traditional division of labour. But what is more interesting, is that the gap between women who are employed (which includes those who work part-time) and those who are not employed, is substantially larger than the gap between women and men.

TABLE 1 Rejection of traditional gender-roles in Britain

Percentages *disagreeing* with the statement: *A husband's job is to earn the money; a wife's job is to look after the home and the children.*

Year	1980	1984	1987	1989	1991	1994
Men		34	28	46	42	57
Women	33	41	36	58	48	61
Employed women	37	59	55	78	66	77

Regarding consequences of a woman's employment, there is an interesting gender difference, as can be seen in Table 2. Men and women's attitudes differ markedly when it comes to items that tap the possible negative consequences for family life and pre-school children in particular.

Men are far more likely to reject the statement that family life suffers if the woman has a job (52%) than they are to deny that the pre-school child is likely to suffer (38%). In contrast, women are fairly evenly split for both items. Thus while men are changing in an egalitarian direction overall, they remain considerably more traditional than women in endorsing the view that children may suffer if the mother works (p < .01).

TABLE 2   Ideas about effects of women's employment

Percentages *disagreeing* that women's employment has negative consequences for family life and children*

	1989			1994		
Disagree that:	Men	Women	Employed women	Men	Women	Employed women
child suffers	29	41	51	38	48	57
family suffers	38	43	54	52	51	60

* With statements:- *A pre-school child is likely to suffer if his or her mother works.*
    All in all family life suffers if the women has a full-time job.

Attitudes concerning the importance of work (both in terms of economic necessity and as a source of independence for women) have been converging with gender ideology over time. Support for the importance of women's labour-force participation has remained relatively steady on a high level since the early 1980s, while gender-role ideology has become more egalitarian. There has been a slight decline over the decade in belief that having a job is the best way for a woman to be an independent person and, by 1994, there is little difference between support for a job as a means to independence and belief that both the husband and wife should contribute to the household income. For both items, about 60% of both men and women agree that women having a paid job can be beneficial. In all, there has been a slow but clear shift in support of women's labour force participation in Britain. Nevertheless, the majority of both men and women are still uneasy about the conflicts that can occur between employment and childcare.

Attitude changes in United States, 1977-1994

In the American General Social Survey, measures of gender-role attitudes have been included since 1977. There have been substantial changes in the last two decades among both men and women, as can be seen in Table 3. Women have, in the main, led the way in the development of egalitarian attitudes over this period and are far more supportive than men of women working.

TABLE 3   Rejection of traditional gender-roles in US

Percentage responses to propositions*, by year.

Men \Yr.	'77	'85	'86	'88	'89	'90	'91	'93	'94
FEFAM	31	49	52	54	57	57	58	61	62
FEHELP	47	63	66	66	73	72	72	76	78
FECHLD	42	53	56	55	58	57	59	59	61
FEPRESC	27	37	42	45	45	44	44	51	49

Women	'77	'85	'86	'88	'89	'90	'91	'93	'94
FEFAM	37	53	53	61	61	61	58	66	67
FEHELP	39	62	63	71	71	70	70	77	79
FECHLD	55	67	67	70	68	68	70	73	76
FEPRESC	38	53	54	58	57	56	58	62	63

*FEFAM   It is much better for everyone if the man is the achiever and the women takes care of the home and family. (% disagree)

FEHELP   It is more important for a wife to help her husband's career than to have one herself. (% disagree)

FECHLD   A working mother can establish just as warm and secure a relationship with her children as a mother who does not work. (% agree)

FEPRESC A preschool child is likely to suffer if his or her mother works. (% dusagree)

Men and women do not differ much when it come to assessing whether the wife should place her husband's career above her own, with the majority of both sexes rejecting such blatant male self-interest. However, women are more likely than men to reject the more neutral statement of gender ideology - that the traditional division of labour is in everyone's interests. Men and women also part company when it comes to assessing the potential negative consequences of women's employment for children, with men far less sanguine than women.

Despite the varying levels of support for the different aspects of gender-roles that are at issue, the *trend* has been in the egalitarian direction, both for men and women. But the pace of change has varied for different time periods, with greater change between 1977 and 1985 than between 1985 and 1994. This is true for both women and men on all four items. This suggests that gender-role attitude change in the United States is slowing down.

In America, the revolutionary changes in views of women's roles occurred in the late 1960s and early 1970s. The women's movement vigorously pursued the goal of creating conditions that would allow women, like men, to be economically independent individuals. The defeat of the Equal Rights Amendment at the end of the 1970s, and the rise to public prominence of the moral majority and the New Right, fuelled speculation of a growing public disaffection with the feminist ideals of combining occupational careers and family life (Mason and Lu, 1988). Support for more egalitarian gender-roles has increased more slowly from the mid 1980s onwards. This may well be due, in part, to changing economic conditions. Since 1980 these have made America's middle class particularly vulnerable and ended the previous decade's high levels of upward mobility. While there is no evidence that the recession brought a backlash against women's labour-force participation the shift in support for egalitarian views has slowed down.

What are the sources of change?

Change can be due to two rather different processes. First, change can be due to historical or period effects, for example the marked changes in labour market conditions that helped fuel the fertility decline and the women's movement. People of different ages may change their views because their former values no longer seem appropriate in the present socio-economic circumstances, or perhaps simply because their attitudes have become out of step with social norms. A second source of change is due to the natural process of population replacement, whereby the older (and usually more traditional) generations die out and their place is filled by new (and usually more liberal) ones. Normally, social change occurring through generational replacement is a relatively slow process and is not rapidly reversed, while the process involved in period change may be more revolutionary.

Breaking down British responses to the question "A husband's job is to earn the money; a wife's job is to look after the home and family" by age shows, as expected, that younger age-groups (of both men and women) are far more likely to reject traditional gender-role ideology than older ones. Eighty-three per cent of women (78% of men) aged 18-27 in 1994 support the pro-feminist position and disagree that the husband should earn the money while a wife's job is to look after the home, compared with only 27% of women (21% of men) over the age of 68. The age demarcation is clearer among women than men, and far more marked in 1994 than 1984. In addition, as Table 4 shows, all age-groups have become more egalitarian over time.

TABLE 4   Rejection of traditional gender-roles by age

Percentage *disagreeing* with statement that: *A husband's job is to earn the money, the wife's job is to look after the home and children.*

Group \ Age	18-27	28-37	38-47	48-57	58-67	68 +
Men 1984	48	54	38	25	19	10
Women 1984	59	59	50	37	17	11
Men 1994	78	70	73	46	34	22
Women 1994	83	70	78	50	38	27

Because the survey points are 10 years apart and the age-groups span ten years, it is also possible to compare how any one age-group might respond, ten years on (for example when those who are 18-27 in 1984 reach the age of 28-37 in 1994). In this way we can compare the change going on because of generational replacement with that due to period effects. Using methods of analysis that are reported elsewhere (Scott *et al*, 1996), it is possible to show that both period effects and generational replacement play a role in the overall change in gender-role attitudes between 1984 and 1994. However, in Britain, much of the change is due to generational replacement, a process that suggests that gender-role ideology will be relatively slow to change.

Cross-National Differences: 1988-1994

The International Social Survey Programme has included a module on women and the family in 1988 and 1994. Even with data from such a relatively short time span, very different patterns of change are emerging in the different nations. Tables 5 and 6 show the percentages of the populations in Great Britain, the U.S., West Germany, Ireland, and the Netherlands who disagree that women's

TABLE 5   Women's employment and family life

Percentage *disagreeing* with statement that: *All in all family life suffers if the woman has a full-time job.*

Family life suffers	Britain	USA	West Germany	Nether lands	Irish Republic
1988	41	50	26	34	37
1991	44	48	37	53	46
1994	51	51	24	38	39

employment has negative consequences for family life and who reject the traditional gender-role ideology whereby the husband is the breadwinner and the wife looks after the home and family.

There is a greater similarity between countries regarding gender-role ideology than beliefs about the consequences of women working on family life. West Germany is the most traditional of the countries considered here, whereas the Netherlands is the most egalitarian (at least with respect to ideology). However, even in the Netherlands, there has been some reversal in the belief about the compatibility of family life and women's employment. In the United States, while there has been a slight shift towards a more egalitarian

TABLE 6   Rejection of traditional gender role ideology

Percentage *disagreeing* with statement that: *A husband's job is to earn the money, the wife's job is to look after the home & children.*

Reject trad. roles	Britain	USA	West Germany	Nether lands	Irish Republic
1988	53	52	36	55	46
1991	45	49	48	66	54
1994	59	59	48	65	53

stance with regards gender ideology, beliefs about the consequences of female employment on family life have remained stable. British attitudes too lean overall more towards the egalitarian than the traditional, in comparison with other countries, but the change is somewhat uneven and not very great.

At the outset, I suggested that gender-roles are often discussed only in terms of women's roles. What are public perceptions of the negative consequences of family life of men being too preoccupied with their jobs? In Table 7 we can see that there is a surprising degree of agreement between the sexes that family life suffers because men concentrate too much on their jobs.

TABLE 7   Negative effect of men's work on family life

Percentage *agreeing* with statement that: *Family life often suffers because men concentrate too much on their work.*

	Men	Women
Britain	62	58
USA	62	57
West Germany	67	64
East Germany	58	55
Netherlands	59	61
Irish Republic	75	76
Norway	69	69
Sweden	50	42
Poland	63	71

Sweden stands out as being the one country where the majority do not concur that men's work is a particular problem. This may reflect, in part, the success of their policy of gender-equality - which introduced parental leave in 1974 and a radical extension of the day care system - in changing behaviour. Yet even in Sweden women's involvement in jobs is clearly shaped by family factors in a way that men's jobs are not (Hoem, 1995).

Discussion and policy prescriptions

Although trend data are somewhat limited in Britain, there is little reason to suppose that the British have changed much in the last decade in their opinions on the importance of women working. Moreover, the evidence does suggest that the ideology surrounding traditional gender-roles is increasingly rejected, even though there is evidence that the pace of change has slowed in the 1990s. There is, however, no evidence to suggest an anti-feminist backlash, although a majority of both men and women are still concerned that maternal employment can cause real difficulties for children.

On the question of difference between men and women, the latter have been much more prepared than men to reject traditional gender-role attitudes. Interestingly, while women draw little distinction between the negative effects of women's employment on family life and on pre-school children, men clearly differentiate between the two and are far more likely to concur that children might suffer if the mother works. In an age of political correctness, opposing gender egalitarianism in terms of children's needs is presumably more palatable than when done in the name of the needs of the family - which includes the husband.

The most distinctive feature of gender-role attitude change in Britain when compared with the United States is the *slow rate* of change, particularly among women. This may relate to the way women juggle home and work responsibilities. The relatively high amount of part-time work in Britain allows married women to contribute to the household income and gain some economic independence, while not posing any fundamental challenge to the traditional division of roles that reaffirm gendered identities (Fenstermaker *et al*, 1991).

Overall, in countries as diverse as Britain, the United States,

West Germany, the Netherlands and the Irish Republic, the public is far more willing to reject traditional gender-role ideology than to endorse the view that women's employment is compatible with family life. In the United States and Britain, at least, it is clear that the main concern is with childcare. Is such concern a convenient way of preserving traditional gender-roles by asserting that the interests of women are inherently at odds with the interests of children or the family? If women, who are usually the primary home-maker, are committing more of their energies to employment, then there is going to be a reduction in time available for home-making and child-care tasks, unless partners take up the slack. While time-budget studies show that men do more in the home than previous generations, there is no evidence that their role-shift is commensurate with that of women. Indeed, in a wide range of countries, the public clearly feels that family life suffers because of the priority men give to their jobs.

This is a topic where feelings run deep and evidence can be used to uphold different policy alternatives. Catherine Hakim, in her chapter, argues that research has proved wrong the belief that modern women reject the role of full-time home-maker and are kept out of work by discrimination. She suggests that national surveys across the world demonstrate that many women, often the majority, actively seek and accept this role (see also Hakim, 1995, and Ginn *et al,* 1996). I do not dispute Hakim's portrayal of the evidence, nor do I dispute the contention that policies which expect everyone to work full-time in the paid waged sector are hardly conducive to freedom of choice. However, it is difficult to discuss choice when society tends to operate on a double standard that expects quite different commitments from men and women towards family life and children. It is also important to acknowledge the way choice is constrained by men's greater power in families and by gendered opportunity-structures outside the home.

The fact that men usually prioritise paid employment while women take time off for child-rearing is often explained by men's capacity to earn more than women. However, this reasoning is clearly circular as part of the reason why women earn less is that they are concentrated in poorly paid part-time jobs that allow them to juggle family and employment responsibilities. Gender segregation cannot be explained wholly by human capital differences between men and women. Clearly discrimination does play a part and it is sustained by a double standard of parenthood (Presser, 1995).

Men typically can choose their preference and, not surprisingly, they generally do not want to do day-to-day childrearing tasks. This is not only because they are unpaid and unrewarded by society at large, but also because they do not want their lives to be constrained to the extent that child-rearing entails. Why should we expect men to volunteer to give up work time for the needs of children? Of course being with children is enjoyable. Playing with children can be fun. Even talking to sullen teenagers can be rewarding sometimes. But caring for offspring day in and day out is a burden for even the most devoted of parents. As children grow they find parents an intolerable constraint. What parent could deny that the feeling is sometimes reciprocated? Surely, where possible, the benefits of parenting (and the benefits reaped by children) are likely to be enhanced if parenting is more evenly shared. The omission of reference to men's childrearing potential in policy discussions is related to a strongly gendered notion of parenthood that is socially constructed rather than biologically necessary.

Increasing women's real choice

It is the double standard of parenthood that policy discussion and future research needs to tackle. We need to consider how societies can best be organised to minimise gender differences in caregiving while adequately serving the needs and interests of children. We need to develop policy alternatives that will actively encourage fathers to participate more in child-rearing when mothers are employed. There is also much that we do not know concerning the practice and implications of equitable parenting. Do men suffer long-term economic costs when they assume equal responsibility with employed partners in the day-to-day activities of child rearing? What are the benefits of greater equity in employment and family responsibilities, for men, women and children? At present, the policy debates tend to focus on easing the parental burden by encouraging more flexible employment practices or increasing non-parental childcare arrangements. Such steps are certainly welcome in that they can ease the employed mother's burden, but they serve to maintain the status quo and do nothing to reduce the double standard of parenthood.

At present women are often faced with the choice between providing a secure, nurturing environment for their children and their own economic security and self-fulfilment. Some women clearly regard full-time parenting as sufficiently fulfilling to risk their economic security - and that of their children - by remaining fully dependent economically on men. An increasing number of others have decided otherwise, both within and outside of marriage. It is unusual for men to have to face such a choice. Clearly many men regret their relative lack of involvement in family life and childrearing. Perhaps, as employment becomes more varied and jobs for life increasingly rare, men may begin to see some advantage in life-trajectories that can incorporate different mixes of full and part-time work and provide a greater balance between expressive and instrumental activities.

Yet if we wait for such change to happen through the slow shift in gender-role attitudes, we will wait far too long. There is an urgent need to tackle the double standards of parenthood that exacerbate the conflicts faced by employed mothers. Gender-roles need to become more egalitarian both in principle and practice. Women should be able to achieve economic security and self-fulfilment without endangering the secure and nurturing environment that children need. The future well-being of society depends on it.

Sexual Divisions and the Distribution of Work in the Household

Jonathan Gershuny

Introduction

Men and women do different things in their daily lives. Men do more paid work, women more unpaid. Both have leisure time in roughly equal proportions, so the differential work pattern is what distinguishes them from day to day. We know a lot about the paid part of this work from official statistics and social surveys, but traditionally the unpaid part is ignored in the official statistics and largely absent from the surveys. This is because of the high status of paid work, which derives from the important role of 'production' in establishing peoples' social status, class identifications, and in the broadest sense, their life-chances. And it is also because of the low status of unpaid work - which in turn reflects precisely the fact that this was in the past unambiguously 'women's' work.

The statistically invisible unpaid work activities of daily life have great importance. In the short term they raise an issue of gender inequity or unfairness. Women increase their participation in paid work while maintaining their domestic responsibilities and thus acquire a 'dual burden'. Or alternatively they restrict their work to the home, and thus lose direct access to the economic sources of status and power. And since in the longer term the accumulated experience of paid work has itself an economic value in terms of potential future earnings, this dual burden, insofar as it leads either to shorter paid work hours, or to a withdrawal from the labour force altogether, means a progressive depletion of women's personal resources ('human capital') relative to men's.

It is plain that societies' views about women's role in the workplace have changed. For example, the table from Scott, Braun and Alwin cited by Hakim in her chapter in this book shows a dramatic growth of public approval for women in the workforce throughout the 1970s and 1980s (Shirley Dex has documented something similar for the UK from the 1940s to the 1980s). It is safe to conclude that, matching the (re)entry of women into the workplace throughout the OECD nations, there has been a shift in opinions of seismic proportions in attitudes to women's paid work roles.

The purpose of this piece is twofold. *First* to show that changes in actual *behaviour*, though in the same direction of increasing gender symmetry, have been rather incomplete, and *second* to suggest some reasons why this has been the case.

Overall time-use patterns

Across the developed world, the second half of the century has seen a very considerable growth in the presence of women in the paid labour force. We are accustomed to seeing evidence of women's presence in the labour market in terms of the proportion of women with jobs. We know that throughout the OECD, women's participation in paid work has been rising since the 1960s (though in Britain latterly much of the growth in women's employment has been in part-time, insecure and intermittent jobs).

The growth in women's employment means that the mid-century male-breadwinner/housewife pattern is no longer the dominant pattern for British households. Table 1, based on the British House-

TABLE 1 Spouses' joint employment status
(Percentages)

	1991	1995
Wife >empl than husband	9	10
Wife ft, husband ft	28	27
Wife pt, husband ft	21	21
Wife ne, husband ft	18	15
Wife pt, husband ft	1	1
Wife ne, husband ne	24	27

hold Panel Survey, gives the distributions of spouses' joint employment patterns from waves one and five of this nationally representative survey. It shows that the more traditional combination of full-time-employed husband with non- or at the most part-time employed wife is still declining (from 39% to 36% of couples in the BHPS over this period), while those couples who both have full-time jobs, or in which the wife is more fully employed than the husband, constitute 37% of the total. (Throughout what follows, 'non-employment' is used inclusively to mean both unemployment and absence from the labour force.) Does this mean that gender symmetry in formal employment status, of the sort foreseen by Michael Young and Peter Wilmott in *The Symmetrical Family* (1974), is emerging as the new norm?

Are we approaching the position in which the economic opportunities of men and women have converged? When we look more widely at husbands' and wives' work overall - ie including unpaid as well as paid work - it emerges that this is not in fact the case. We discover, or rather *rediscover*, since this is found regularly wherever we look in Europe and North America, that the growing resemblance between husbands' and wives' work lives is only superficial. Wives may be working in full-time jobs, but they still maintain a disproportionate responsibility for the unpaid work in the home. Wherever we look we see the same rather sad statistics. Full-time employed women continue to carry a 'dual burden': their husbands have, in effect, one job where they have two.

One view of the UK position, drawn from the paid and unpaid working hours questions in the BHPS, is set out as Table 2. (I should mention at this point that the BHPS, as does the Government Labour Force Survey, asks respondents to estimate their total work hours, and it uses the same questionnaire-based estimate technique for domestic work time. The results are less reliable than those from the 'time diary'-based techniques such as those used by Young and Willmott, which we will discuss in the next section - but the BHPS for the moment provides the most reliable nationally representative picture of the gender distribution of the total of paid plus unpaid work.)

The results do not on the face of it seem too extremely unfair - after all, the total hours of paid and unpaid work for full time employed women are only slightly longer than for their similarly employed husbands. But consider: the women in apparently full-time jobs are actually working much shorter hours in those jobs than their husbands, and are (on average slightly more than) compensating for this by doing unpaid work at home. Their differential responsibility for housework (and also childcare and shopping, not included in the BHPS housework total) means that they have less time (and presumably attention) for their paid work than their husbands do. And this, combined with the fact that the wives are much more likely to take time out of their paid jobs for childcare and to cope with family crises, may go some way to explain why women still do markedly worse than men in terms of pay and promotions.

TABLE 2   The dual burden 1995, Version 1

	Work hours per week					
	Husband's work hrs			Wife's work hours		
	paid+ travel	house work	total p/wk	paid+ travel	house work	total p/wk
Wife> employed than husband	3	10	13	31	16	46
Wife ft, husband ft	50	5	56	43	14	57
Wife pt, husbnd ft	50	4	54	20	22	41
Wife ne, husbnd ft	50	4	54	1	26	27
Wife pt, husbnd pt	18	5	24	15	17	32
Wife ne, husbnd ne	0	9	9	0	23	23

This implies that the 'full-time/part-time' categorisation is somewhat uninformative when it comes to estimating work burdens. It appears that these words mean different things for men and women: contrast the average 50 hours per week of full-time husbands work-plus-commuting with the average 43 hours-per-week for wives. The meaning of the standard employment status classification differs between the sexes. So instead of the spouses' joint employment statuses, consider the classification scheme used in Table 3, which looks directly at the *paid work-time balance* between the husbands

TABLE 3 Spouses' paid work time balance
(Percentages)

	1991	1995
Wife > than husband	12	13
Wife approx = husband	10	11
Husband 5-20hrs> wife	14	14
Husband 20-40hrs> wife	16	15
Husband 40+hrs> wife	24	21
Neither has any	24	26

and wives. Once we look at the *actual hours* worked in paid jobs we realise that, despite the quite large number of wives in nominal full-time work, in fact fewer than one quarter of all wives spend as much time in paid work as their husbands do, while around one half of all husbands spend substantially longer working at their jobs than their wives do.

TABLE 4 The dual burden 1995

	Work hours per week					
	Husband's work hrs			Wife's work hours		
	paid+ travel	house work	total p/wk	paid+ travel	house work	total p/wk
Paid work time balance						
Wife> husband	12	9	21	37	15	51
Wife approx = husb	43	6	49	42	14	56
Husb 5-20hrs> wife	47	5	52	35	16	51
Husb 20-40hrs>wife	52	4	56	24	21	44
Husb 40+hrs> wife	52	4	56	5	25	30
Neither in empl	0	9	9	0	23	23

Now (see Table 4) the real weight of the wives' dual burden becomes apparent. Relatively few wives work as many hours in their jobs as their husbands do. The most straightforward interpretation of this table is that the full-time-employed wives' continuing differential responsibility for the home as well as the job acts as a constraint on their paid work. They work shorter hours, we might infer from Table 4, in part at least, *because of* their extra unpaid work. And in the relatively rare couples where the wives' *paid* work time is approximately the same as their husbands', **their total work week including unpaid housework is some nine hours longer than their husbands'.**

Changes within couples over time

One explanation for the dual burden phenomenon is simple gender politics. There are issues of power, deeply embedded and central to the way men and women relate to each other. Not just in the developed world, but also in less developed societies studied by anthropologists, men always appear in the dominant economic positions. Indeed, the dual burden evidence identified one of the crucial mechanisms that might maintain this. Through our careers we build up work experience and evidence of effective performance, which let us get better jobs: in this context wives lose out twice over.

On one hand, if it is the wives who must go home and cook and clean (and leave work early if the child is sick) they have less time and energy to devote to their paid jobs, and appear *less* dedicated to their employers. On the other, the husbands have wives to do these things for them, and appear *more* dedicated to their employers. It is not so much the glass ceilings that hold the employed wives down, as the dirty floors in their *other* jobs.

However the more recent work of sociologists such as Arlie Hochschild (1990) suggests another and perhaps ultimately less pessimistic view.

We learn how to be husbands and wives from our parents. We may expect - not consciously, but in a deep and unconsidered way - that our wives and husbands, and that we *as* wives and husbands, should in turn resemble them, despite the fact that the material circumstances in our present lives may be quite different.

Consciously we husbands may recognise that our high-powered wives ought to be able to expect something different from their husbands, but, in the unconsidered practices of daily life this recognition doesn't really get made effective.

The results of this are manifestly unfair. Some wives put up with it, and perhaps give up their jobs. Others may give up their husbands instead. Yet others persuade their husbands to improve their behaviour to some degree. And wives also adjust and lower their housework standards, despite the fact that this may challenge their received views of wifely responsibilities.

We are socialised as children: as adults we are partially *re*socialised. The gender ideologies that we develop in our households of origin are challenged and modified in our marital homes. And our children are as a result and to a limited degree differently socialised.

This second view suggests that there should be some progress in the direction of gender equity. The effects of this process will be gradual. Women enter employment. The contradictions emerge. There is a lag, then things start slowly to change. They do so over decades, generations But however slow, we can already see some evidence of this gradual shift.

TABLE 5 Hours of paid and unpaid work per week.
Husband and wife both employed full time (controlling for family size)

	1974/5		1997	
	Husb.d	Wife	Husb.d	Wife
Paid work	45	36	41	33
Unpaid work	12	25	15	24
All work	57	61	56	57
wife's % of unpaid work		68		62
wife's % of all work		52		50

Table 5 is based on time diary surveys in which couples record exactly what they are doing continuously through a whole week.

These diary-based studies are much more burdensome for respondents than the 'estimate' questions discussed in the previous section, and for this reason such surveys are difficult to find, and often on a smaller scale than the more straightforward questionnaire surveys. Nevertheless they do in principle provide more reliable estimates of time use. The 1974/5 data used here come from a national diary survey carried out by the BBC Audience Research Department (including approximately 1200 couples); the 1997 data come from a special diary-based study of the BHPS pilot sample (a small national sample including approximately 350 couples).

Table 5 suggests that actual hours worked for pay in two-full-time-job couples have declined somewhat between 1975 and 1997. (This is not what we would expect from the official questionnaire-based work-time statistics - but there is evidence that these sources substantially overestimate the paid work time of people working above 40 hours per week: Gershuny and Robinson 1994) However, what is important in the table is that it places the change in unpaid work time (here including, as well as cooking and cleaning, also 'odd-jobs', shopping and childcare) alongside the changes in paid work time. In 1997 the husbands do rather more unpaid work during the week than in 1975, the wives a little less.

TABLE 6 Wife's % of domestic work time
By couples' joint employment status (controlling for family status)

	1974	1997
Both ft	68	62
Husband ft, wife pt	78	64
Husband ft, wife ne	81	72

Table 6 shows the same process of slow convergence also applies to couples with a more traditional distribution of jobs. Where the husband is full-time employed and the wife part-time or non-employed, the 'reacting to unfairness' mechanism that works in the two full-time job couples is unlikely to operate. But there is another process, a sociological snowball effect. The effect of more and more men being seen to take serious responsibility for domestic tasks, is to make it, statistically speaking, normal. Our views of what we should do to be husbands and wives reflect, not just our childhood socialisation and our private domestic arguments, but also what we see in other peoples' lives. The statistical fact that more men are doing housework, as it becomes more widely known, is in effect a normative sanction for *more* husbands to do more (and for more wives to allow themselves to do less).

Individual level change

So far we have just considered change at the aggregate level. We see that on average over recent decades, couples' distribution of unpaid work becomes somewhat less unequal. The pessimistic interpretation of this evidence is that it shows no more than a 'cohort effect' - the consequence of younger, less unliberated men succeeding older generations with more gender-segregated views of work responsibilities. But the reality may be a little more promising.

We can now adduce some evidence of change at the individual level. The BHPS looks at the behaviour of the same people in successive years. So we can use it to examine what happens to the distribution of domestic work as the couple's employment situation changes. Table 7 takes successive pairs of years, and looks at the effects of husbands' and wives' movements into and out of the labour force on changes in the amount and distribution of housework. (It derives from a straightforward linear regression, but the coefficients are translated into 'effect parameters'.) So the first row shows that over this period, men's housework time increased overall by just one tenth of an hour per week per year, while women's housework declined by about three-tenths of an hour per week per year.

However, if the wife moved from non-employment to employment in the course of the year (line 7), her housework time will have declined by an average of 7 hours per week, while her husband will have increased his housework by 2.4 hours per week to partially compensate for this; and the woman's proportion of the couple's total housework declines by about 10%. If the husband moves out of employment altogether, his housework increases by nearly 5 hours per week, while the wife's decreases by nearly 3 hours per week and her housework proportion declines by 13%.

TABLE 7 Cross wave annual change in weekly domestic workhours and women's proportion of couples' housework time.

MCA effect parameters: BHPS waves 2-4 (1993-1994)
(Controlling for respondents' ages and age of youngest coresident child)

	Women's % of housework	Men's housework hours	Women's housework hours	N cases
Grand Mean	-1%	.1	-.3	5599
Wives' year-on-year employment change				
1 Ft to ft	0%**	-.2*	-.2	1530
2 Ft to pt	3%	-.4	1.9	140
3 Pt to ne	**9%****	**-.5**	**6.8 ****	139
4 Pt to ft	-3%*	.1	-1.3*	148
5 Pt tp pt	-1%	.0	-.3	1290
6 Pt to ne	5%	-.7	2.8	199
7 Ne to ft	**-10%***	**2.4**	**-7.0****	68
8 Ne to pt	-2%	-.0	-3.8	251
9 Ne to ne (ref)	0%	.2	-.3	1834
Husbands' year-on-year employment change				
11 Ft to ft	0%*	.1	.3	2804
13 Ft to ne	**-13%****	**4.8 ****	**-2.7 ****	139
15 Other	0%	-.0	.1	1128
17 Ne to ft	**10%****	**-3.7 ****	**.4**	88
19 Ne to ne (ref)	0%	-.5	-.4	1440

* significant at .05   ** significant at.005

Notice particularly the four rows in bold type in Table 7. The effect of the wife's movement backwards and forwards between full time and non-employment (rows 3 and 7) on her unpaid work time are pretty much symmetrical, about seven hours per week in each direction. But the effect on the husband is asymmetrical; he increases his housework by about two and a half hours per week when she takes on a full-time job, but only decreases his housework by about half an hour when she makes the move out of employment. And similarly for the husbands' employment change (rows 13 and 17): he increases housework by 5 hours when he quits a full-time job, and decreases it by 4 hours when he takes on a fulltime job; she by contrast decreases her housework by approaching three hours when he quits the job, but increases her housework by less than half an hour per week when he takes on a full-time job.

This is a clear ratchet effect. The consequence of changes in a couple's joint employment status is overall that he learns from his experience of her employment to do more housework, and she learns from her experience of his non-employment to do less housework.

Decreasing gender polarisation

The changes we have been discussing are small ones. Women still do the bulk of all unpaid work. And women who choose to work as long at their jobs as their husbands do, do substantially more housework than their husbands.

But nevertheless the changes are regular, and small as they are, they are regularly in the direction of increasing gender equality. That equality is still some way off, perhaps, on the basis of the trends we see here, as much as 30 or even 50 years away, perhaps two full generations. And indeed the pluri-generational time scale is, on the basis of the arguments advanced here, inevitable, since children who grow up in households with an unequal division of housework will of necessity incorporate this as part of their own gender ideologies. But we can also see evidence of changes in the direction of gender equality within particular generations, changes that take place within the course of an individual life. So the successive generations grow up in households that are increasingly egalitarian in this respect, and the gender polarisation decreases, slowly, both within and between generations.

These British results are representative of changes across the developed world. Wherever evidence is available over historical time, we find overall that men are increasing their unpaid work and women reducing it. But the process still has a considerable way to go. Full time employed wives with similarly employed husbands are still doing more than three-fifths of their household's domestic work. Even if their total of paid plus unpaid work time is pretty nearly the same as their husbands, still they spend much more of their work time outside the paid labour market. And every week that this happens, their husbands gain a further competitive advantage in the career stakes. So the gaps between men and women in earnings and promotion prospects, which are found in virtually every country, which reflect the extent of lag of change in domestic organisation behind change in the workplace, can be expected to persist for several generations, while men's and women's unpaid work burdens slowly converge.

New Ties to Bind

Rosie Styles

It could be argued that the contract between two adults is never more critical and crucial than when that partnership has produced a child. It doesn't matter whether the partnership has the legal force of a marriage behind it or not. The way in which these two adults now behave - towards their baby, towards each other and towards society as a whole - is the critical factor which will play a vital and far reaching role in the growth and development of that child.

In the past, child rearing was to a certain extent 'protected' by marriage and the extended family. Children need a minimum of sixteen years in which to mature and many need considerably longer before they can truly fend for themselves. The quality of the care they receive during their formative years will go far in determining their capacity to form relationships with others and their ability to function as balanced and responsible adults.

The parents will provide the example from which the child learns about caring, trust, tolerance, generosity of spirit, loyalty and all the other worthy qualities which go towards a binding intimate friendship. Their attitudes towards money, work, the community, the environment and their concepts of right and wrong, will all have an effect upon their child. With the decline of the extended family, many parents these days feel they have no support system to help them bear the load.

Parenting without marriage

Not only is the extended family now a rarity. Marriage has declined dramatically in the last few generations and over a third of all births nowadays are to couples who are not married to each other, though the great majority are cohabiting. An unmarried father has no legal parental responsibilities for his child unless the parents take certain steps and clearly it is in the interests of society that all fathers, married or not, have responsibility for their children.

The family as a unit has become a fragile entity. About 40% of marriages end in divorce, often when the couple still have dependent children. Many adults now spend their lives in a series of families, rather than in just one. While this may suit the adults, those who counsel children during a breakdown of the family describe the suffering and pain of those children as nothing less than bereavement.

The emotional and economic cost of family breakdown is so great that society simply cannot sit by and give up on marriage, or the commitment that a marriage is designed to embody. Given that we cannot turn the tide back, one way forward is to focus on parenting, since it is increasingly detached from marriage.

The formation of the Baby Naming Society[1]

1994 was designated the United Nations International Year of the Family and in preparation for it many organisations planned conferences, seminars, workshops and the like to explore family life in the nineties. There was much talk and lamentation about the loss of traditional values and about ways in which family life had broken down. What seemed in short supply were practical ideas which could be implemented to provide some new support for families; a new way of focusing on parenting and recognising that our children represent society's hopes for the future. Within this framework, Michael Young launched an organisation called the Family Covenant Association. It was one step towards recognising that society needs new ties to bind.

The 'Covenant' had two elements. Firstly, a welcoming or naming ritual for children in which the parents promise to care for the child as it grows to maturity. Secondly, the recommendation that a child's future could be further safeguarded if parents take certain legal actions. These legal actions are important for married parents, but they are of even greater significance if the parents are not married. The word 'covenant' was chosen because it means a binding contract. Sadly, because the title did not explain what the organisation does many people thought it was to do with giving money to families. In September 1995 the name was therefore changed to the Baby Naming Society. The society is a completely independent body with no religious, philosophical or political affiliation whose services are available to any parent or family wishing to celebrate a new child.

The decline of baptism

The idea of incorporating parental commitment into a naming ceremony was timely. The incidence of baptism had been dropping steadily since the turn of the century and quite dramatically since the 1970's. Britain is now a multi-faith society with an increasing number of people marrying outside their ethnic or religious origins. Within this context, even parents who profess a faith often now wish to leave their child free to follow his or her own spiritual path through life. Regular church attendance has declined in many denominations. Within the Church of England, this has given rise to an unwillingness on the part of some clergy to baptise babies simply at the parents' request. Many priests now ask for the parents to attend church and a series of preparation talks, so that they fully understand the significance of baptism. While the Baby Naming Society would never try to persuade anyone away from a baptism, the simple fact is that far fewer than half of all babies now have a proper ritual to welcome them into society.

The need for ritual

Rituals are not just occasions for collective celebration or mourning. They are occasions which re-define our social relationships and which help people to acknowledge what they are taking on. One purpose of a marriage ceremony is to declare to one's friends and family that circumstances have changed; the two people have become a couple and make promises regarding their future together, in front of others who are important in their lives.

Occasions which gather relatives together help to re-knit family solidarity. For some families, especially if they are large families scattered geographically, births, deaths and marriages may be the only times when the whole family congregate, so these rites of passage assume even greater value.

In some ways a child welcoming ceremony is more important than a marriage or funeral. Parenting is the most important task that anyone can be called upon to perform. A ritual which can strengthen the parents' commitment, by making promises of support explicit and public, is surely to be welcomed. A ritual in which *other* adults can promise a network of support, for both the parents and the child, could provide the back-up which so many parents need with their family and relatives often far away.

Many people describe birth as miraculous - a natural occurrence, yes, but nevertheless one which inspires wonder and awe. Those who witness birth are often reduced to tears of overwhelming emotion. Parents often say they want an occasion to reflect upon these emotions and to celebrate the joy which a new child can bring. If the traditional rituals are no longer suitable or appropriate for many, rather than simply lamenting this what we need is an alternative, infinitely flexible and adaptable ritual to fill this gap in society.

The ceremony

Witnessed ritual, with carefully chosen words, can serve to enhance and reinforce relationships and create binding ties. What matters most about a baby naming ceremony is that the parents - and other adults, if desired - enter into a commitment of their own choosing which reflects their own intentions for the child. The fact that the parents choose what to promise enhances their capacity to keep the promise. Making these promises in front of their nearest and dearest is another way of encouraging them to maintain the commitment. In deciding what to promise, parents have to ponder and discuss their hopes and aspirations for their child's future. They have to reflect upon their new-found responsibilities. They have to confront the possibility that the baby is someone whose needs must be put before their own whims or desires.

A very important element in the ceremony is the appointing of other supporting adults in the role of godparents, although a different title might be chosen. It is apparent that parents choose these people with immense care. Taking the opportunity to explain to their guests why they have chosen them, the following phrases have been used; 'for his sensitivity and spiritual depths', 'she lives her faith through her actions and will be both a spiritual and practical guide', 'because he is such a good listener and can often help us to see things from a different and more useful perspective'.

It may be significant that there is no evidence of a cynical choosing of those who might provide the child with financial or worldly 'blessings'. Promises which any 'godparents' might make are not prescribed, so they too have to decide what they can realistically offer to be and do for the child. Therefore these also should be promises which are possible to keep.

In the absence of the extended family and in days when families separate while they still have dependent children, the role of godparents could be of more value than ever. They can provide an extra anchor for stability. They can provide the additional influences and dimensions which would once have been provided by the aunts, uncles and cousins. They can be an ear to turn to, a shoulder to cry on. The fact that they have offered this support in public, must strengthen their ties to the family and make it easier to seek their help when needed.

Another option within the ceremony is for the parents to re-state their marriage vows. Realistically there is no reason to assume that just because a vow has been made twice it will be kept. But the very fact that some couples choose to do this, demonstrates that they realise the importance of sustaining the marriage while the child is developing and has need of both its parents. Those who are not married can use the ceremony to make a declaration of commitment to each other. Again, we cannot assume that such a promise would be kept, but its very making shows that the parents hope they will stay together and are prepared to say so.

Legal actions to safeguard children

A naming ceremony has no legal force, but the Society promotes a series of actions which do have the force of the law behind them and which can help to safeguard the future for children. These are; the writing of a will, appointing legal guardians and, where applicable, the making of a joint parental responsibility agreement.

Writing a will

When we are young, we don't usually like to think about the fact that we might die. However, we read every day of tragedies to young parents. If a married person dies intestate, a spouse will have statutory rights to at least some of the estate. If there are children, the surviving spouse receives the first £125,000 (at 1997 levels) plus Goods & Chattels, plus a lifetime interest only from half of the remaining estate. The rest passes in equal shares to the children. If you are married with a child, the only way in which you can change this is by writing a will.

Unmarried persons have no such entitlement. They need to be particularly aware of their situation, which may not only involve finance, but also the family home. They are definitely in need of a legal 'tie to bind' - albeit in the face of death.

Legal guardians

It is very important that parents appoint guardians rather than leaving it to a court to decide who will care for their children if the parents die. For married couples, a guardian will be needed if both parents die simultaneously, say in a car accident, or if a surviving parent dies while the child is still dependent. For unmarried parents the situation is more complicated.

Some parents mistakenly assume that appointing godparents is sufficient and that these adults will be allowed look after a child if it is orphaned. They will only be able to play this part if they have also a legal role and have been appointed as legal guardians. The simplest way to appoint a legal guardian is in a will, though a solicitor could draw up a Deed of Appointment.

According to the Children Act 1989, only a person with parental responsibility can appoint a guardian. So if a mother and father are not married to each other and have not made the necessary agreement, then it is the mother *alone* who can appoint a guardian. Without a joint parental responsibility agreement an unmarried mother must consider if the father should be appointed as guardian in the event of her death.

Joint parental responsibility agreements

Cohabiting parents can suffer from legal disabilities without knowing about it. Surveys have documented ignorance and misunderstandings. Many unmarried parents seem to think joint responsibility is automatic, or followed if the child took the father's surname, or because the father had registered the birth along with the mother. On all these counts they are wrong. Unless parents take action, an unmarried father has no parental rights - whether the parents are living together or whether they have separated. Unmarried fathers can find themselves denied contact or residence with their children if the parental relationship breaks down.

Parental responsibility is defined as 'all the rights, powers, authority and duties of parents in relation to a child and his property'. This includes determining where the child should live and with whom he should have contact, his education and religious upbringing, travel abroad, consent to medical treatment, appointment of a guardian and rights over the child's property.

For unmarried parents, unless they have taken action, it is only the mother who has these rights. Obviously it is very desirable that the father as well as the mother is fully responsible for their children. There are several ways in which a father can acquire parental rights:

- he can go to court for a parental responsibility order
- he can go to court for a residence order
- he can marry the mother
- he becomes the child's guardian
- he and the mother can take out a special agreement

Clearly it is preferable for the mother and father to agree, rather than the father having to apply to the courts. The Children Act 1989 made provision for unmarried parents to take out a joint parental responsibility agreement which gives them equal rights over their children, but until now this has been little used.

In 1992, there were 215,225 babies born outside marriage (31.2%). Of these, 76% (163,571) included the name of the father on the birth certificate. 1993 figures showed a slight increase, about 32% of babies born outside marriage of which nearly 77% of unmarried fathers co-signed at registration. The joint parental responsibility clause of the Children Act 1989 came into force in October 1991. By the end of December 1993, two full years later, over 300,000 unmarried fathers would have signed their children's birth certificates, yet only 7,611 joint parental responsibility agreements had been lodged at the Principal Registry of the Family Division.

The Baby Naming Society suspects that the general public is still ill-informed and is addressing the urgent need to correct the misunderstanding.

Where now?

It would be very desirable if, in a few years' time, the Baby Naming Society could undertake some research on the families which have opted for a naming ceremony. Have the parents ever stopped to recall their promises? If so, under what circumstances, and what difference has it made?

Have the 'godparents' been as supportive as hoped? If the child had a special book, has it been read? What follow-up has there been for the child? What has been the effect *on the couple themselves* of making a joint commitment? If we could show that these new types of ties have served some purpose beyond the ceremony itself, we could be on to a winner.

However, to make the ceremonies accessible to all rather than just the financially privileged, the Baby Naming Society has been funded through grants. Generous though these have been, they are increasingly difficult to come by and the future of the Society is far from certain.

Yet there are many indications of growing public interest in these issues, in the US as well as UK. In an effort to reduce divorce rates, we now have *Prepare* - a computer aided pre-marriage examination which is already mandatory in some American States and is being used by a number of clergy in Britain. A further American initiative is the 'marital covenant' - that word again! A binding promise. Begun in Louisiana, and a radical alternative to the 'no fault' divorce which Britain has adopted, it provides mandatory pre-marriage counselling.

If the marriage breaks down, a divorce can only be obtained if unreasonable behaviour can be proved, which includes conviction for murder or serious crime, adultery or abuse, or after two years of separation. Supporters of the scheme think it will be readily adopted, not least because partners would find it difficult to justify anything less than a lifetime of love and commitment before getting married.

There is still much more that we can do to restore commitment between parents and to provide children with supportive homes. On a personal note I would suggest, though it may not be fashionable to do so, that the best scenario for a child's future would be firstly that the child grows up with both parents who are in a committed and loving relationship with each other. Secondly, that for the first few years, the child is looked after by its mother, not a child minder. No matter how good that child minder may be, she's not mummy.

Thirdly, that the father is not excluded from the child-rearing years by unreasonable demands at work and an ethic which thinks 'you can't be any good unless you're putting in the hours'. Finally, that the child has opportunities to form relationships not only with other children but with other adults who have the child's interests at heart and can provide an extra dimension to the child's understanding of what it means to be a 'grown up'.

On the part of the state, we need more support for ordinary parents. There seems little point in pouring government money into elaborate systems for childminding to encourage mothers back into work. Many find themselves in low paid part-time jobs which barely cover the cost of the minding. Why not make the money available to provide new mothers with a choice of being their own baby's minder? Yes, some will opt to go back to work. I suspect the majority feel it would be better for their children if mum was at home for a few years.

Recreating personal commitment

Among parents themselves, we need to encourage an attitude which says 'I am responsible for my relationships'. A 'no fault' divorce system allows us to make mistakes, shrug it off as 'not my fault' and move on, sometimes to make the same mistake again. Somehow we need to empower people to make wise choices in their life-partners.

We need a morality that says fidelity and loyalty are desirable and usually necessary for a lasting relationship. And we need to find a way in which couples are able to have children without too much financial deprivation and a system which allows them to devote themselves to parenting in the best possible way.

Above all we need to develop new types of ties between men and women whereby couples feel committed to their relationships, yet not constricted within them. The most promising way to start may well lie in concentrating on how to bind parents more strongly to their children, so that the children of tomorrow grow up with the security of unconditional love and a sense of their own worth. These are the 'ties to bind'.

FUTURE MODELS & OPTIONS

Diversity and Choice
in the Sexual Contract:
Models for the 21st Century*

Catherine Hakim

All policy analysis rests on underlying assumptions, often unstated, about the nature of the social world and social processes. One of the most problematic assumptions currently underlying all European Commission reports is that women are a homogeneous group with a single set of well established preferences: to combine lifelong employment with child-bearing and child-rearing. All European Union policy analysis is written on the assumption that all workers are self-supporting primary earners who have a full-time lifelong career which is only interrupted, if at all, temporarily and involuntarily by the need to care for young children or the elderly, and that part-time work is taken by women mainly or exclusively when caring for others (European Commission, 1995b: 21, 138-141).

The European Commission has so far refused to recognise the existence of secondary earners in the workforce, notably married women and full-time students with jobs, and it has only recently and reluctantly accepted that part-time workers constitute a permanent, substantial and growing part of the workforce in most Western European countries. Similarly, EU discussion of the minimum wage does not take account of the expanding numbers of secondary earners: it insists that all wages should be adequate to provide for a reasonable standard of living for an adult, or complete family, ignoring the fact that wage-earners differ qualitatively in work orientations, job priorities and financial needs.

* This is a revised and updated version of a paper first published in March 1996 in the *British Journal of Sociology* under the title 'The sexual division of labour and women's heterogeneity'. I thank Routledge and the London School of Economics for permission to reprint the material.

The European Commission's perspective is problematic because it is demonstrably untrue, and rests on the Commission ignoring its own research reports as well as substantial research evidence for member countries. Policy-making is of course easier if one has to satisfy only one group or one objective. Policy-making becomes infinitely more complex if one has to take account of diverse preferences and allow genuine choices. For this reason alone, male-dominated trade unions have not welcomed female members and have played down the differences in their work preferences and interests, such as a marked preference for part-time rather than full-time jobs (Hakim, 1997).

However all the available research evidence shows that, even by the 1990s, the majority of women in Britain, and across Europe more generally, did not seek continuous lifetime careers but continued to give priority, to varying degrees, to family activities. New research on socialist countries also shows that social engineering did not succeed in replacing this diversity of preferences with what feminists would regard as 'egalitarian' sex-role preferences. Policies for the 21st century thus need to recognise, and permit, this diversity of sex-role preferences and family lifestyles instead of seeking to impose one single model on everyone.

The feminist myth of a common goal

A substantial proportion of women, as well as men, still accept the sexual division of labour which sees homemaking as women's principal activity and income-earning as men's principal activity in life. This acceptance of differentiated sex roles underlies funda-mental differences between the work orientations, labour market behaviour and life goals of men and women (Hakim, 1991, 1994, 1995, 1996a, 1996b, 1996c, 1997; Blossfield & Hakim, 1997). The proportion of women who accept the homemaker role varies from half to two-thirds, depending on the precise formulation of the sexual division of labour presented to them in interview surveys (Hakim and Jacobs, 1997). It is true that attitudes and expectations are changing, among both men and women. But not as fast nor as completely as some commentators would have us believe. It is precisely because changes in attitudes are partial, uneven, moving at different speeds in different social groups and cultures, that we now have a heterogeneous and polarising population of adult women in the relatively affluent Western industrial societies.

A few women have rejected the sexual division of labour. Apart from the isolated defiant souls that occur in all societies and all times, such women are generally the most highly educated, most highly motivated women who are the cause of a sudden sharp increase in the female share of professional, managerial and other highly-paid occupations in Britain and Europe more generally in the 1980s (Hakim, 1992: 136; Rubery and Fagan, 1993). They are found everywhere, in all countries, East and West, but the size of the minority varies from the invisible few thousands to the more vociferous minority that gets its voice heard. However, most women still go along with the sexual division of labour, many actively preferring it and colluding with men, others not sufficiently inconvenienced by it to be willing to make a stand against it. Whether they are labelled as the victims of false consciousness or not, or simply foolish, is a matter of intellectual taste. The acceptability of the sexual division of labour clearly owes something to the fact that most women choose to spend a part of their life producing children and rearing them, and they prefer to be supported financially by someone else while they are doing it, either a husband or the state.

Another reason is that the sexual division of labour can be efficient and mutually advantageous, as rational choice theorists keep pointing out (Becker, 1991: 54-79). Whatever the reason, it is widely accepted, and not only by the men who gain from the arrangement but also by women, because they too perceive themselves as gaining from it.

Feminists have argued that modern women reject the role of full-time homemaker; that they seek to participate in the labour market on exactly the same basis as men, so that sex differentials in work rates or within the workforce can be read as the effects of discrimination rather than personal choice; and that as soon as the barriers come down, women will flood into wage work on a full-time basis if at all possible (Hakim, 1996c).

I held this view once. My own research proved me wrong. National interview surveys across the world demonstrate that many women, often the majority, actively seek and accept the homemaker role. A large amount of female employment is driven by economic necessity rather than by egalitarian attitudes. Feminist arguments about the causes of sex differentials in the labour market, and the impact of sex discrimination, fail on the evidence (Hakim, 1995).

The modern sexual division of labour

Surveys have often measured attitudes somewhat crudely by acceptance or rejection of statements that propose a complete division of labour between wives and husbands, in the sense that income-earning is presented as an exclusively male function and home-making as an exclusively female function. This approach is illustrated in the International Social Survey Programme's item 'A husband's job is to earn the money; a wife's job is to look after the home and family' which is often treated as a measure of 'modernity' in attitudes. Throughout the 1980s and into the 1990s this statement (or equivalents) attracted roughly 50% of men and women disagreeing and 50% agreeing or indifferent, in the USA, Britain and other European countries, with attitudes fluctuating over time but broadly balanced (Witherspoon, 1988: 189; Scott, 1990: 57; Alwin, Braun and Scott, 1992; Kiernan, 1992: 97-99; Scott, Braun and Alwin, 1993: 34; Haller and Hoellinger, 1994: 102; Braun, Scott and Alwin, 1994; Scott, Alwin and Braun, 1996). In Germany, Italy, Austria and Hungary, support for the statement is stronger than disagreement. For example only one-third of German men and women reject the sexual division of labour compared to half in Britain (Table 1). Attitudes to the housewife role are less ambivalent and more positive, with a majority of women as well as men agreeing that it can be just as fulfilling as working for pay; only one-third in Britain and Germany and even fewer in the USA reject the idea (Table 1).

However the complete separation of roles has been updated in the post-war decades to accept wives going out to work as a secondary activity. An interview survey carried out in 1986-87 showed that the domestic division of labour is now relative rather than absolute; that attitudes to income-earning can change at a different, faster pace than attitudes to the homekeeping role; and that there are qualitative differences between the work orientations of women working full-time and part-time (Vogler, 1994: 45, 55; Hakim & Jacobs, 1997). The majority of part-timers regard

TABLE 1   Western views on the roles of men and women

Percentage *disagreeing* with these two statements:

A   *A husband's job is to earn the money; a wife's job is*
   to look after the home and the family
B   *Being a housewife is just as fulfilling as working for pay*

	A (Separate roles)		B (Housewife job)	
	Men	Women	Men	Women
Britain	47	58	33	36
USA	47	52	22	21
Irish Republic	40	50	17	24
West Germany	33	35	29	32

Source: 1988 International Social Survey Programme data reported in Scott, Braun and Alwin (1993: 30-1).

breadwinning as the primary (but not exclusive) responsibility of men, and see women as secondary earners whose *primary* (but not exclusive) responsibility is domestic work and homemaking. The majority of women working full-time reject both these propositions in favour of symmetrical roles. In addition, women with part-time jobs and non-working women are almost identical in their sex-role preferences; together they form the dominant majority group in favour of separate roles for wives and husbands. 'Egalitarian' women are a minority of all women aged 20-60 years (Table 2).

One EC Eurobarometer survey provides a unique measure of support, across Europe, for the *modern* sexual division of labour, which falls half-way between the completely equal sharing of income-earning and domestic functions to separate and parallel roles (Table 3). Roughly one-third of the EC population supported each of three family models. The egalitarian model attracted most support in Greece, Denmark, Italy and France, followed closely by the Netherlands and UK. The complete separation of roles attracted most support in Luxembourg, Ireland and Belgium. But in all countries there was a wide spread of support for all three models of

Rewriting the sexual contract

TABLE 2   Attitudes to the sexual division of labour in Britain

---

	Women working			Women not working	All women	All men
	Full-time	Part-time	All			
The female partner should be ultimately responsible for housework % agreeing	44	74	59	81	67	65
The male partner should be ultimately responsible for bread-winning % agreeing	30	59	44	70	54	59
I'm not against women working but the man should still be the main breadwinner in the family % agreeing or indifferent	49	69	58	64	60	56
In times of high unemployment married women should stay at home % agreeing or indifferent	27	35	30	48	38	46

Source: Hakin & Jacobs (1997: Table 3) reporting analyses of 1986 and 1987 SCELI data for men and women aged 20-60 years.

the family, none receiving majority support, with the single exception of Greece's majority support for the egalitarian model. This suggests that the 'modern' egalitarian family is really a reversion to a pre-industrial model which required the labour of all family members, including children sometimes, for survival. Overall, a two-thirds majority of European men and women favour the idea of the working wife, and a two-thirds majority also favour the wife retaining all or the major part of the domestic role. Within countries, differences by sex are negligible except in Greece, Italy and France where men are distinctly less favourable than women towards the egalitarian marriage (European Commission, 1984: 9). Age has by far the strongest influence on attitudes (Table 3) reflecting generational differences as well as the impact of aging and

TABLE 3   European views on the sexual division of labour

Percentage supporting each of the three models:

		Egalitarian	Compromise	Separate roles
Greece		53	23	25
Denmark		50	33	17
Italy		42	28	30
France		41	27	32
Netherlands		41	27	32
UK		39	37	24
Belgium		35	25	40
Ireland		32	26	42
West Germany		29	38	33
Luxembourg		27	23	50
Men	15-24 years	49	33	18
	25-39	40	38	22
	40-54	28	36	36
	55 and over	26	28	46
Women	15-24 years	60	25	15
	25-39	45	32	23
	40-54	36	34	30
	55 and over	31	29	40
Total for EC of 10		38	32	30

Notes: The question asked:-
People talk about the changing roles of husband and wife in the family. Here are three kinds of family. Which of them corresponds most with your idea about the family?

- A family where the two partners each have an equally absorbing job and where housework and the care of the children are shared equally between them.
- A family where the wife has a less demanding job than her husband and where she does the larger share of housework and caring for the children.
- A family where only the husband has a job and the wife runs the home.
- None of these three cases.

Percentages have been adjusted to exclude the 3% not responding to the question and the 3% choosing the last response.
Source: Derived from the Eurobarometer report by European Commission, *European Women and Men 1983*, (1984)

life experience (Scott, Alwin and Braun, 1996). The key contribution of this survey is that it shows, for all European countries, that people who reject the complete separation of roles for men and women do not necessarily accept egalitarian or symmetrical roles: at least half only go as far as supporting a secondary earner role for the wife, who retains the larger share of domestic and childcare work. Attitude surveys have often presented people with a false dichotomy which failed to recognise the modern version of the sexual division of labour, a compromise that stops a long way short of truly egalitarian attitudes (Table 3).

Equally diverse attitudes and behaviour are reported in other EC reports. There are huge differences across the EC in the percentage of wives who state they are not working because of 'family reasons' even when they have no child, ranging from 20% in Portugal and Denmark to 80% in Holland and Italy (European Commission, 1995: 142). Similarly, there are large differences between countries in the percentage of married women without children who work full-time, ranging from 60% in Portugal to 20% in the Netherlands (European Commission, 1995: 142). Part-time work is almost non-existent in all southern European countries whereas it is a common (rather than atypical) form of employment for women in most Northern European countries (European Commission, 1995: 142; Blossfeld and Hakim, 1997).

Perhaps most important, several recent studies have shown that across Europe one-third of all women who work full-time would in fact prefer a part-time job in an ideal world (Thomson, 1995: 74; European Commission, 1991: 115). Among mothers working full-time, the great majority would in fact have *preferred* not to work full-time but only part-time or not at all while their children were young (European Commission, 1991: 47-48; Wolcott and Glezer, 1995: 81). We cannot assume that women working full-time hours are invariably doing so from choice, are career-oriented and hold modern attitudes. Economic necessity continues to be an important determinant of female employment, as it always has been (Braun, Scott and Alwin, 1994).

The limits of social engineering

There have been three important attempts to eliminate the sexual division of labour and impose symmetrical sex roles: in the Israeli kibbutzim, in Sweden and in China. All three have been only partially successful, revealing that there are limits to what social engineering can achieve. Tables 4 and 5 display the relative success of Sweden compared with other European societies and of China compared with other Far Eastern societies. The attitude statement in Table 4 proposes the complete separation of roles; the statement in Table 5 does not completely exclude wage work for wives.

In 1993, one-quarter of women aged 20 and over in Britain, France, Germany and the USA agreed with the rigid separation of roles in the statement 'The husband should be the breadwinner, and the wife should stay at home' (Table 4). In Japan and the Philippines two-thirds accepted the complete sexual division of labour. The long-term trend is for declining acceptance and a decade earlier, in 1982, acceptance of the idea was invariably higher, except in the Philippines, even though the earlier survey was limited to women aged 20-59, excluding older women who are usually more conservative in outlook.

Sweden demonstrates that energetically 'egalitarian' policies, which in this context means policies promoting symmetrical roles for men and women and supported by vigorous fiscal and social security rules to prevent backsliding, can substantially change social attitudes: the vast majority (around 85%) of women reject the complete separation of roles. However there remains a stubborn minority of women (16% in 1982 and 13% in 1993) who still accept this design for living, albeit a lower proportion than in the rest of Europe (Table 3). While these results show how malleable attitudes are at the aggregate level, they also point to small minorities of women across Europe whose perspective has not changed, for whom the complete separation of domestic roles remains entirely satisfactory. China demonstrates both these points even more sharply.

China implemented the most determined social engineering policy aimed at eradicating the sexual division of labour and associated attitudes. The Marriage Law of 1950 laid down the principles of equality between the sexes, monogamy, freedom to choose marital partners and the right to sue for divorce, marking a break away from Confucian patriarchal values which supported an essentialist conception of the difference between the sexes and

TABLE 4
The sexual division of labour: East and West comparisons

Percentage of women agreeing with or indifferent to the statement:
The husband should be the breadwinner,
and the wife should stay at home.

	1993	1982
Sweden	13	16
UK	21	28
France	24	...
Germany	29	38
USA	27	35
Korea	33	...
Japan	62	76
Philippines	67	56

... = Not available

Notes: Results from nationally representative random samples of 1000 or more women aged 20 and over in 1993 for all countries except Japan where results are based on a nationally representative random sample of 2000 women aged 20 and over interviewed in November 1992. Data for 1982 relates to women aged 20-59 years. The survey covered West Germany only in 1982 but the whole of unified Germany (including East Germany) in 1993.

Source: Calculated from Figure I-35, in Tokyo Metropolitan Government, 1994: 78.

sharply segregated roles for men and women (Stockman, Bonney and Sheng, 1995: 141-154). The successes and failures of this largest-ever real-world social experiment are immensely valuable to social scientists, particularly for the study of women's position in society. Success was greatest in eradicating centuries-old perceptions of sex differences in ability and in the practice of male dominance in the household.

There was also substantial success in eradicating the sexual division of labour: a low-wage full-employment policy made it necessary for all adults to work and hence for couples to share domestic work as well. However, in 1988, after the economic reform programme begun at the end of the 1970s had introduced a new climate of opinion, there was a major public debate over a new trend for women to withdraw from wage work and their reasons for doing so. A survey carried out in Beijing in November 1993 showed that one-quarter of all women, one-third of wives and two-fifths of men accepted the sexual division of labour as the ideal to aim for (Table 5).

The attitude statement here was worded sufficiently vaguely as not completely to exclude wage work (social labour in China), but the relatively large minorities of women (especially wives) agreeing with the sexual division of labour is still remarkable. Respondents to the survey were aged 20-69 years (typically 30-50 years) and resident in Beijing, thus including the most educated and most cosmopolitan groups in Chinese society, 40 per cent of them professionals and senior administrators, who had lived in a communist society for virtually all their adult lives. Half the wives had earnings similar to or higher than their husbands.

The policy of one child per family meant that in 1993, and for the foreseeable future, the great majority of couples had only one child to raise, and they had access to good socialised childcare facilities staffed by professionals.

Yet even in these most favourable circumstances, a consistent one-third of wives in all age groups (varying slightly 27%-40%) preferred to stay at home as a housewife if their husband earned enough money to permit it. Similarly, acceptance of the sexual division of labour as the ideal was found in all age groups, varying only from 20% for people in their 60s to 38% among people in their 30s.

It might be argued in this case that people were simply reverting to traditional patriarchal values which had been suppressed but not abandoned. This might have been so in some rural areas, but not in urban areas, let alone Beijing. The 1993 survey found strongly egalitarian attitudes on all aspects of family roles and relationships. For example over three-quarters of husbands and wives in all age groups stated that family decisions were made jointly, whereas the husband dominated decision-making in Bangkok, Seoul and Fukuoka, the three other cities surveyed.

Acceptance of the traditional family division of labour was lowest among people in their 20s, but also among people in their 50s and 60s. It was only among people aged 30-50 that acceptance rose to two-fifths, clearly linked to childcare concerns. Four-fifths of men and women in all age groups thought women should stay at home when a child is young (Ma *et al*, 1994: 122-133, 344-363).

TABLE 5   Far Eastern views on the roles of men and women

Percentage agreeing with each statement:	Beijing		Seoul		Bangkok		Fukuoka	
	Men	Women	Men	Women	Men	Women	Men	Women
There are no significant differences of abilities between men and women	70	77	62	67	87	90	55	54
The ideal is for men to have a job and for women to take care of the family	40	24	69	51	68	71	72	60
If my husband earned enough money I would rather stay at home as a housewife *	...	35	...	...	...	...	...	...

Notes: ... Not available   * Asked only of married women

Source: Calculated from Figures II-5-1, II-5-20, III-6-1 and III-6-2, in Ma et al (1994: 122, 154, 344). The surveys were carried out in 1989 (Fukuoka), 1991 (Seoul), 1992 (Bangkok) and 1993 (Beijing), with representative samples of N=1736, N=1608, N=1570 and N=1920 respectively.

This is strong evidence to support Becker's argument that the sexual division of labour in the household can be accepted voluntarily as efficient and mutually advantageous rather than as something imposed on people by custom and patriarchy.

The other side of the coin is that only one-third of wives (one-quarter of all women aged 20-69 years) would prefer this option; two-thirds of Chinese wives rejected it firmly, despite the extra burden of combining wage work and domestic work, with consistent views on related topics (Ma *et al*, 1994; Stockman, Bonney and Sheng, 1995: 141-154).

The impact of social engineering in China is highlighted by comparisons with almost identical surveys in Bangkok, Seoul and Fukuoka (a large town in central Japan with attitudes closer to the national average than to those of Tokyo residents) carried out in 1989-1992 (Table 5). Acceptance of separate sex roles is much higher in Bangkok, Fukuoka and Seoul than in Beijing. The Thai case shows that this is not necessarily related to beliefs about sex differences in abilities, as the Thais do not believe there are any significant differences of ability between men and women, whereas in China this belief had to be eradicated. It appears that the complete separation of roles between men and women will continue to attract support, even if minority support, because it does, as Becker argues, offer certain concrete benefits to couples. The modern version of the sexual division of labour, which is relative rather than total, attracts even greater support.

The increasing importance of preferences in the 21st century

There is no evidence that attitudes cease to be important once women gain access to higher education and better paid jobs. If anything the opposite is the case, as women can afford to choose between competing lifestyles, given homogamy (Table 6). A two-

TABLE 6   Employment rates by sex role attitudes

Sex role attitudes	Percentage of each group in employment		Distribution of sample	
	Highly qualified	Other women	Highly qualified	Other women
Modern	92	76	23	14
Ambivalent	84	66	63	67
Traditional	64	54	15	20
All women 20-59	82	65	100	100
Base = 100%	746	2700	746	2700

Notes: The highly qualified have tertiary level qualifications, beyond A-level; other women have no qualifications or only secondary school qualifications. Sex role attitudes were scored on the basis of nine attitude statements, including the ISSP sexual division of labour statement shown in Table 1 of this paper.

Source: Calculated from Tables 6.21 and 6.22 in Corti et al (1995: 69) reporting 1991 survey results from the British Household Panel Study.

thirds majority of women, whatever their level of education, hold ambivalent views on sex roles, with minorities firmly accepting or rejecting the sexual division of labour. It is well established that higher education qualifications are associated with higher work rates - a 'mark up' of 17 percentage points in Table 6 (65% versus 82%). But the impact of sex role attitudes is greater, especially among highly qualified women, producing a 'mark-up' of 28 percentage points in employment rates when modern and traditional women are compared (64% versus 92%).

As I have pointed out elsewhere (Hakim, 1996a: 132-134; 1996b: 14-15), universities and higher education qualifications have a marriage market function as well as vocational value. Qualifications can be acquired as an 'intellectual dowry', to ensure a girl marries a partner of at least equal status, rather than marketable skills. In this case the returns to education consist of the husband's earnings potential rather than personal earnings potential. It cannot be assumed that all women obtaining higher education qualifications plan careers in the labour market; many will aim for two-person careers, supporting their husband and working, if at all, primarily as a hobby (Hakim, 1996a: 133, 205).

Throughout history, the non-working wife has been seen as a sign of affluence, and the wife who only works part-time is the modern equivalent.

Policy implications

Most European countries have social customs and public policies that favour, directly or indirectly, a single form of the sexual contract: either 'egalitarian' symmetrical roles (as in Sweden) or else a clear division of labour within the couple (as in the Netherlands or West Germany). Britain has such contradictory policies that it is impossible to classify. Policy development in the European Commission is based on the premise of rapid convergence on the egalitarian model of the sexual contract.

Yet there is no evidence that this is happening at all. On the contrary, there is increasing diversity in the models of the sexual contract that find favour. The egalitarian model is supported by only a minority of women as well as men. The majority preference is for continuation of the sexual division of labour in the family and separate sex roles, to varying degrees. If attitudes are converging, it is not on the egalitarian model, as assumed by the Commission, but on the modern sexual division of labour in which wives retain their primary homemaking role but also participate in the labour market as secondary earners, often in part-time jobs.

Policy-makers may find this inconvenient, but we need to cater for an increasing diversity of sex-role preferences in the 21st century and allow people to continue making real choices between different and possibly incompatible lifestyles. But in a civilised society, difference and diversity are positively valued.

Promoting Women's Economic Independence[1]

Ruth Lister

The case for women's economic independence through their ability 'to earn their own subsistence, independent of men' as 'enlightened citizens' was made back in 1792 by Mary Wollstonecraft (1985). It was central to early twentieth century campaigns for women's social and economic welfare.

At the end of the twentieth century, despite their increased labour market participation, many women still do not enjoy full economic independence (Lister, 1992; Joshi *et al*, 1995). While the extent and degree of their economic dependence varies over the life-course and between different groups, the constraints of women's continued responsibilities for care, the low paid part-time work which many, mainly white, women undertake and a benefits system which still, in part, reflects an outmoded male breadwinner model all combine to undermine women's economic independence. Moreover, even those who are economically independent heads of households can be affected by the ideology of women's economic dependence which still influences women's overall labour market position. Thus, for instance, African-Caribbean female heads of households and lesbian women can still be affected, although the issue of economic independence is likely to figure in different ways in their lives than in those of women who experience direct economic dependence. It is the latter who are the primary focus of this chapter.

It begins by arguing the case for the importance of women having an independent income. It then discusses how state policies can facilitate access to the two main routes for achieving this: the labour market and the social security system. This then leads to the dilemma that an independent income through the social security system might undermine access to such an income through the labour market. The answer to this dilemma, it will be argued, lies, at least in part, in a redrawing of the boundaries of responsibility for care work between women and men.

The case for independence

The case for women's economic independence can be made both on practical and on more philosophical grounds. The philosophical case rests primarily on the importance of autonomy as an essential element of human welfare and as a prerequisite for full substantive citizenship.[2] This autonomy, provided that it is not misinterpreted as a form of atomistic individualism, is compatible with the recognition of human interdependence; indeed, it is, I would contend, a precondition for genuine, non-exploitative, interdependence. The unequal power relationship that, as I argue below, underpins women's economic dependence means that the interdependence of which it is a part is skewed in favour of men. The latter's dependence on women for care and servicing, which facilitates their own independence as workers and citizens, is conveniently obscured (Pateman, 1989; Cass, 1994). This formulation problematises men's economic independence as being built on freedom from the caring responsibilities that still spell economic dependence in varying degrees for many women. The implication is that a strategy to promote women's independence means not the destruction of interdependence but its reconstruction on more equitable lines.

The relationship between autonomy and economic independence is spelt out by Tove Stang Dahl in a treatise on feminist jurisprudence. Within a framework of the central values underlying 'women's law' - those of justice, freedom and dignity - she contends that 'a minimum amount of money for oneself is a necessary prerequisite for personal freedom, self-determination and self-realisation'.

Conversely, economic dependence represents the negation of freedom. From a human rights perspective, women's economic dependence on men is, she contends, 'a moral problem both on an individual and a societal level'. Dahl thus argues (1987: pp91,97,111) that 'access to one's own money should be considered a minimum welfare requirement in a monetary economy....An independent income of one's own is a prerequisite for participation in and enjoyment of life, privately as well as publicly. Lack of money, on the other hand, gives a person little freedom of movement and a feeling of powerlessness'.

The practical implications of this more philosophical case relate to the poverty and powerlessness that economic dependence can spell. Heather Joshi et al (1995: p61) found that just under half of mothers living in a partnership do not have an independent income sufficient to meet minimum everyday needs as defined by the income support scale rates. Without child benefit, this proportion would rise to three-fifths. They are, therefore, the authors observe, 'at risk of poverty if resources are not shared, or if their partnership were to break down'. There is a growing body of evidence (e.g. Pahl, 1989; Vogler, 1994) to indicate that resources are not always shared fairly within families to the detriment, in the main, of women and children.

The economist A.B. Atkinson observes (1991) that, if poverty is conceptualised in relation to a 'right to a minimum level of resources', 'we may question whether the dependence of one partner, typically the woman, on the other, is acceptable'. Another, Stephen Jenkins, develops this further (1991) to suggest that a feminist conception of poverty 'concerns the individual right to a minimum degree of potential economic independence'. Ultimately, it is as individuals that people experience poverty, albeit in the context of their relationships to others. Both the actuality and the ideology of women's economic dependence serve to make them more vulnerable than men to poverty. The long-standing failure to recognise the family as a site of income distribution, reflected in the typical measurement of poverty at the level of the family or household, means that the poverty of some women, fully or partially economically dependent on their male partners, remains invisible.

The distribution of resources (including work and time as well as money) within the family is, partly, a function of power relationships which, in turn, reflect the relative economic resources that each partner commands independently (Okin, 1989; Pahl, 1989; Blumberg, 1991). Research in the UK has demonstrated how the unequal power relationship typical of full or partial economic dependence is experienced by many women as a lack of control over resources, a lack of rights and a sense of obligation and deference (Pahl, 1989; Burgoyne, 1990). It indicates the importance attached by many women to an independent income, especially from paid work. A study of young Muslim women of Pakistani origin, for instance, found that paid work was 'valued for offering women a measure of independence and a sense of self-confidence' (Brah, 1996: p140).

Lack of control over money can be a factor in relationship breakdown and some lone parents report that the poverty of lone parenthood can be preferable to the lack of control over resources that they experienced in a partnership with a man (Graham, 1987; McKay & Rowlingson, 1997). This power relationship has been analysed using Hirschman's model of 'exit' and 'voice' in which 'exit' refers to the possibility of leaving an unsatisfactory situation and 'voice' to the ability to change it. Access to an independent income from either the labour market or the state strengthens women's voice and their opportunities for exit (Okin, 1989; Hobson, 1990). An independent income within marriage or cohabitation promotes 'voice'; knowledge that it is possible to support oneself and one's children outside marriage or cohabitation facilitates 'exit'. Moreover, those who already have an independent income within marriage are better placed to exit. The ability to exit is especially important for women in violent or abusive relationships.[3]

The role of government in promoting access to an independent income

From the perspective of both 'exit' and 'voice', Government has a role to play in helping women to achieve an independent income, either from the labour market or the state or as a combination from both.

The Labour Market

Starting with access to the labour market, there are a number of aspects to the government's role. First, it can help to provide the necessary infrastructure of training and child and adult care facilities. Training and opportunities for life-long learning are now firmly on the policy agenda. They can be of particular importance for women who have spent time out of the labour market providing care. They need to be extended also to women in part-time work who tend to lose out on existing training opportunities.

Until very recently, in the UK childcare was treated as the

responsibility of individual parents, and to a lesser extent employers and the private sector, in the great majority of cases. As a result, the UK has come bottom of the publicly funded childcare league in the European Union (Moss, 1990; Bradshaw, 1996). One welcome result of the change of government has been a recognition of the importance of childcare, including out-of-school care. Harriet Harman, the Social Security Secretary, has described it as 'a fundamental part of Britain's economic infrastructure, on a par with transport or communications'.[4] In his first Budget, the Chancellor, Gordon Brown, announcing a national childcare strategy, declared that 'from this Budget forwards, childcare will no longer be seen as an afterthought or a fringe element of social policies but as an integral part of our economic policy'. Leaving aside the implication that social policies are subsidiary to economic policies and the inadequacy of the resources committed so far, this does mark an important shift in approach to one that acknowledges that childcare is a public as well as a private responsibility. As the care of older people also increasingly constrains women's labour market participation, better community support services to enable carers to combine care with paid employment are also needed.[5]

It is generally women who provide care in the public as well as the private sphere. This highlights the fact that government also has a role to play in promoting women's economic independence as an employer in its own right. A number of studies have emphasised the role of the welfare state as employer of women's labour in enhancing women's economic independence, although it is often on the lower rungs of the employment ladder, especially in the case of black and minority ethnic group women. The expansion of public health and welfare service provision thus opens up opportunities for women's employment; conversely, women are especially vulnerable at times of contraction.

Government can also take responsibility for regulating the terms and conditions under which employment is taken. This does not have to imply an over-regulated labour market, but what the Commission on Social Justice called 'intelligent regulation' (1994). Examples of intelligent regulation that are necessary to safeguard women's employment rights are: policies to prevent discrimination against part-time workers; effective equal pay, anti-discrimination and anti-harassment legislation; a minimum wage; and what are now commonly called 'family-friendly' employment policies. The last include:

i   improvements in maternity leave;
ii the introduction of parental leave and leave for family reasons;
iii carers leave; and
iv flexible (and shorter) working hours that meet employees' and not just employers' needs.

However, as I shall argue below, 'family-friendly' policies need to be directed towards men as well as women.

The State

Women who are able to conform to male employment patterns will normally qualify for social insurance benefits in their own right during periods of unemployment or sickness, although entitlement to those benefits was eroded under the Conservative Government. This process was taken furthest with the replacement of unemployment benefit, paid for 12 months to those who had paid sufficient contributions, by the jobseeker's allowance which is paid for only six months on a contributory basis. After that an unemployed married or cohabiting woman has to rely either on her male partner or on means-tested income support for financial support.

If one member of a couple is in full-time work, as defined by the DSS, the other cannot claim income support. Even where a claim can be made, entitlement is affected by a partner's income. This is one factor behind the high proportion of 'work-poor' couples in which neither partner has a job. Although technically either member of a couple can now claim income support on behalf of the family, in the great majority of cases it is still the man who claims.

A general problem of means-tested benefits for women in heterosexual couples is that, even where they are the claimants, their individual income needs may not be met because entitlement is based on the couple's joint income and on the assumption that that income is shared fairly between them. As noted earlier, research indicates that this assumption can be at variance with the actual distribution of income within families. However, the alternative assumption that resources are not shared at all is as, if not more, likely to be unrealistic, which makes it difficult to assess means-tested benefits on an individual basis.[6]

It would, though, be possible to split the benefit payment, once entitlement had been assessed, and allow women to draw their own (and possibly all their children's share) independently. This has been suggested by a number of people; a report for the Equal Opportunities Commission, for instance, argued that it would 'significantly increase the independent incomes of women who previously had very low incomes' (Duncan *et al*, 1994: p22).[7] Although on the surface this proposal holds certain attractions as a way of putting more money directly into the hands of low-income women, research on the distribution, management and control of income within low-income families indicates that there may be dangers. This research suggests that social security benefit recipients tend to operate a 'whole wage' system of family finances, whereby the whole of the benefit payment (minus frequently some personal spending money for the man) is passed to the woman to manage (Pahl, 1989, Morris, 1990). In this context, while a system of split benefits would mean that the woman was guaranteed some money in her own right, it is possible that she could end up worse off, if her partner then treated his share as personal spending money, leaving her with the same expenditure responsibilities but less money to meet them.

The difficulties involved in providing married and cohabiting women with an independent income for themselves through means-tested benefits suggests that a strategy for enhancing their independent benefit income is best pursued through non-means-tested contributory and categorical benefits.[8]

There are three main options within the present structure of the social security system:

i reform of the contributory system so as to improve women's access to it;

ii the abandonment, or at least easing, of the narrow contributory principle which ties benefit entitlement to individual contribution records;

iii the development of the categorical benefits, in terms of both improvements in existing benefits and the introduction of new ones.

Aspects of each of these options were advocated in the report of the Commission on Social Justice. The Commission envisaged a modernised social insurance system better tailored to today's employment patterns and family needs. It was particularly concerned to address the exclusion of large numbers of part-time workers; at the latest count, about two million women earned below the lower earnings limit that acts as an entry threshold to the national insurance scheme. Among the specific recommendations made by the Commission were:

i   the extension of social insurance membership to people employed for an average of at least eight hours a week, with possible exemption from payment for those on very low incomes, as in Ireland;

ii the introduction of a part-time unemployment benefit;

iii the development of parental leave insurance;

iv the incorporation of categorical income replacement benefits for disabled people and carers into the social insurance system, which would involve raising their levels to the same level as the insurance benefits;

v   that consideration should be given to the possibility of long-term care insurance.

All these reforms would do much to improve access to an independent benefit income for women who are part of the labour force. A more difficult issue is how to do the same for women who are outside the labour force, for a period at least, because of their caring responsibilities. The invalid care allowance provides such an income for those providing full-time care for adults, although its status as an independent benefit is compromised by eligibility criteria that link it to the receipt or non-receipt of other benefits by the care recipient and by its low level. The Government is to examine the possibility of introducing a second-tier citizenship pension for those unable to build up a contribution record because of time spent out of the labour market in caring activities.

Lone parents are entitled to income support until their youngest child is aged 16, although the modest additional help they receive as lone parents is to be phased out. Income support provides no more than a poverty line income. There is a good case for making it more generous. There is also a case for querying whether it is in lone parents' best interests to assume that they will remain on income support until their children have grown up. The UK is very unusual in not requiring lone parents to register for work once their child has reached a certain age.[9] The shift in policy towards encouraging and supporting lone parents of school-age children to take paid employment is therefore welcome. Its success will depend on whether the infrastructure of child care and training is adequate to meet their needs.

This still leaves the question of what support, if any, should be provided for women (or men) in couples who stay at home to care for children. The introduction of paid parental leave could cover the first year of a child's life, as in Sweden, for those who have already been in paid work (the great majority). After that, one option that has been put forward is for a benefit to be paid to those who stay at home to care for young children.[10] The problem with this is that it is likely to encourage women to take longer periods out of the labour market that could disadvantage their situation within it. An alternative approach, that reduces this risk, is to pay a benefit to all those raising children, after the end of any parental leave period, in recognition of the costs - including 'time costs' - incurred by raising children, regardless of the parents' employment or marital status. However, in the current context of welfare state retrenchment the idea of such a universal benefit seems something of a pipe dream.

At present, the only independent income most married and cohabiting women at home caring for children receive is child benefit, and, if their husband is low paid, family credit. Even though these benefits are primarily to meet the needs of their children, they are important to women as a source of income over which they normally have full control. In this context, the Chancellor's interest in replacing family credit with an in-work low income tax credit, as signalled in his first Budget, could have an adverse impact on mothers, as resources are transferred from them to their wage-earning husbands.

When family credit was first introduced, it had been the Conservative Government's intention to pay it through the pay-packet as a work incentive to low-earning men. A coalition of anti-poverty groups, women's organisations and the small business lobby (whose members did not want to be responsible for making the payments) defeated the Government and it was forced to make the payments direct to the caring parent, who is normally still the woman. The question of who receives cash benefits for children has always been a sensitive issue in the UK and earlier attempts to pay family allowances through the wages system also failed.

The introduction of an in-work tax credit would also almost certainly mean a return to the joint taxation of couples. Independent taxation was introduced in 1990 as a response to growing criticism by married women of a system which denied them privacy and independence.[11] The alarm bells are ringing that the Chancellor's interest in the integration of the tax and benefits system could jeopardise this reform. One of the criticisms of negative income tax type integrated schemes, which, in effect, deliver means-testing through the tax system, is that they institutionalise the couple as the tax and benefit unit, thereby undermining married and cohabiting women's access to an independent benefit income. This would be at a time when the European Commission (1997) is encouraging the individualisation of benefits 'in line with the general trend towards a greater autonomy of the individual'.

In contrast, the alternative approach to the integration of tax and benefits - a citizen's or basic income scheme - is premised on the principle of independent benefits. This would provide all adults (and children) with an income in their own right. One of the arguments put forward by many citizen's income supporters is that it would provide all women with an independent benefit and would be a way of valuing caring work.

The danger is that, without other changes in the labour market and in the division of unpaid caring work between women and men, it might be seen as an encouragement to women to stay at home. Indeed, one supporter, Hermione Parker, has accepted (1991: p4) that 'mothers with babies would tend to stay at home longer before going back to work'.

Moreover, it would not value caring work as such, as it would also be paid to those at home not providing care. There is considerable support for citizen's income across the political spectrum and a growing international movement behind it. Nevertheless, doubts remain about its political and economic feasibility in the foreseeable future and it does not appear to be on the formal political agenda at present.

Reconciling 'difference' and 'equality' models

Citizen's income brings us back to the dilemma, referred to a number of times already, of how to promote women's independent income through the benefit system without undermining their access to an independent income through the wages system because of the disincentive the former might create. We are, in effect, faced with two different models for promoting women's social citizenship rights which reflect a long-standing tension in feminist thought.

The first is the 'equality' model which offers women equal rights with men by promoting their access to the labour market on equal terms with men as 'citizen wage-earners'. The second is the 'difference' model which offers women social rights, as 'citizen-carers', in recognition of the value of the caring responsibilities that they undertake. The problem is that neither model on its own is adequate. The challenge is how to combine the two. The answer, as a number of feminist commentators have concluded, lies partly in shifting the sexual division of labour between paid work and unpaid caring work so that both women and men can be treated as citizen-earner/carers (e.g. Pateman, 1989; Phillips, 1997). In a recent European poll, when asked how to iron out continued inequalities between women and men, the most popular response was the greater sharing of household responsibilities.[12]

Jonathan Gershuny's chapter deals with this issue in greater detail. Here, I will simply draw out briefly some implications for government policy. The European Council of Ministers has proposed that 'Member States should promote and encourage, with due respect for the freedom of the individual, increased participation by men (in the care and upbringing of children), in order to achieve a more equal sharing of parental responsibilities between men and women'.[13]

Only Scandinavian governments appear, in fact, to have identified shifting the sexual division of labour as an explicit policy goal. It is possible to learn from both their successes and failures. There have been three main, interlinked strands to the strategies adopted: parental leave, working time and public education programmes.

Their experience indicates that, if men are to be encouraged to make use of parental leave provisions, a period needs to be reserved for fathers. Another source of encouragement is full or nearly full wage replacement, as otherwise it still makes more sense economically in most cases for the mother to take all the leave. Significant also is changing the workplace culture so that family-friendly employment policies are regarded as relevant to men as well as women. Policies on working time that enabled parents of younger children to work shorter hours if they so wished (as in Sweden) and that tackled the long hours working culture that has taken hold (especially in the UK) would help, as would public education programmes directed primarily at men and boys.

Conclusion

This discussion of the kinds of policies needed to promote women's independent income points to the need for multi-faceted policies on behalf of government. However, while it is for government to take the lead, change also needs to take place among employers and among individual men and women, if women are to gain an independent income as both earners and carers.

The achievement of an independent income is crucial for the autonomy and citizenship of women whether or not they live with male partners. It is time that politicians looked beyond their preoccupation with public dependence on the state, which for some women, in fact, spells independence, and addressed this issue of private dependence within the family, in the name of genuine human interdependence.

The Case for a Ministry of the Family

Shirley Dex & Robert Rowthorn

There has been increasing discussion in Britain about provisions and policies to enable parents to combine employment and family responsibilities. This discussion has mainly revolved around women. Women have joined the labour force in growing numbers, but still shoulder the main responsibility for child care and domestic work within households. This double burden has been viewed as a problem by many commentators and statistics reveal women to have higher levels of stress than men (Corti, 1994). However, equality in the workplace is still some way off so the pressure is on women to work harder and longer to match men's contribution. Men for their part are being encouraged to take a greater part in caring and domestic labour at home, but most appear to be resisting.

The issues raised by this discussion do not concern only women, but also men and children. There are matters of general public interest involved and government policy has been drawn into the discussion, although only in a somewhat piecemeal fashion. Overall, there is a lack of coherence in thinking about these issues which in our view can be best rectified by focusing on families rather than just women. This would bring into consideration some important elements which the existing discussion has missed out.

There has been little concern with the role of parents in the upbringing of children, and the issue of how much parental time is optimal for child development has been largely ignored; likewise, the implications of child care and employment patterns for the welfare of children and the stability of family life have been neglected. The labour supply incentives set up by various public provisions and fiscal regimes are discussed at length, but there is little discussion of the incentives created either for or against marriage, family stability and committed parenting. We appear to think that we can buy love and care for our children in unlimited quantities as a perfect substitute for our own care.

This paper argues that policy discussion should take a broader and more integrated view of these matters, that our primary aim should be to establish a favourable environment in which our children can grow up, that parenting should be viewed as valuable and vital to the health and welfare of society, and that public policy should be designed to facilitate commitment and mutual support within families. The paper considers some of the partial views we have encountered and provides arguments *against* such views and *for* the position we have just outlined.

Partial views

The DfEE's (1997) consultation document on *Work and Family: Ideas and Options for Childcare* is an example of the partial view on these issues. It represents a laudable effort to stimulate public discussion of child care needs in a context where employment for women is widespread. It makes good points regarding the general principles which should govern child care policy. However, the paper is narrowly focused and unbalanced. Its primary concern is with the role of women as paid employees, and the emphasis is on how child care arrangements can be modified to encourage the paid employment of mothers. The document recognises the legal rights of parents to care for their own children at home, but this option is not taken seriously. A one-sided emphasis on child care arrangements for mothers in paid employment is also present in much of the literature produced by the Shell sponsored organisation *Employers for Childcare*. This literature conveys the implicit message that looking after one's own children is inferior to paid employment, and is an option which is only taken when there is an absence of an affordable professional childcare.

The DfEE document gives the impression that there are masses of mothers out there desperate to get a job but hindered by the lack of child care provision. It would be useful to examine to what extent this is the case. In Britain in 1993, for mothers with a child under 10 years of age, 17 per cent were employed full-time, 35 per cent part-time and a further 5 per cent were unemployed. This gives a total of 58 per cent who were economically active, 42 per cent being economically inactive (Brannen *et al*, 1997). Getting an accurate figure for how many of the latter are genuinely hindered from taking a job by the lack of child care is difficult. We estimate that approximately one tenth of economically inactive mothers fall into this category.[1] This is equivalent to 3-5 per cent of all mothers with a child under 10. These figures show that the problem is small. Moreover, as we point out below, there are many mothers now in employment who would prefer to stay at home if they had more money.

Another group who are claimed to want to work are lone parents. The TUC *1997 Budget Analysis* says 'Even though most lone parents want to return to work, many are unable to do so because child care provision is currently poor and patchy' (p6.) It is often said that 90 per cent of lone parents wish to work. This claim is misleading since it refers to the proportion who would like a job *at some time in their lives*. The proportion of lone parents who wish to work now or 'soon' is 28 percent and 63 per cent 'later' when the children are older or grown up (Morgan, 1995: p110).

Clearly, there are some mothers who fit the DfEE's assumptions but they are estimated to be a small minority. Moreover, even those who say they would like to work if affordable child care were available might have a different response if they were offered the additional option of receiving money to look after their own children. We should also ask how many mothers who are currently employed would prefer not to work if they had more cash available? The evidence on this topic is sparse. However, 23 per cent of employed mothers with a pre-school child would like to reduce their hours; these are mostly employed full-time. Also, 37 per cent of employed fathers who have a pre-school child said that they would prefer to work shorter hours (Dex *et al*, 1995). These figures are much higher, approaching 50 per cent, where mothers and fathers work more than 40 hours per week. There are, of course, some who would prefer to increase their hours although the extent to which this is motivated by financial considerations is not clear.[2]

The DfEE paper also fails to give serious consideration to the implications of different child care regimes or employment patterns for the welfare of children or the stability of family life. Politicians and the public at large are becoming increasingly concerned about the welfare of children and the extent of family breakdown.

Employment patterns and child care regimes have important implications in this field. Part of the problem here is that the welfare of children is the brief of other government departments; for example, the Department of Health has responsibility for the physical development of young children; DSS for poverty, family breakdown and child abuse issues. Concern has been voiced by some child development specialists that neglect of children is an issue, and that attachment between babies and their mothers fails to develop when mothers are often away when the child is young; these both have undesirable consequences on child development and mental health (Belsky and Rovine, 1988; Barglow *et al*, 1987; Scarr and Eisenberg, 1993). It is undesirable that links between employment patterns and child care regimes should fall outside the scope of every department's remit, not least because it will then be possible for one department to advocate child care policy which runs counter to government aims in the sphere of family life and child welfare.

We suggest that the overlaps in these important issues warrant the establishment of a forum for discussing and devising a more coherent set of family policies. We elaborate below more of the issues such a forum would need to consider. The Labour government has appointed a part-time minister for women. This implies that the issues in question concern only women, and that only women's views on these issues are relevant. In fact they concern all members of society no matter what age, sex or parental status. The Labour government should recognise the wider interests involved and appoint a full-time minister for the family.

The hours children spend in non-parental care

On average in 1991, employed fathers worked 46 hours per week (main job + overtime + second jobs). Travelling to work added a further 4 hours per week on average to father's working day. Married women with children were employed on average 24 hours per week in 1991 (including overtime and second jobs) and added a further 4 hours per week travelling time if they worked full-time, less if part-time. British men are working longer average hours than other men in Europe and hours of work have been increasing in Britain. In addition, there has been growing insecurity at work; more jobs are temporary and self-employed (Dex and McCulloch, 1995). There has been a growth in full-time male/part-time female partnerships in families with children, but also a significant and growing phenomenon which one commentator has called 'workaholic couples' who put in long hours for high pay and depend heavily on paid domestic help and child care (Brannen *et al*, 1993). On the other hand there has been a growing proportion of so-called 'work-poor' households which do not contain anyone with a paid job (Gregg, 1994). Some of these are lone parent households.

If we encourage parents to work when they have young children, it must mean that they see less of their children. It is reasonable to argue that changes in hours of work mean that children see fewer total hours of their parents than they did in earlier generations. In terms of the longer perspective, however, it would be possible in the 1990s for children to be seeing more of their father than they would have in the 19th century, but probably less of their mother. The more recent changes, increasing women's full-time employment participation, must mean a sizeable reduction, at least since the mid-1980s, in the time some pre-school children spend with their mothers and a less pronounced reduction in the time mothers spend with their school-aged children. Is the father compensating for this reduction in the mother's time with the child? The evidence is mixed but suggests, on the whole, that the answer is 'No'.[3]

Will not a smaller amount of 'quality time' suffice, where the parent gives the child its full attention? We think not. Children need to develop both a sense of security and a sense of self worth. 'Quality time' may well help with the development of self-worth. It will not be able to provide the foundation for security since that will come from 'quantity time'. If the family is meant to shape children's attitudes and behaviour through loving and stable relationships and introduce them to ideas of personal responsibility and mutual interdependence it will be difficult to achieve in one hour per day of a tired mother's time and even less of a tired father's.

We think, therefore, that policy should recognise the need for parents to spend time with their children. There needs to be a recognition that a father's role in family life is equally important to a mother's role and that this cannot be carried out without spending time at home. There are various possible options which would help. More part-time jobs which are not just low-paid jobs for mothers and fathers. It might be useful to have restrictions on the hours of the working day and/or week of parents of very young children.

Education and its link to caring

To what extent should non-parental caring for children be encouraged? Evidence from the Thomas Coram Research Unit in the UK, supported by much American evidence, suggests that care by external centres or child minders is not in general as good as care provided by parents or relatives in a number of respects (Morgan, 1996). Children who attend day care have much less one-to-one interaction with adults than do children cared for at home; their care is less continuous because of staff turnover; the commitment of the carer is often less, and the amount of information they learn is less. Paid nannies who come to the house have many advantages for children, in particular more one-to-one attention. But they still have a high turnover, and they are very expensive and beyond the means of many households. This suggests that there are educational and emotional reasons for limiting the daily hours of non-parental care that young children receive.

In the case of very deprived parents, young children may get considerable benefit from an intervention programme involving attendance at a centre outside the home, but this is normally for only a part of the day and may involve a considerable input of time by the parent. This is not a form of custodial day care which frees the mother for paid employment.

More generally, most young children will benefit from attendance for a few hours a week at some form of pre-school education, but once again this is not the same as day care, since the length of time is short and parental involvement may be required. As far as regular day care is concerned, even top quality professional care is no better than what is available from the typical mother, and for very young children it is often worse in both educational and emotional terms.

The DfEE consultation document on child care further suggested that school effectiveness for older children was related to out-of-school care, but not to parental input after school. There appears to be little evidence on the topic and what there is points in the opposite direction (Franks, 1997).

The costs of child care

There is currently much talk about the need to provide 'affordable' child care. This objective is often justified by citing survey data that report the existence of mothers who would seek employment if (affordable) child care were not a problem. The conclusion is that professional child care should be subsidised. Such a conclusion is unwarranted. The child care lobby is driven by three forces: employers, employed mothers who wish to continue working, and a certain type of feminist. Employers support subsidies for professional child care because they want cheap labour. Employed mothers who wish to continue working have an interest in restricting child care subsidies to those in employment, since the inclusion of non-working parents would absorb funds which they might otherwise get. Some feminists think that all women should be employed and usually full-time, since it will emancipate women from dependence on men both currently and in old age.

Survey responses are only part of the picture, and possibly a misleading part at that. Mothers are normally asked to choose between the status quo (staying at home on present income) and the unique alternative of taking paid work whilst the children are cared for virtually free of charge by highly subsidised professionals. Faced with such a choice, it is not surprising that women from hard-pressed families choose the professional child care option. Their answers might be very different if mothers or fathers were simply offered a fixed amount of money and told they could spend it how they liked. Some would prefer to spend it on full-priced professional care, but many would use it to boost family income whilst caring for their own children since it is financial necessity which drives many mothers of young children to take paid work (Harkness *et al*, 1995; Martin and Roberts, 1984).

If an important motivation for women to take paid jobs when they have young children is the need for money, then allowing them the choice of looking after their own children, whilst receiving a cash equivalent, could have benefits all round. Policies of this kind operate in Sweden and Finland where it is popular to take the cash and care for one's own children. We think the same option should be offered to men who want to stay at home and care for their children.

Fiscal incentives

It is vitally important that the behavioural incentives of any policy be considered and in a comprehensive way. Long hours in paid employment by both parents can leave young children emotionally damaged. It would seem undesirable, therefore, for government policy to encourage this form of parental behaviour. Proposals to give childcare vouchers to mothers who want to increase their hours of work appear to be just such a perverse incentive (see DfEE consultation document). Paying Family Credit only to mothers who have paid jobs is another such incentive, as are the current financial incentives to lone parents to leave the benefit register to take up full-time jobs.

Lone parents are a particularly difficult group. The breakdown of marriage often leaves lone parents, mainly women, in poverty. It is often uneconomic for them to take a part-time job since they are better off on benefit, given the total benefit package they receive (cash plus subsidised housing and other bills), than they would be in a low paid job paying for child care themselves. This obvious and increasing drain on the exchequer's spending has provoked a policy discussion on how to get these women into jobs. Apart from doubts as to whether the economics will work to the Treasury's advantage[4] we need to consider the children. These children have already been deprived of one parent in residence. For the lone parent to take up a full-time job will leave them further deprived of parental time. In the process, it may also reduce the employment opportunities for many poor couples who are struggling to keep their family together. We do not under-estimate the isolation and poverty of lone parents in all this, but other ways of tackling these problems should be found which do not leave the children more vulnerable than they already are, and damage other families.

The first budget of the new Labour government raised the childcare allowance for many lone parents to £100 a week in order to encourage them to take a paid job and reduce their dependence on state benefits. At the same time it increased the tax burden on married parents. Here we make the additional point about the incentives implicit in this policy with regard to marriage. The policy will send out a signal to women considering marriage and family formation that the state will make it easier for them to bring up children out of wedlock so long as they are prepared to have a job and not care for the child themselves. The weight of evidence shows that children brought up in lone parent households do less well and have more problems than children brought up by two parents (Burghes, 1994; Utting, 1996). Thus, the new policy will create incentives which work against marriage and against the most favourable environment and conditions for bringing up children. Moreover, by encouraging lone parenthood, it will exclude an increasing number of men from the responsibilities and satisfactions of family life, thereby adding to the marginalisation of males which is such a worrying feature of modern society. Designing a tax and benefit system which helps the vulnerable without creating incentives for lone parenthood is a difficult problem which should be given high priority.

Discussions about affordable child care have been taking place largely without any simultaneous consideration of the way the tax system has been treating families with children. Here again is another example of a partial view whereby one government department can be considering offering benefits to families for child care on the one hand, and another taking more tax off families. The burden of taxation on couples has increased much faster than the tax burden on single men. The percentage tax on the average earnings of a couple with one main earner (plus two children after mortgage relief) has increased from 12 per cent in 1979 to 20 per cent in 1994/95. This compares with an increase from 23 to 26 per cent for a single man over the same period (Morgan, 1995). This change has increased the pressure on families with children to have two earners. Such a policy would be reversed by a family policy which made children's needs its major concern.

Benefits for the economy?

It is often argued that the time women spend at home looking after children and performing other household tasks is largely wasted. It would be economically more efficient to put the children into professional care centres and for their mothers to take up paid employment. This would increase gross domestic product (GDP) and allow an improvement in the overall material standard of living. We need to consider carefully the components of this calculation.

We examine first the idea that a vast amount of talent is wasted at home which could be better used outside. This may be true in the case of some professional women who withdraw from the labour force or go part-time. In the case of most mothers, their talents and education are no greater than average and their potential contribution to the economy is no greater than average. Moreover, as some feminists recognise (Gardiner, 1996, p245 citing England, 1992) running a home involves extensive managerial skills. One could argue that this is a period when the human capital of many women is augmented, and it is merely prejudice which prevents this benefit being recognised. It may also be the case that the skills of professional women are transmitted more effectively to the next generation if they raise their own children, than if these children go to full-time day care and are looked after by less skilled care workers.

To the extent that there is an economic case for widespread day care, this can only rest upon the existence of economies of scale. If a care worker can look after more children than a mother, then it is conceivable that leaving the children in day care may reduce the total time which society spends upon child care and other household tasks, thereby increasing the amount of time available for other tasks. At first sight this argument is attractive, since the carer to child ratio is often much lower in day care centres than in the home. However, such a comparison is misleading since the full costs involved in this option have not been considered; namely, the enormous cost of high quality child care, the additional expenditure on travel to work, convenience foods and other work-related items, and the time spent travelling to work. These items embody human labour, and a full time-budget would include this labour as part of the social cost of the mother going out to work. When such items are taken into account, the efficiency arguments for day care are not persuasive.

Table 1 shows how the entry of a mother into full-time employment might affect the allocation of time in a hypothetical couple with two children under five years old. The figures are based on what we consider to be reasonable assumptions about working time. In particular, they assume that where the mother is not employed, the total working hours of both partners are equal.[5] If the woman is not employed, she spends on average 66 hours a week on household tasks (childcare, cooking, cleaning, shopping etc.). The man spends 46 hours per week in his job, plus 4 hours travelling to and from work, plus another 16 doing household tasks such as gardening, DIY and childcare, making a total of 64 hours in all. Thus, there is an equal division of labour and the combined hours of the couple are 132 hours a week. When the mother enters full-time employment this situation changes in two ways. The total amount of labour performed by the couple increases dramatically - by 20 hours a week, and this increase is borne almost entirely by the mother, whose additional hours of work and travel greatly outweigh any reduction in the time spent on household tasks. The resulting division of labour is unequal and is also stressful for both partners. Even if tasks were equally shared, the additional hours would still impose a heavy burden on both of them.

Table 1
Comparison of family time budgets and contributions to GDP

How time used	Hours spent by			GDP (units)	male % of time
	father	mother	total		
mother not employed					
Household tasks	16	66	82	0	19.5
Commuting	4	0	4	0	
Job	46	0	46	46	
Total	**66**	**66**	**132**	**46**	**50.0**
mother in full-time employment					
Household tasks	20	41	61	0	32.8
Commuting	4	4	8	0	
Job	46	37	83	83	
Total	**70**	**82**	**152**	**83**	**46.1**
Increase	**4**	**16**	**20**	**37**	

The table also shows how these changes affect gross domestic product (GDP), which is the measure often used to indicate the economic progress of a nation. By convention, this measure covers only those activities which are performed directly for money, so that labour performed within the family and the time spent travelling to and from work are not included. In the table we assume that labour is of uniform quality, so that each hour spent in paid employment creates the same value of output, and hence increases GDP by the same amount. Comparing the two situations, we see that total parental hours increase by 20 when the mother takes up full-time employment and her job creates 37 units of output which are included in GDP.

Where does the extra output go?

Thus, getting mothers into full-time employment gives a large boost to GDP. This is often cited by its advocates as a major economic benefit, but such an interpretation is misleading. Most of the apparent economic gains are the result of accounting conventions, which ignore 'output' produced in the home and focus exclusively on what is produced in exchange for money. If an activity such as child care is transferred from parents to outside professionals, this is classified as increase in GDP even though nothing real may have altered.

Table 2 illustrates this phenomenon in more detail. When the mother takes up full-time employment, she performs 37 hours of paid work per week. We assume that her entry leads to a reduction of 5 hours in the amount of labour performed by other workers, so the overall increase in paid hours in the economy is 32 per week, which creates 32 additional units of GDP. The exact composition of this total depends on the nature of substitute child-care. The table assumes that a high quality Swedish-style day care system is in operation, which involves an average of 3.5 children for each professional child care worker.[6] Thus, to look after the two children in day care requires 21 hours of professional care. In addition, we assume that to supply meals, clean and maintain the nursery buildings, and produce these buildings requires a further 4 hours of labour. Finally, we assume that another 3 hours per week are required to supply and maintain the means of transport (car, bus or train), the additional convenience foods and other items which are utilised as a result of the mother's entry into full-time employment. These are only rough estimates, but they indicate the orders of magnitude involved.

When these various items are taken into account, the picture changes radically. Taking into account the probable displacement of

Table 2   Where do all the hours go?

How time used	Time (hours)	GDP (units)
Mother's job	37	37
Displaced workers	-5	-5
Overall increase		
in paid employment	**32**	**32**
Additional costs:-		
Professional childcare staff	21	21
Childcare buildings, supplies etc	4	4
Convenience foods, transport etc	3	3
Total additional costs	**28**	**28**
Surplus	**4**	**4**

some other workers, then the overall increase in GDP resulting from the entry of the mother into employment is 32 units. Of this total, 28 units consists of the additional goods and services required to support the new pattern of family activity. This leaves a surplus of only 4 units of GDP available for other purposes. Thus, the entry of the mother into full-time employment leads to a large increase in the total amount of labour performed by the family, may damage other workers by reducing their employment opportunities, and produces only a small net addition to GDP.

From the family's point of view the situation is even worse than these figures imply. Suppose there were no taxes and subsidies, so that the family received all of the mother's earnings and purchased day care at full cost. Then, in return for a very large increase in their combined hours of labour, the family would receive a modest increase in its income net of work-related expenses. In reality, however, income is normally taxed and the subsidies on day care are small.

Under these conditions, any net increase in GDP may be entirely appropriated by the state, and the average family may actually be worse off as a result of the mother's entry into full-time employment. The gross monetary income of the family will be higher, but all of the gain may be absorbed by taxes, day care fees and other work-related expenses.

The full cost of dual earning

This is the reality which fuels the campaign for day care subsidies. Apart from highly-paid professional women, there are few mothers whose post-tax earnings are sufficient to cover the full costs of high quality day care for several children and other work-related expenses. Many employed mothers find acceptable child care in the form of friends or relatives, but others have no option but to rely on inferior, low cost care from childminders or understaffed day care centres. For this group there is no doubt that child care subsidies or tax allowances would be of great benefit, providing them with either more disposable income for their families or superior care for their children. However, such a solution presumes that day care subsidies are the best way of helping families, whereas in reality cash may be a more welcome alternative for low income families.

For professional families to purchase high quality child care at full cost may be advantageous since the earnings of the mother are much greater than those of professional carers. However, even a dual earner professional family may feel considerable stress, and the mother's return to work after childbirth may be motivated by her fear of losing her place on the career ladder, rather than any positive desire or immediate economic benefit. Here also solutions other than mothers of young children returning to full-time work may be preferable; for example, greater availability of part-time work in professional jobs for both men and women; or provision for longer career breaks.

What do mothers really want?

Evidence from public opinion polls and observed behaviour suggests that there is a wide diversity of preferences amongst women. Some are certainly desperate to get paid employment as soon as possible, some become depressed if they stay at home. But there is a large number who would prefer to stay at home when their children are younger, or work part time for a period of years. There has been a tendency in discussions and policy documents to assume that all mothers want to work, whatever their circumstances. We think that far more recognition should be given to the diversity of views and preferences. Many married women in employment say they work primarily for money (Harkness *et al*, 1995). If offered cash in lieu of professional child care, one or other partner might well choose to stay at home or greatly reduce their hours of paid employment.

Some feminists believe that it is demeaning to be a full-time mother, because of the "dependency" on men which is involved, or because it does not allow women to achieve their full potential. Quite apart from the condescension involved, this does not accord with evidence from the Nordic countries where women have achieved the highest level of equality in the world. After some years of experience of combining parenting with paid employment, and sustained propaganda in favour of this combination, a Swedish government poll in 1987 revealed that '80 percent or more of mothers regarded it as ideal to be able to care for their children at home, at least until they were three' (Leach, 1994: p72). The revealed preference of mothers in the Nordic countries for either no employment or part-time employment cannot simply be dismissed as false consciousness. Nor does it mean that they wish to withdraw from the labour force permanently, but many would like to do so for a time. This is not surprising, given the stress involved in dual earner families with children, and the satisfactions of motherhood. There is no case for denying mothers freedom of choice.

Conclusions

In conclusion, we think that Britain needs a co-ordinated and coherent set of family policies. These are vital for healthy family life and for servicing the needs of an advanced industrial economy. On economic, personal and social grounds the case for subsidising professional child care at the expense of the cheaper and better alternative of family child care is weak. The outcome would be more hours of labour for the family, little increase in GDP net of work-related costs, and the possibility of unemployment for those displaced in our work-short economy. Universal, accessible, afford-able, high quality professional child care is impractical on grounds of expense; it has no obvious benefits for children, and may be harmful for many of them; it may also be against the wishes of many mothers or fathers who would prefer to use the money to support themselves whilst they look after their own children.

Putting Families at the Centre for Women

Dame Angela Rumbold

One of the minor irritations of having lost my seat at the last election is that the new House contains many more women. It would be fascinating to be there now to see both how those with children cope (and I am sure that for many it will prove hard), and also, more generally, how their presence may influence the way in which the interests of women in the country as a whole are represented.

I suspect that I may have a better understanding of women outside of politics than many of the new career parliamentarians. For it was largely by accident that I went into politics at all. My interest in family life is strong, and it was only when my children no longer needed my constant attention that I even considered spending long working hours away from them.

Putting motherhood first

I have always thought that women fall into two categories when it comes to making the decision about whether or when to have children. Those who think motherhood important, but not the primary force in their lives, make the choice according to the position in their central career when it would be least intrusive. For the other category, in which I place myself, children are the main desire and the career is always a supplementary drive. Thus when I married at just 25 there was no question about whether or not I should have a family. I wanted children because I saw it as my first priority to establish a family, and also because I like small children and indeed still enjoy their company greatly. I have an almost unlimited supply of patience and take great pleasure in watching each stage of development.

It was when the youngest of my children reached the age of

nursery school - three survivors although a fourth was born and did not survive more than a few months - that I was prompted to make a move. My mother announced that I was a great disappointment to her, because I was allowing my brain to atrophy. I ought to sort myself out and get a job.

The comment hit home and I almost immediately enrolled to take a further degree course. I had already obtained a law degree at the age of 20, and now wanted to study Art History. I happily engaged on such a course thinking that I would eventually teach, and this would both be compatible with my growing family and also satisfying to me because of the intellectual stimulus and my own urges to communicate with other people.

Politics, when it arrived, was an accident. I had become very active in a charity looking after the interests of children in hospital. Indeed, I had accepted a part-time job as the Chair and Chief Executive at the same time as I was pursuing my second degree course. It was a chance meeting with a friend who was standing as a local Councillor which set me on my way. I was drawn on by my personal irritation with the local library that never seemed to have heard of the books I wanted, and with the size of the rates as they then were - which made me ask what on earth Councils did to justify their existence. I was asked to stand in a no-hoper seat, and won! Nine years later I was asked to fight a by-election for parliament which no one thought was winnable, and won again. In both instances luck was the main factor in my success. In no way can I present myself as a successful product of the woman's movement.

Personal freedom and family breakdown

I think that much of the basic force in the woman's movement springs out of the desire, which all young people feel to some extent, to be free. But the way that this developed in the 1960s has led to fundamental changes in family life itself. The advent of the contraceptive pill, combined with the impact of books like Germaine Greer's *The Female Eunuch*, has had a major impact on the structure of our society. The freedom from the consequences of sex outside of marriage heralded a whole new experience for young women. For the first time they could behave like men, and the psychological impact has been so great that it has changed the nature of marriage and the response of the female sex to their own biology.

Every generation of adolescents experiments outside the family *mores*. Today, where even the *mores* of the family are in question themselves, experimentation has moved on from sexual freedoms to the freedom to express emotion through whatever medium is available. Today it can be soft drug use, harder substances and certainly alcohol, free sex and tobacco. All these experiments, some inside the law, others outside it, pose challenges to young people to establish their own strength of character and disposition. Fortunately the vast majority are not naturally drawn to addictive behaviour, although many will try things out.

As adolescents progress into adulthood, the majority settle for less adventurous lives, by choosing jobs and lifestyles that are dependent on careful economic management - which in turn acts as a disincentive to the more expensive forms of self abuse. However, although many will also form strong relationships and will marry with the intention of settling permanently, the climate has moved away from longstanding marriage. There is now an emerging pattern of cohabitation, followed by marriage, then perhaps by divorce. Occasionally the whole sequence is repeated once or even several times.

The emotional consequences of such shifting familial behaviour is well documented, not only for the individuals participating in the break up of relationships, but particularly in the lasting effects it has upon any children of the partnership. It is also interesting I think to look at the *different* effect that these relationships may have on men and women, as this is influencing how peoples' expectations of each other and *mores* are changing.

Men tend to become less involved emotionally and behaviourally as the stress of a difficult relationship impinges on their career outside the family. This causes them to withdraw from the disturbances that the break-down of a relationship inevitably brings in its wake. But women react in a different way. Whilst their immediate reaction can be one of emotional distraction, the end result is often a hardening of the will, to prevent such an emotional battering from occurring again. These experiences are often described seductively as 'better for both parties to recognise that their relationship has broken down', and 'so much better for the children not to live in an atmosphere of continuous battle'. But they produce a widening of the gap between men and women and an increased reluctance to work at any relationship beyond a certain point. They result in an increase in self-reliance and self-support rather than a sharing of both emotional and economic activities.

The move towards full social equality

It would be wrong to imply that all of these changes just flow out of the freedom from fear of pregnancy for women, or even out of the introduction of the concept that women should expect as of right an equality of treatment at work and in the home. There have been many other reasons for changes in life expectations; and over the last few decades the desire of women to be more independent has become bound up in a much more complex way with running new forms of, not just reacting against, family life. Increasing involvement in work has been important to this.

The 1960s brought a growing number of women who expected to enter the professions and to make careers for themselves in business, industry and the financial world. Education had improved their view of their own potential, and they were rightly encouraged to expect, if not equal pay, that at least their careers would not be hampered by outmoded custom and practice.

Media interest was also moving away from the themes of freedom and 'the beautiful people' towards more adult images of equality. Through the 1970s we saw the advent of power dressing and of the woman who if not exactly looking like a man, certainly was expected to have the same high aspirations. Margaret Thatcher became the first woman Prime Minister, and although women continued to talk of the 'glass ceiling' they were steadily rising in numbers in powerful jobs and the professions, and equal pay became a reality for some.

The women's magazines were full of articles about how it was possible to have both a happy loving family and a highly successful career. The Prime Minister had managed it and so could every other ambitious woman. Initiatives to encourage women to succeed abounded. Political parties stepped up the campaign to get more women into Parliament. The 300 Group was launched, rapidly followed by other similar groups dedicated to attracting women into the Mother of Parliaments. Government itself devised policies to ensure that more women were climbing the ladder to success in the Civil Service, and the Public Appointments Unit was urged to lift the percentage of women appointed to boards of directors and public offices.

Through the 1980s women continued to prove themselves capable of doing the jobs that formerly were entirely the prerogative of the male of the species, and at the same time to be mothers with happy families and well-managed homes. Of course childcare became an issue. Workplace nurseries were set up in business parks and close to large cities so that the working woman could take her offsping safe in the knowledge that they were being professionally cared for until the evening when they were collected. By this time, too, many of these children did not have a second parent living at home. So the mother would return and take the child home, usually to face the tasks that would in years gone by have been completed during the day. Sometimes there was a role reversal, and the father stayed at home and looked after the children. Occasionally the father was the lone parent himself - working, relying on daytime childcare, and trying to manage household chores in the evenings and at weekends.

Economic factors also became an imperative. Where previously one earner could provide adequately for his wife and children, the pressures of the economy lead both partners to work. The price of mortgages, the cost of living and the rush to run up bills on credit meant it became essential to have two incomes to make ends meet.

Then came the recession in 1991. The full effect of this hit comfortable middle England and the comparatively rich South in a way that had not been experienced for well over seventy years. Jobs disappeared. Middle-aged men were made redundant. Homes lost their value and left their owners with 'negative equity'. Credit was called in and many lost all their savings. Many families suddenly found themselves facing a much lower standard of living and the uncertainty of unemployment. All too often the husband or male partner lost his job and security whilst the woman continued to be the breadwinner. The economic burdens falling on many women's shoulders proved very great, and outside of their previous experience.

Rediscovering families

Slowly the economy has recovered, and job security has improved. But the shock of change has been profound, and many women in the nineties, instead of seeking to compete in the business world, have begun to recognise that they have another even stronger urge. That is to fulfil themselves and their biological functions of motherhood through the experiences of bringing up their young children. After twenty years of competition in the male world of business and industry they could see that the part of their lives which was gone forever were the joys of the early years of their children growing up. It is not the same when Nanny or Granny sees the first steps, hears the first words, notices the first teeth or watches the rapid changes that take place in the first five years of life. Once gone those years are never recaptured.

A new balance needs to be found again. This is recognised by those well educated and highly skilled women who also want to ensure that their children have the security and love that can only be given by a mother and father in a family setting. Some changes in the expectations of employers will be needed, to ensure that women who wish to have a career after their children have left home are not unduly penalised. But society as a whole also needs to reconcile its belief that women should be encouraged to equal men in every aspect of achievement with some acknowledgement that a more secure future lies for a country that bases its values on the importance of the family.

The woman who is willing or wishes to give up work for the time that her children are young should not lose out by seeing the family unit being taxed more heavily than if she were a single parent. She should not lose her pension rights but should be encouraged to continue to keep in touch with work so that her value does not decrease with time off. Home working is increasingly possible these days, and more flexibility by employers is essential if we are to manage/balance/reconcile both the necessity of a second income with the immense long-term benefits of allowing mothers to be the prime carers of their young children. The impetus towards this balance is becoming self-sustaining as more and more successful women leave their careers to bring up their children. The way forward, to help make this welcome move a major change for the benefit of society at large, must come through finding ways to reconcile the twin demands of the need to work and the need to care.

Representing what women want

This brings us back to the role of politicians. Many of the new generation of women Labour MPs, Blair's Babes, are childless. This will certainly make it easier for them to manage the demands of the House - and in some cases it may have meant that it was less of a grind getting there in the first place. But it does not make them the best voices for women in the country as a whole although that, very widely, is precisely how they are being presented.

There is a great responsibility now on all those in the public eye, and throughout the media, to listen to what women actually want for themselves and their families. The power of the press and television to influence change in today's world is immense. But the loudest voices for the last few decades have been the strident feminist writers and broadcasters. Perhaps the best chance for lasting change will come when those voices are exchanged for more mature female representatives of what women of today and tomorrow want to make them feel most comfortable with their lives.

The procedures which I drew up for selecting Conservative MPs should one day guarantee a crop of women better disposed towards the interests of families. But this is bound to be some years away, and much needs to be started right now. So perhaps our best hope has to be that there are now enough women career politicians in the House for *some* of them at any rate to actually listen to what ordinary women say. The days when just *being* there meant that they could claim to represent womankind are over. They might even have to compete with each other to be able to speak *for* women. If they do this is bound to help put families back firmly at the centre where they belong.

The Politics of the Family

Clive Soley MP

When politicians dabble in family values, beware. John Major's ill-fated back to basics campaign foundered when various Conservative MPs were found to be engaged in a wide range of relationships not normally associated with traditional family values. This should be a salutary warning to politicians of all political persuasions and is one of the reasons that politicians should resist the temptation to preach or to use their own families in the political process, especially in any attempt to garner votes.

Politicians who preach about traditional family values are just as likely to lapse from time to time as anyone else - perhaps more likely given the link between sex and power. Yet politicians are under pressure to "do something" about the supposed decline in the family and in standards of behaviour in society.

Whether or not standards really are worse than in previous times is debatable. There can never have been an age when the older generation and their leaders didn't bemoan the lost values of their own past. The fact that we no longer enjoy 'the crispy bacon we had before the war' may have more to do with our ageing taste buds than with real change and the same principle applies to other aspects of human behaviour.

In reality we cannot know with any certainty whether the family is in greater crisis than in past historical periods. The difficulty of making any reliable historical comparison should not however prevent us from examining the problems facing families today. Above all it should not stop politicians and decision makers from looking for ways in which family functioning can be improved. The reason why politicians should debate the family is because it is such an important institution and crucial to the happiness and effective social functioning of individuals. If families are not functioning well then not only do individuals suffer but also the society in which they live has to pick up the consequences of family breakdown, whether in the form of mental illness, crime or simple failure to maximise the individual's potential in life.

Recognising diversity

The debate cannot be value free but it can start with a recognition that families come in all shapes and sizes. Ask most people what their mental image of a family is and they are likely to conjure up a picture of husband, wife, two children and in all probability a dog and a car! In fact, families are far more varied in their makeup. The adults will frequently not be married or have been married before. The family may be of an adult child living with an elderly parent, two sisters or brothers living together. The variety and complexity of family life is too great for simplistic legislation or prescriptive moralising.

This is not some fine academic point. I saw a constituent recently who had fathered a child and the mother then had two other children by another man with whom all three children lived following her death. Because the deceased mother had felt the second father was not capable she had asked the first father to stay involved. He did so and in fact goes to the home several times a week to cook, wash and iron. Where does this family fit in the conventional wisdom of the moralists and who is going to be so bold as to criticise the morality involved?

From time to time governments around the world have attempted to prescribe family structure. Governments of both right and left have dabbled in this and it almost invariably ends in tears and sometimes catastrophic failure.

The latest manifestation of this desire to prescribe family form is the growing tendency to associate marriage with family. This latest form of politically correct thinking holds that if we encourage marriage then family functioning will be improved; politicians from both parties have therefore suggested altering the tax system to benefit marriage. But why this should necessarily produce happier or better parents is not immediately obvious. In fact it is the quality of the relationships within the family that is likely to determine its success, not the legal framework or the financial payments made by the state. You cannot buy love and you cannot buy good relationships.

None of this should be taken to mean that marriage is unimportant. It is important precisely because over many centuries and in a wide variety of religions and cultures it has been used as a way in which people publicly express their committment to each other. The structure of marriage has been through many changes over the ages and between cultures but in modern Britain its importance lies in the desire of two people to have a public ceremony where they express and record their act of commitment to each other and perhaps to any children of the union. Its importance to the couple is why it must be treated with respect and why state and churches should create the circumstances where the marriage ceremony can be a rewarding and enjoyable experience.

We do need to encourage stable and happy family relationships, preferably with both parents present. Single parents have to carry a far greater burden of work and responsibility; when there are two parents, the child has two role models as well as two sources of support and friendship. What we must give greater recognition to is the enormous significance of becoming a parent.

There is a danger that churches will emphasise the importance of marriage because it protects and enhances part of their function, but given the increasing number of childless adults the real emphasis should be on the needs of children. Why do we emphasise and research marriage, yet spend so little effort on studying the father's commitment to parenting and the way society undervalues the paternal role? I suspect that focussing on marriage and the churches' role enables us to duck the far more difficult question of support for parenting, and particularly fathers, across society as a whole.

If family policy were to be restricted to helping and preparing couples for marriage we would be failing to address the problems that beset families except at the margin. So what should family policy be about? It is this question which politicians have failed to address. We know that the social and economic structure of the state affect family functioning but it is such a complex area that it is easier for the political process to ignore its impact on family life and for the politicians and other commentators to focus instead on moralistic statements. But condemning for example single parent families neither explains the growth of such families nor helps parents cope with the problems of rearing children alone. Nor does it address the double standards of some male politicians, editors, religious leaders and other opinion formers who moralise about single parents while leaving the 'wife' at home to bring up the kids while they get on with the 'serious' business of running the country.

A crisis in men's roles

The barely concealed agenda here is that if man can get on with hunting and gathering then woman can get on with running the home. For better or for worse, modern society is no longer like that, and changes in technology and the economy make it an unsustainable system even if it was ever desirable. Many men are facing a crisis of identity because the roles that were ascribed to them in the industrial revolution began to fade away with the collapse of heavy industry and left them uncertain - are they hunter gatherers or parents? Are they the dominant male or the co-operative partner? What if their greater physical strength is devalued and intelligence and dexterity given a higher reward and the woman turns out to be better equipped to survive in this brave new market? If the male is not much use at earning an income because the modern market doesn't value his strength and macho style and if he's not much use round the house or with the kids what is his role? Is he to be valued only as a stud but not wanted on the journey? How do we prepare men for these more complex challenges?

The picture I am conjuring up may be a stereotype but it is an outline of what has happened in many of our regions where heavy industry has gone and the unskilled male is left jobless and without value. Whether in the inner city or in the areas where the old male dominated industries existed the redundant male has yet to find a role and it should come as no surprise that these are the situations where women are more likely to be single parents. And how easy it is for politicians to scapegoat these women! It's so much easier than addressing social change.

It is hard to overstate the importance of the social and economic structure as a determinant of family structure and of family functioning. Shortly after the Meadowell riots of 1991 I visited the area (a housing estate near Newcastle) and met an action committee set up by the local residents to improve the estate. The members of the committee were all women - about 15 of them - and as I recall, none was under 35. When I asked why there were no men I was told they were out fishing or down the pub. Although these women were taking the lead they were not going to allow the men to be criticised: they summarised the situation by the statement "they use to have work in the pits and in the shipyards. They've got nothing now". Estates on the periphery of big cities like Meadowell confront society with the problems in stark terms. Unemployment is high, poverty rife, opportunities for advancement very limited. The riot that took place was conducted primarily by young males. It says a lot about the relative roles of men and women that men commit crimes much more commonly than women but women receive treatment for mental ill health much more commonly than men. Or, to put it in other words, men externalise their problems while women internalise theirs.

So the question of the role for men in a modern market economy is a crucially important one. If they are no longer going to be the metal bashers and the unchallenged leaders of commerce and industry what do we expect of them? Men have begun to answer this more than we might suppose and certainly more than legislation allows for.

In South Wales estimates vary but at the height of the last slump (1988 to 93) about half the main carers of children at home were men. Meanwhile the women were increasingly employed in the assembly of electronic goods where they enjoyed the advantages of manual dexterity and an absence of any need to assert their dominance as males. More importantly still they were cheaper to employ. Differential pay rates can be a major factor in deciding who stays at home to look after the children. How different from the days when the Welsh economy was dominated by the miner coming home to a hot bath prepared by the wife and with the expectation that he was the final arbiter of punishment of the children. For better or for worse there is no going back!

It is tempting for a politician of the left to assert that the eradication of poverty and the creation of full employment would be the best family policy. Certainly it would make family breakdown less likely. But even in societies where there is significantly less unemployment and poverty, such as the Scandinavian countries, there are still problems about family identity and male/female roles.

What politicians can and cannot do

Politicians need to be realistic about the limits of policy and they need to be clear about attainable objectives. We cannot predict the way technology and the economy will affect the family and work roles in the 21st century. There may be much more home working. But if so will parenting be shared or will it still be primarily a female role? Or will men be come more marginalised and have even more difficulty competing with women in certain occupations? Will men still keep women below the glass ceiling?

It is because prediction is so difficult that a better approach to policy formulation is to make no assumptions about different roles between the sexes. What we need to focus on is the viability of the family and the effectiveness of parenting and this we can do without moralising and without having to second guess technical and economic change.

The aim of the policy maker should be to create flexible systems that allow the individuals within the family to select their roles and the state and private companies need to ensure that flexibility. The now accepted term of 'family friendly policies' is the appropriate term in my view. Attempts by the state or by companies to apportion roles will fail not least because families do make their own decisions. Who is to say which parent is to look after the children and during what stage of their lives? Such questions have to be decided within the family.

It is all too often assumed that it is the woman who wants children or that there is some rational choice made about parenting. In fact the choices that are made are extremely complex. The man may want children more than the woman. The relative desire of one parent for children may change after the children arrive. The choice is not always made with equal enthusiasm by both partners and in a way that lasts through the full period of parenting.

So if we are to help parents and families we need policies that allow flexibility. Politicians cannot realistically be asked to create legislation which prescribes some mythical 'best' family or 'best' role for men and women. They can and should however be asked to create legislation and policies that allow parents to determine the roles that best suit them in bringing up children. They can and should be asked to create the legislation and policies that give the best chance to a child, in whatever family structure, to maximise their potential.

These policies are possible and can be appled in the light of existing social and economic structures and practices. In particular this means nursery education, child care facilities at work and in residential areas, paternity leave to encourage bonding soon after the birth of a child and to give support to the woman after birth. It includes some aspect of relationship education in the school curriculum to allow youngsters to learn more about sex education, child rearing and interpersonal relationships generally. It embraces counselling for families and relationships in difficulty. These are the areas where policy can be particularly helpful.

The failure of the moralistic approach and of the prescriptive roles approach is that it fails to recognise the complexity of the real world of relationships. This is aggravated by systems of Government which departmentalise policy in such a way that it is difficult to devise a coherent family policy.

Co-ordinating policies

Attempts to address this problem have focussed on ideas like a Ministry for Women or for the family or for children. I no longer think such approaches work. I would prefer a sub committee of the Cabinet, chaired by a senior Minister, to have responsibility for family policy. It is not ideal but it would enable some coordination to take place. It was the failure of the last government in this respect that led to the main recommendation of the All-Party Parliamentary Group on Parenting in their report that the Government should improve co-ordination between Government departments, local authorities and health authorities.[1] Despite the new Government's stated commitment to the family, I see no evidence yet of that wish being translated into action by setting up the necessary co-ordinating machinery.

Until we do get effective co-ordination at Government level we are unlikely to get the leadership necessary to ensure family friendly policies in either the private or public sector. A few companies are leading the way and both local and national government are beginning to realise the importance of this area of policy, but it is slow at present and limited to important but discreet areas like nursery provision. Nursery provision is vitally important but is anyone asking why we still have housing policies which result in families being in emergency accommodation for years? Or which puts families with young children in high rise flats where the children have to stay in all day or play outside unsupervised where they can drift into vandalism and crime? What are we doing with transport policies that make parents fearful of letting their children walk to school or play in the street through fear of accidents? Above all, who is preparing men, especially the less skilled, for family responsibility?

It is these policy areas that governments can influence and in doing so would improve parenting and family functioning. If we simply try to second guess the direction of social and economic change, and if we try and prescribe the form of family structure, then we are likely to fail.

Declaration of Peace between the Genders

Michael Young

The old war between the genders has lost most of its ferocity. Victory has gone to women, not yet fully on the ground where the war is still being waged, but on the battlefield of ideas. The claim for equality is no longer being denied, at any rate in public. Men are still protesting in private, and still hold on grimly to their positions of power in politics, industry, academia, the media. But they began to lose their advantage, of physical strength, from the moment the Industrial Revolution produced the machines which have by now largely replaced muscles. They no longer declare their right to superiority with any force, and once the legitimacy of their claim to predominance is no longer asserted, it will not be all that long before equality in one sphere after another becomes a fact and from there on the superiority will be the other way round.

What's wrong with that? The beginning of the third millennium would see justice done to the no-longer-weaker sex as some compensation for all the injustice of the second millennium and the first. The wrongs of two thousand years to trillions of Marthas would be righted, and, considering the pace at which events are moving, the final verdict in favour of women could be handed down quite soon.

Girls born now could see it all happen by the time they decide not to marry.

Difference without inequality

What then? Men won't like it, and more militant resistance and abuse will become the order of the day. They will draw more pungent and bitter attention to the numbers of men who are unemployed and to their more subservient role at home when there is a home. They will try to turn the tables again. But I maintain that in this they will have no chance of succeeding. Without right on their side, they cannot win. The only way to win is not to win. The only way to win is to move the goalposts, and play another game in which both genders win, in which the drive for equality is succeeded by something more fundamental, the drive for difference.

There are two reasons why, after a few more decades, this is how things will begin to move. The first is because people would perish if the differences between the genders ceased to count, as could happen if women were indistinguishable from men in work and men indistinguishable from women in the home, and more indistinguishable in general. We would be far too much the same and it would be extraordinary if fertility did not fall away as a consequence.

The greatest threat to the developed world, homogeneity, goes further than being a threat to fertility. The same basic industry, the same basic media, the same sports, the same way of life cluttered up with the same material goods. We are only saved from being drowned by abundance by the weekly potlatch when the refuse men (not yet women) march up to throw the weekly excess into the champing teeth of their pulverising machines. Fly from Osaka to Orlando, from Orleans to Osnabruck, from Oklahoma to Orrefors, from Ontario to Orvieto, and soon we will hardly know we have moved further than next door. Next door will be so much like the door at the other end of the world.

Life would be intolerable if to all this enveloping homogeneity was added gender homogeneity. The bitter protest of the old order - the desperate heaving over the genital differences between men and women in the last half of the 20th century - would be quieted. It could not survive a fundamental homogenisation of men and women. We would be called on to celebrate the great victory - that at last men and women were the same - and we would lie down not to follow the *Kama Sutra* but, without the stimulus that difference produces, to yawn our way to a dreary, dreamy death. But I believe that long before that happens, people will realise that it is going to happen and take action to ward off being overcome by boredom before they actually are.

The second reason is that, miserable as many men have become as the scales of justice have tilted against them, the chief sufferers have not been men but children of both sexes. Boys have suffered more than girls as more men have lost their confidence and hence their magnetism as role models. But both girls and boys have by and large had more miserable childhoods. The hard work of their parents has obtruded too forcefully into their domestic lives; the work of mothers and the work or non-work of fathers has carried the dominant hurry sickness into the homes. Children have been timetabled, their slow rhythms of growth and world-discovery made subservient to the more mechanical rhythms of the office and the factory. Machines have entered into the heart of the family, and against it, and prepared children for the driven life they are going to have to lead.

Some of the children will submit to being plopped down from an early age in front of TV sets and videos of *Thomas The Tank Engine* and telephones that play *Three Blind Mice*. Many others, and I think an increasingly large minority, will not put up with it. The little darlings will become the wild savages of a technologically ever more marvellous world, but a world that for the victims will have ceased to scintillate. Global warming will be accompanied by emotional chilling too cold to bear unless first a few, and then a few more, and then many more, start off in a new direction.

Time for valuing diversity

What direction would that be? It cannot be towards a future which is better for women alone or men alone, or at all for the one at the expense of another. It has to be a future which is better for both. To my mind, it has to be a future in which the hurry sickness is abated, in which the acquisitiveness for material goods is abated, in which material gifts to children are no longer thought to be the symbols of love, in which the pressure of work is lessened if not lifted, in which the increasing productivity brought by technology is taken out in real leisure and the slow appreciation of each other and of their children.

The search for riches and more riches has often been denounced as self-defeating. However much people have, they are supposed to want still, still more or, better put, hectic, hectic more. They are all taught, we are all taught, to believe in more. The case against more has often been made before, most recently by ecologists, and never heeded; but the coming crisis in the relationships of men and women, and of both of them with their offspring, will give it a new urgency and cogency.

Reduce the salience of work and the edge would be taken off the competition between the genders. The inferiority of one or the other in that sphere would matter less. Men and women could be gradually relieved of the cultural imperative to step up their incomes on a steady gradient every year. They could have time to be with each other without the harassment of a get-rich society and to cultivate and appreciate their differences. Some of the most important qualities and differences of the human race are femininity *and* masculinity.

They could have time to be with their children. They could stop being tied to one particular identity and explore other sides to their own complex natures, which are so much more complex than their roles. They could enjoy more individual lives in a more meaningful collective.

It would help if a start were made to rephase the life cycle, retiring later but with both genders having five years off paid work. They would be paid after the birth of children in order to take unpressured delight in their children when the children are at their most delightful, and they are at their most loving. If nowhere yet does not become somewhere soon; if there is no moral substitute for the war between the sexes, there is not going to be anything to celebrate when another century comes to an end. There will be none but technologically sophisticated and emotionally barren savages to celebrate it.

A Manifesto for Men[1]

Jack O'Sullivan

As men, we know we could get a better deal. We look at women and see modernity: expansive people exploring new roles, conquering the world. Quietly, secretly, we admire the gathering pace of their achievement. And we say to ourselves: what about us? Isn't this how we are supposed to be, bright, confident, going places?

So what is getting in our way? There is no point in blaming women, stoking up a sex war. This remains, after all, a man's world. If we knew what we wanted, we could enact it. No, the problem is our lack of imagination. Ask women what they, as women, want and they'll tell you: equality. Men? We haven't a clue. And the reason is simple. We have failed to understand the opportunities of this century's greatest and most enduring social movement, the collapse of the sexual division of labour.

Women know the demise of the old order makes them more powerful, because it provides economic independence. So they have shed the past with enthusiasm. But we are confused. We think that because the old order gave us economic power over women, the world must have been designed to meet our specifically male needs. So we see change as a source of loss, not gain, and desperately hang on to the vestiges of the past. While women surf the tide of history, we seem to be drowning.

We're making a mistake. The past ill-served our real needs. It forced us into a narrow sense of ourselves as workers, which fell apart when we were sacked, retired or fell ill. It drove us out of our homes and made us strangers to our children. It meant we sub-contracted our physical, emotional and practical needs to women. They fed us, nurtured us, gave us access to their feelings, mediated a social world for us. They did our private labour, just as we did their public work. For all the adult behaviour we demonstrated outside the home, we remained children within it. It left us, particularly the elderly, half-dead, living sad, limited lives, often stuck in soured relationships.

We can change all this. And it isn't just wishful thinking. A fair wind was behind women's liberation: in a few decades they gained control of their own fertility, while the economy demanded a vast expansion in the labour force. Even conservative men couldn't stop them.

Likewise technological change is on our side. Today's information revolution - and the job flexibility pioneered by women - allows many of us to bring work back into the home. Low birth rates, female income-earners and improved life expectancy for women free us from simply being breadwinners. The way is open for us to cast aside our fathers' dependence on women. Indeed, it is possible today for a man to father his own child via a surrogate mother and raise it without having a relationship and without having a woman around. Most men would not seek this arrangement, but the possibility is a liberation. Soon, though we will still love women, we will no long need them in the traditional way.

The first step must be for us to break our silence. Hence this manifesto.

1 Just imagine how we might be

When the sexual division of labour underpinned notions of being a man, we defined ourselves in three ways: as breadwinning workers, as the opposite of women, and as fathers who did what mothers did not do. Each notion rules out a vast sphere of activity and stifles men. We must rewrite these definitions.

2 Work is not the promised land

When people ask me what I am, I say I'm a journalist. Not a man. Not a father, not a husband, not a son, not a brother, not a citizen, not even a combination of these; a journalist. Like many men, I am my work. When work's OK, I'm OK. Everything else might be falling apart, but success at work sustains a man. It provides status, power and a means to be a breadwinning father. The women's movement has only further emphasised the paramount status of work and that, by implication, domesticity and child-rearing is drudgery.

Yet expecting work to support our sense of self so fundamentally is a mistake. Many self-definitions survive the passage of time. Job isn't one of them. It's too insecure. One day we know we'll get fired, sick or retire. For those who are young and can't get a job or are dumped on the scrap heap at any early age, failure at work leads to depression, crime, violence and, in some cases, suicide. Must a man go mad before he discovers a sounder way of valuing himself? We have to realise that putting faith in work is a con.

3   Man is not the opposite of woman

When women were seen to be weak, we had to be strong. We did what women didn't do, but now there's hardly anything women won't do. They play sports, earn money, attend football matches, fly RAF fighters and initiate sex. Yet we persist in thinking of ourselves as the 'opposite' of women. At this rate, we'll end up defined as the people who do the few activities women don't want to do: rape, murder and abuse.

4   Fathers, too, can fulfil all a child's needs

We remain limited by the traditional image of fathers as providing income, discipline and, in some cases, a playmate for a child. Physical and emotional intimacy with children have been the prerogative of women and largely continue to be so. Today many men want to be closer to their children and are active fathers. We enjoy it and are competent. But some women refuse to treat us as equals. History exposes these attitudes as nonsense. As Adrienne Burgess shows in her new book on fatherhood (1997), in the 19th century there were many more lone fathers, because of high rates of maternal mortality and because custody of children was automatically granted to fathers after separation. These days, the supports available to modern parenting - manufactured baby milk, child minders, nurseries - mean a father can do everything a mother does.

Yet we have failed to challenge an anti-father culture. Schools ignore a boy's potential to become a father and offer no training. At antenatal appointments, health workers look straight through expectant dads. When a child is born, there is no state entitlement to paternity leave. Employers don't usually expect to make concessions to fatherhood (such as looking after a sick child). Most men can forget trying to go part-time: that way lies redundancy. And a divorced father can expect only very limited access to his children, while an unmarried one may have no rights at all.

In the past, the only relationship many mothers had to the working world was to keep their husbands going by cooking and washing for them. We regard such notions as outdated. Yet most British institutions still act as though a father's family role is to earn money so his wife can bring up the kids. And while the Equal Opportunities Commission exists to support women's rights in the workplace, there is no equivalent to encourage a man's rightful place at home with his children. The Child Support Agency chases dads to pay up, but does nothing to help us father our children.

5 All men should aspire to the spirit of fatherhood

The importance of reclaiming fatherhood goes beyond men with children fulfilling the potential of their role. The 'father' concept is a way we can generally modernise ourselves. As the father of a baby daughter, it allows me to be caring and emotional without being judged wimpish or gay. It's a grown-up role, freeing me from what might otherwise be a narcissistic, Peter Pan existence. It's a channel for my male desire to be protective. And I'll always be a dad, whether or not I've got a job.

I'm not suggesting every man should throw away the condoms and start breeding. But men should be encouraged into fathering-type roles and attitudes - particularly to young people. This new image could begin to solve the crisis for young men. Children under 11 spend most of their time in the company of women - at home, in nursery, at school. Boys, especially in single-parent homes, have little access to men. It's hardly surprising they seem so lost. They need us to be more involved with them, mentoring them, helping them in sports, at school and generally growing up. We could teach boys assertiveness and self-defence, so they learn non-violent ways of expressing themselves. We could provide them with a safe place to talk. Boys these days worry that they will say the wrong 'sexist' things - better to stick to the computer. If high-status jobs were created for men to work with children, it would help men themselves and give boys their missing role models.

6   Equality begins at home

In many homes men are passive, allowing women to organise our personal lives, letting them act as gatekeepers of the home, determining which friendships are maintained, how involved the couple is with family. Many of us find it difficult to take the initiative or to say no to women at home, because we never learned how to say no to our mothers.

7   Good sex involves negotiating what we really want

Our passive and reactive nature is often reflected in our sexual relations with women. As young men we develop much of our sexuality in a secret way, through masturbation, for example. And many of us never get past this furtive style of exploration. We never realise that it is OK to ask, indeed argue with women for what we want. Many of us remain in awe of our lovers, as we were of our mothers. We fear disapproval and, above all, contempt. The popularity of pornography marks, at least in part, our failure to be honest with our lovers about our desires.

We are also confused about what women are asking for. They seem to despise 'sensitive' men, but don't want the old-style, buttoned-up tough guys, either. And the rules of courtship seem to change all the time. We need everyone to be straight about what they really want.

8   Public institutions should look at men in a new light

Take the NHS. The creation of women's services shows that gender can influence health needs. In Australia significant gains are additionally being made by targeting men. The NHS may have been created by men, but that does not mean it serves our needs as well.

9   Respect comes from self-respect

The negative image of men has sprung from surrendering the public debate to those who are pissed off with us: women. We owe it, if not to ourselves, then to our sons, to correct the record.

10 Men must start doing it for themselves

Successful men must take up a leadership role. Too often they stay quiet because they have least to gain from rethinking their roles. Their jobs are relatively secure, with high status and power over women. They have some control over their working hours, can often work from home and afford child care. They can still have it all.

So they hang on to what can be salvaged from the old order, and close their minds to reshaping the world in a way that better suits all of us. The men's movement is thus often inhabited by angry, inarticulate men who lack an intellectual framework for understanding their dilemmas. Intelligent, educated men could lead the way. We need them to start thinking, fast.

What Do We Need Men For Anyway?

Fay Weldon

It is often said these days that men are becoming redundant. But redundant to what? Women can get by without them, true enough, and always could, and often had to, and so can men without women, come to that. But where's the fun? When it comes to the children women have always had to manage as best they could, with or without men's help. It is very nice when women can bring up their children and have a partner there who will help out. But if no man is around a woman will do it. She has to. There they are, the little howling dependent things, and you do what you can. Nature insists. This is rather less true the other way round in my experience. If women are not there men will, because they have to, look after children. But there usually is a woman around, both because there are more women than men - or used to be - and because nature cuts in more savagely with women than with men. Men *do* bond, but less usually than do women. It is more natural in the man to drift off, driven by the selfish gene.

My own childhood is a case in point. My father left home when I was five and I was brought up in a household composed entirely of women. I went to a girls' school and very seldom met a man. And this went for lots of my friends too. The children of such homes usually consort with children in a similar situation. You always discovered, when you looked round your friends, that they had the same sort of background. You mutually vetted one another, in the hope that others could understand your predicament - which was that you were 'not as others were'. This was in New Zealand in the thirties when mine was a rather unusual situation. By tradition most men worked, and women stayed at home and envied them, whereas my mother was alone and went out to work and supported us.

I was in touch with my father, though, and would visit and stay with him. He was a doctor, and an extraordinarily competent, good and charming doctor. When we stayed with him we would often go out with him on his rounds. We lived in a rural area, and he didn't like to leave us behind. We kept him company on his rounds. He was a very interesting and remarkable man and I admired him very much.

He was always full of ideas. I remember he put on a production of Ibsen's *Peer Gynt* for the local people in a tiny little ghost-, former gold-town. There was a group of energetic people in New Zealand at the time, bent on bringing drama to the outback, and they would all be putting on these community plays, up and down the length of the country. He was always great fun, an admirable person. However he was never a good provider, and no, I wouldn't say he was a useful and reliable member of 'a family'. But he was to the community.

At the time men didn't see 'parenting' as much to do with them. I can see that this was in some ways women's fault. Women of my mother's generation would say to men if they stepped into the nursery and picked up the baby 'Oh, don't drop it!' This kind of relegated men to non-fatherhood, for ever. The wilful driving out of the father meant that women's lives were more circumscribed than they are now.

Women ran the nursery and kitchen and men went out into the world and brought back news of what was going on. And as a division of labour it was not all that bad, for many women, perhaps even for most women.

It was what many of them wanted. Women liked men to be providers - and still do, even if the state has to take over the role of those individual men who are absent. In myth men were the effective ones but in practice, as far as I could see, women did everything - as they do in most societies in the world. I don't think it ever has been different and I have given up insisting that women complain about it since it seems endemic to the female nature to do absolutely everything, and in men's nature to be idle and decorative. Show me a man having a bad time and I'll show you a woman having a worse time. So let us just get on with it. But women are changing their notion of what they require of men; which is why some say there is a crisis in men's roles.

The gender-switch

Women have always hoped to be able to do more for themselves. But while men controlled women's fertility, which they did, a woman's life was out of her own hands. As soon as you get to the pill the whole structure of society changes. Women in the sixties gained control of their fertility, and more were able to earn, and could support themselves without having to be dependent on men. Men fought back at first and were truly horrible to women, and were amazingly insulting to them, through the sixties and seventies. And indeed, women were not yet accustomed to speaking in public or being in charge of anything, and were in the habit of presenting themselves as rather foolish creatures, and often were. Why should men not notice?

But then, at certain levels of society, women got fed up with it, and feminism arrived. Women began to be horrible to men in their turn. Gender, it turned out, was a two-way street. Women began to speak well of themselves and badly of men, lost their capacity for adoration; and suddenly everything changed at once - attitudes, social structure, and a technology fitted to female labour. Since the invention of the typewriter there has always been something bitsy and boring outside the home that women can do. But now women needed men for support less than they did. The same kind of things, with variations, were going on in other countries.

There are demographic factors too. There are now more men than women. So if men want sexual partners they are in a client situation, as women so often used to be - especially after a war, and men rather liked wars. The men who survived had a larger pool of women to choose from. Worth the risk. Women had to compete then to please men, and now men have to compete to please women.

All this has gradually led to a turn-around in man-woman relations. A sort of gender-switch has occurred, which was not quite what women wanted. Women are now in a way as nasty to men, and as rejecting of them, as men ever were to women. We've had a switch from a patriarchy to a form of matriarchy; from a Father God and wicked witches to Mother Nature and abusing fathers. We have therapism, the whole healing-by-talking business, which is anti-rational and so traditionally female, and divisive in families and society: inasmuch as we've evolved a cultural habit of putting blame on others. There's a whole new belief abroad as to what people are. We have New Labour, a touchy-feely form of politics, caring and sharing. In our former religions there was a sense of sin: the idea that you were born imperfect, striving to be good. There is now a sense that we are all born perfect - bright, beautiful, good and intelligent - and if we are not then it is somebody's fault. Somebody out there is to blame. Our spouse. Our teacher - if we don't get into university. Someone.

We now need ten million extra houses because 28% (growing, and expected to rise to 30% any minute now) of households consist of only one person - which seems to me not what people were designed for, or necessarily what makes them happy. Feminism is just one element in all of this, but may indeed have triggered off a whole lot of other things. But as to what is cause and effect, what is the disease and what is the symptom, perhaps we are still too close to be able to say.

Whatever the precise links may be, and however things fit together, all our lives have been changed as a result of the feminisation of our culture. Women are affected as well as men, or perhaps even more so. Many now prefer not to have children, which they may well regret when they get to their sixties and seventies and older. But who at thirty ever thinks they'll get there, or if they do, will be living, feeling, regretting sentient beings. Some women will come to feel it terribly, and a lot of people won't or will deny it. Look around today and you see lots of women without children, who wouldn't dream of having them they're having far too nice a time. They look at those who do have children, who have a terrible time, and who don't have enough disposable income, and feel sorry for them. The childless have good sex lives, and no doubt will continue to do so - but the having of children is what pulls marriages, partnerships, apart.

I used to think wilful childlessness was rather shocking. I used to have all kinds of pious and virtuous feelings about having babies - that only by having babies did you ever learn to be unselfish or to discover what you are yourself. Nowadays I couldn't think of one good reason to discover who you were. Better be blind to it, say I.

More women are relying on their careers for their major satisfaction in life. And this may be a mistake for many. Careers are very interesting until you are thirty or thirty five, and then they begin to pall because other, younger people are doing more or better than you in those same structures. You have done it all before anyway and there are no surprises. And just as with men, only the one man got promotion, rose to the top, so with women its' only the few. The point of the race is that all but one get left behind. What happens to all the others? At the age of fifty most men still have the family, the history, the relations, the life, the Golden Wedding party and all that. Women who have remained single don't have that. They have their friends. But friendship goes, just like marriages go. Then they can find themselves in a very difficult situation. It isn't fair, but life never was.

I have many friends like this. They get to a certain age and sometimes they are very successful and sometimes they are not. And then they wish they had not had that abortion, they wish they had married this man, that man, they wish they had not been so picky. They wish all kinds of things. But then again you meet married women of the same age who say 'Oh I wish I had never had that son. What a waste of orange juice!', or 'I have been married to this terrible man all my life. I wish I was you and unencumbered.' I think that a lot of this is simply temperamental, and very little to do with gender. We want what we don't have. But I would think, by looking at it, that by the time a woman gets to fifty or sixty it is better to have had children than not. On the other hand, you are never going to get everything.

A role for men after the revolution

It is impossible to say how things will turn out in the future. But I think that it may be leading to a new role for men, or for those who can adapt to what women want. There was a revolution - a feminist revolution, though it was also more than just that - and I fear we'll lose a generation as a result. Everything has changed, society has been turned upside down, and as happens after any revolution, yes, you lose a generation. They are lost, lost, lost. We have become self-centred while we mill around one another, inventing new social structures and trying to create new ways of living and being, and so far failing.

But the human race is extremely ingenious, and will find ways of making life comfortable for itself. The society of the future, I suspect, will do without concepts and merely seek the authenticity of its own emotions, which will be seen as without moral content. 'Good' and 'bad' are on their way out. 'Caring' and 'selfish' are on their way out.

The generation of women which comes after us may well look at those without children, these barren twigs on the tree of life, this stunted growth, and cry "Not for us! Let me have six children and you, husband, go out to work or, indeed, you husband look after the children and I'm going out to work." And such people might very well manage to marry in new ways - as young people are beginning to, I find - with gentler men marrying confident women who are good at earning, while men look after the babies and are perfectly happy. I think this is happening already. If you go to the school gate now you will see men, waiting and gossiping; if you go to the shops you see the men with babies. How did you react to that word, 'Gossiping'? Did you think but that's what women do, not men? Gotcha!

I think that if my father were living in Britain now he would be very like my son Daniel, who is making and producing films *and* is also a very good family man. But then he's married to a woman who will allow him to be a father. Dan is a born impresario, but he is also dedicated to his children. Today's society allows men to be involved in parenting. Because he lives in a different culture, he is a reasonable provider and an involved father. Women want this now, and so I believe do men, and it is I hope the way that society will presently settle down after so much turmoil and strife.

The Androgynous Generation

Helen Wilkinson[1]

At the dawn of a new millennium, we find ourselves in the middle of an historic change in relations between men and women as rapid demographic, technological and economic changes combine to unravel many of the assumptions not only of two hundred years of industrial society but also millennia of traditions and beliefs.

This revolution, not yet complete, has been far from painless. Indeed, it has been more painful than most because it challenges our very sense of self, our very identity. At work or at home, men and women often seem like gender warriors engaged in a civil war that shows no signs of abating. From rising divorce rates, to escalating harassment claims at work (from both men and women) the gulf of understanding between the sexes has never seemed so vast, and the bitterness never greater.

A contract under strain

The evidence of a contract under strain is not hard to identify. Over the last three decades, as women have entered the workforce, men have exited it. Shared breadwinning has become the norm, and in some cases, especially at the less skilled, less educated end of the spectrum, female breadwinners are actually displacing male breadwinners altogether. Instability in the workplace is mirrored by instability closer to home. Women are increasingly calling the shots in relationships - often parting ones - as men struggle to adapt to the new expectations women have of them. The divorce rate continues to rise (with women initiating the majority), marriage rates are in historic decline, birth rates have slumped, whilst the number of women choosing to remain child free has dramatically increased.

But these are only symptoms. The underlying reasons for these stresses and strains are economic and cultural. The old style sexual contract was role-based - loosely defined here as one in which men were to be breadwinners, and women were to be homemakers - and it was modelled on the needs of the industrial era, an era when physical strength was important, when our manufacturing base was strong and when routine jobs for unskilled and semi-skilled men were abundant. Equally important was the fact that the cultural politics of the time reinforced and legitimated the emerging sexual division of labour.

However that era has gone, torn asunder by globalisation and rapid technological change, to be replaced by an information-based service sector economy. The skills that were once central to the domestic economy - flexibility, inter-personal and communication-based - have moved centrestage to the economy as a whole, displacing many men from their role as sole breadwinners in the process and leaving them to share the task with the partners in their lives. Technological change crucial in driving many women from the paid labour market in the late eighteenth and nineteenth centuries is now by contrast a source of male joblessness and a driver of female employment.

The economic and technological revolution, combined with shifts in women's values, has ripped through our culture. This is the *genderquake*. It has brought in its wake huge instability in relationships, family life and the workplace. In particular, it has subtly transformed the balance of power between the sexes - in the bedroom with the advent of the pill, in the kitchen as technological advance has freed women up from domestic chores, and in the workplace as technology begins to break down the distinctions between work and home. But perhaps most important of all, the influence of feminist ideas has so permeated our culture that the very legitimacy of the old style sexual contract has come under unprecedented challenge from the majority of women who now reject the idea that a man's place is at work and the woman's at home.[2]

Rewriting or modernising the sexual contract?

Taken together all these forces have called into question the legitimacy of the existing division of labour between men and women, and the debate that now rages at the end of the twentieth century is fundamentally about how far the disparate parts that make up the old style sexual contract can be welded back together again; how far this is ethically appropriate; and perhaps most important of all, how sustainable this is in the light of people's daily experiences and their shared values.

In this chapter, I argue that the old paradigms for sexual relations are rapidly becoming obsolete because of the deep-rooted forces described here - economic, technological and cultural - which have steadily undermined the old social order and which will continue to do so. In my view any attempt to rework the *existing* contract is bound to fail. We require nothing less than a thorough modernisation of the sexual contract, if we are to achieve a gender division of labour which resonates with and fits the underlying social and economic forces for change.

Forces of resistance

It goes without saying that this process of modernisation will not be easy. The sheer pace of change has produced major social dislocation. The faultlines from the genderquake - crises in the family, gender tensions at work, and the wholesale destabilising of male identity it has precipitated - have led many to react to these changes with despair. Certainly there is no shortage of people (on the left as well as the right) warning of imminent moral and social breakdown and looking to blame someone or something whether it be single mothers, feckless fathers or the legacy of the 1960s. The way in which these issues is debated shows just how uneasy many people feel about this power shift, and how it threatens long held assumptions about the family, gender roles, the nature of work and power itself.

But that is only half the story. Many people are uneasy, because instead of seeing progress, they see only costs. And it is in this context that the consensus on which British society was implicitly based has fractured, both by gender and generation. We are left with a society divided about the roles of men and women, torn apart by children's rights and needs, anxious and insecure about changes in the world of work and uncertain about the future for relations between the sexes.

Men's unease with these changes is hardly surprising. Within the space of a generation, many of the certainties which they have grown up with, and been socialised into, have been torn asunder. Masculine identity defined for almost two hundred years through the task of breadwinning is now under threat by global economic forces, and by the rising power of women. To many men, the deep rooted 'feminisation' of our society must seem all pervasive.

The unease that many men feel is especially acute for older generations, those who pre-dated the feminist struggles of the 1960s and 1970s, and those in their forties and fifties who have been in the frontline of the sex war. Steeped in the old ways, they have been ill-prepared for the changes that now confront them on a daily basis. Almost inevitably they have had less time to adapt. They have a more fixed mindset, having built lifestyles and families around a guiding set of principles which now seem to be crumbling to dust.

Popular culture has best captured these shifts. In the hit Hollywood movie, *Falling Down*, Michael Douglas plays a white middle class middle aged male, a victim of 'downsizing', who is estranged from his wife and his child, and whose journey through the wasteland of inner city New York becomes a metaphor and *cri de coeur* of white male middle America. When, at the end of the film and after scenes of violence and death, he finds himself confronted by an armed police officer he bemusedly asks "Since when did I become the bad guy?", capturing the mood of literally millions of men the Western world over - middle class as well as working class - who have been left reeling from the shock of the transformations that they have experienced.

In the broad historical scheme of things, the decline of the old order has brought new opportunities for many women, and women seem to be more at ease with the changes of the last few decades than men, and more optimistic for the obvious reason that they are less attached to the old system and so have less to lose by its disintegration.[3] And although a younger generation of women are entering the economy at a time of great uncertainty, insecurity and fluidity, their status compared with their mother's generation has dramatically improved. [4] They are more likely to be in fulltime jobs than previous generations of women, and higher up the occupational scale. Young women today are more educated, better qualified, and have much greater freedom and choice than ever before, and perhaps not surprisingly are also more optimistic.

These gender differences are important. But it is the generational faultlines which may prove to be the most significant. Almost inevitably the generation people have been born into helps define the way in which they interpret the future and the past. Older people are less relaxed about these changes, more traditional in their values and more strongly attached to the old style sexual contract.[5] Older women (especially those in their sixties and above) like their male counterparts are more anxious about what is going on, partly because they have more energy and identity invested in the old system, having relied on their partner to be the breadwinner, whilst they have been the homemaker.

It is in this climate that we are witnessing a rebirth of political ideas and movements predicated on notions of sexual difference - whether it be within the feminist movement or the fledgling men's movement or among social conservatives. This retreat to old ideologies, this return to basics pervades the political spectrum. Ironically, it is as if a kind of 'gender fundamentalism' has taken hold at the very time that effective sexual differences and distinctions are being rapidly eroded in our economy and culture.

The androgynous generation

To Theodore Zeldin (1994) this pattern is not surprising. He notes that in times of transition while the old and politicians scurry back to old beliefs and old ideas, the young in contrast are nibbling at new ideologies. Certainly, young men, as well as young women, are more at ease with the emerging sexual contract. This is partly because the generations born since the 1960s, whom we at Demos have called 'freedom's children', have inherited a culture of freedom and an unquestioning commitment to equality between the sexes. In a very real sense, they are the 'switch generation', the generation which finds itself in the midst of a historic transition, bridging the old world and the new.

In their values and their behaviour, young people today are increasingly androgynous. Demos' research and a vast array of data clearly charts the convergence of values between young men and women - women's masculinisation and men's slower but steady feminisation. Young men and women today share many values in common, they want to flirt with their masculine and feminine sides, and are far more likely to reject gender roles, whether it be in the home or at work. They are also more willing to acknowledge that they are attracted to members of the same sex, more relaxed with homosexuality and lesbianism, and less hung up on gender itself, with young people being far more likely than the old to say that they would not mind being born again as a member of the opposite sex.

Less bound by tradition, and less attached to the old way of doing things, young men, like the young women who are their peers, are far less attached to the old order, and the old sexual contract. They too have less vested in the old system, and are already seeking wider outlets for their energies, judging success by their capacities as a good lover, nurturing father, and best friend as well as being the main breadwinner, partly because the latter was never an automatic assumption for them.

This generation is at the forefront of coping with multi-faceted gender identities, and more at ease with the society we are moving towards - a society of flexible, interchangeable gender roles where sexual differences are obliterated in most areas of our lives, and where a new ethic of shared responsibility is beginning to emerge. Today's schoolchildren are even further down that track.

The evidence of their androgyny is perhaps best illustrated when we look at the relationships that young men and women are forming today. Amongst younger generations, we see a clear move towards greater equality in the home and an unravelling of the old gender division of labour with just 8.4% of women under 25 agreeing that 'a husband should earn and the wife should stay at home.' Most young couples believe they should take joint responsibility for household chores and should share financial management and purchasing decisions.

We may also be seeing the advent of flexible androgynous relationships predicated on the idea of greater partnership. The bonds that young people are forming today are less constrained by traditional roles and more focused on friendship, love and mutual respect. Indeed, studies have suggested that in the way they live their daily lives, heterosexual young couples today seem to be sharing many of the qualities that characterise gay and lesbian relationships today and in the past, particularly in their rejection of role-based ties. With children too, there is a more flexible relaxed attitude. Young people are far more likely than older to agree that children should have the right to participate in family decision-making.

It is perhaps the belief in the individual's freedom to choose how they live their life which defines this generation, and it appears to permeate all areas. Young women today are less bound by traditional definitions of women's liberation, and are thus more likely than older women to agree that a women who stays at home to look after her children is as liberated as a woman who goes out to work, implying a resistance to over-prescriptive dogmatic agendas of any persuasion. Women and men in their twenties also almost unanimously agree that everyone has to find out for themselves what life they want to lead, and that it is up to individuals to work out their own set of references.

For this generation then, notions of separate spheres for men and women, of male breadwinners and female homemakers, and even assumptions about innate gender differences are being questioned and rejected, at the same time as they are under assault from wider economic, technological and cultural forces. 'Freedom's children' have grown up assuming that sexual equality is their birthright. They value their freedom to choose and their right to express their individuality, and are ill-at-ease with dogma. The old style sexual contract holds little legitimacy for them.

The foundations of a new sexual contract

What then are the defining characteristics of the newly-emerging contract? Whereas the old pattern was defined by sexual difference, the new one is encapsulated in the idea of androgyny, and the ambiguities of gender distinctions. Whereas the traditional template was role-based, and prescriptive, the emerging model is deliberately flexible, inter-changeable and adaptive, a response to the fact that the flexible economy requires flexible families.

But if the emerging contract is to succeed, it needs to be nurtured and supported. The language of collaboration and consensus needs to replace the language of conflict and war. We need to move away from counterposing masculine and feminine qualities, and we need a rhetorical shift away from the language of gender warriors to one of fellow travellers. Our goal should be to minimise sexual difference and instead emphasise the common traits, and shared concerns of men and women.

These rhetorical shifts are vital and are already beginning to occur. But we must go a step further. If we are truly to modernise the sexual contract, and give people genuine choices, we must reform the institutions which have supported and nurtured the old one, and which continue to prop it up. At the moment, we are left with remnants of an infrastructure which was designed for an era when men's and women's lives were separate and marriage was essentially an economic contract. Those times have gone. We must lay the foundations for a new civil society which can accommodate and facilitate a new model.

What might this mean in practice? Our marriage ceremony and its rituals must be updated to better fit the values that underpin the partnerships that are being formed today.[6] The welfare state, family policy and policies for the workplace will need to be adapted to recognise the social and economic realities of a dual earning economy. We will have to put into place policies which support parents, rather than simply mothers, through commitment to measures like paid parental leave[7] and through reform of custody laws to promote co-parenting in all possible cases. Policies which foster economic independence will need to be combined with a coherent strategy for lifelong learning which equips all our citizens - male and female - from their early years and throughout adult life to acquire the mix of feminine and masculine skills that they will need to cope in the workplaces and families of the future.

But perhaps most important of all, the principles underpinning a future contract will have to embrace individuality, choice and diversity if it is to secure its legitimacy with younger generations. It must be a personalised and individualised contract, and the role of the state should be to facilitate these choices. Democratisation and the principle of subsidiarity - handing decisions down to the lowest possible level - are therefore an indispensable precondition of modernising the sexual contract.

Looking forward to diversity

So what would life in the twenty-first century look like if such a set of conditions were achieved? In many ways, my guess is that it would not look radically different from today. No doubt, a substantial minority of couples would still opt for a more traditional way of life, preferring the certainties of the role-based contracts described by Catherine Hakim in her chapter to the ambiguities of more flexible, more androgynous models. But alongside the now familiar traditional model, we should also expect to find entirely different ideas, and entirely different arrangements, with couples multi-tasking at home just as they have to do at work. Indeed, if the new sexual contract is truly a democratic one, we should expect to see an array of variants, individually and democratically negotiated between the people involved, which meshes with the differences and diversity of our multi-cultural, multi-faith society and reflects the individuality of our younger generations.

Indeed, the central feature distinguishing the new order from the old will simply be this diversity. As far as possible, these choices will have been freely made. Individual decisions will not have been circumscribed by a culture and infrastructure which imposes rigid and artificial distinctions on men's and women's roles. The political culture instead of resisting change will embrace it, and instead of limiting men's and women's opportunities it will be encouraging people to expand them.

So whilst sexual differences may continue to thrive in the new order, those who wish to experiment with flexible and inter-changeable roles, those who wish to break down the boundaries that divide men and women from each other, will have the freedom and support from the state to do so. *Vive la différence!*

Rebuilding the African-Caribbean Family in Britain[1]

Sharon James-Fergus

Relationships between men and women are still the cornerstone of the African-Caribbean family and community. Love that leads to long-term, fulfilling and secure relationships is what most individuals aspire to. However, there is a disproportionately high number of families within the African-Caribbean community led by a single parent. Is there a problem with relationships in which African-Caribbean people are involved? If there is, why has it arisen for us, and what can be done about it?

These issues have been the subject of lively discussions within the African-Caribbean community for many years. There are many complex issues involved. Some white people assume that single parenting is an African-Caribbean tradition. But this involves a misunderstanding of our culture. I would argue, on the contrary, that British society has produced influences which have pulled apart black men and women and make it difficult to keep up black family life. I will look here at how differences in the experience of black men and women in Britain have changed their personal relationships and perspectives on family life. Then I will consider what we can do now to rebuild black families and strengthen our community.

The elevation of black women

African-Caribbean women are at the forefront of family life. Ever since they came here in the 1950s and 1960s, they have been married, working, running the home and raising the children: a tower of strength for their family. Their source of strength was religion. They were faithful members of their church and faithful wives. Even today black churches are full of these women. They respect the husband, as they try to live within biblical principles.

However, in recent years African-Caribbean women have embraced the ideology of white women. They are still working, running the home, and raising the children, but they are demanding more from their partners. Historically they were happy to bear the whole responsibility of their home and family, working for low wages, poor terms and conditions and having on average four children. Has the liberation of women and equal opportunities initiatives really emancipated black women?

The women's liberation movement ideology began to bear fruit within the African-Caribbean community when the first generation of British-born black women were finishing their school education. Many left school literate, numerate, and with various qualifications. Their family life was very much based upon the old African-Caribbean traditions including teaching girls to be fully competent in running the home, well disciplined, respectful of their elders, with a religious foundation, and able to adapt to the needs of their family and the system.

They were their mother's helper whilst their brothers were waited on. They worked hard whilst accepting the value of their work in the smooth running of the family home. This foundation gave girls the ability to cope with complex tasks and circumstances from an early age.

In the 1970s these girls were ready to join the workforce. There was an abundance of jobs with organisations such as local authorities, banks, hospitals and private companies. They were able to learn quickly, disciplined and humble: no job was too small for them. They were viewed by their employers as non-threatening and flexible, therefore a welcomed asset to any team. The Commission for Racial Equality carried out studies which showed that they experienced racism. But the black woman's drive, ambition and force did not allow them to be unproductive under such practices.

As they moved into the 1980s it was recognised that black women could only get low paid, junior posts. Black men were rioting because of inequalities in many aspects of life, and this contributed to the development of equal opportunities initiatives. As these programmes began, articulate, skilled women were given the opportunity to progress. The policies offered some protection from harassment, and better terms and conditions of employment. It was possible to have a baby and return to work. As a result, many black women progressed successfully, and in the 1990s there are many professional high-flying African-Caribbean women who have prosperous careers. Black women have been emancipated.

However, this financial emancipation has been achieved at a cost. Their elevation into a successful career has meant that they are more likely to have senior posts and higher earning power than their prospective or actual black partners.

Because they are economically independent career women, their child's father may feel that it does not matter whether he is an active parent or partner. Furthermore the time they can spend with their family has been reduced. So overall the working black woman is experiencing a lot of pressure.

Paying the price in relationships

This group of women are finding it difficult to maintain long term relationships. The harmony in the home has been threatened. Some partnerships are able to move with the new challenges that the women's new career responsibilities bring. However, a great number fail, due to the different life expectations of the couple. Although general household duties still remain the woman's domain, the man is required to assist in the home, mainly with childcare; taking and collecting the children from school and nursery. If he fails to help he is resented by the woman and seen as a burden.

Black women tend to have higher expectations of their men than men have for themselves. Many cannot empathise with the black man's experiences in Britain and expect him to achieve more to lighten her load. Black women are bombarding men with their demands to bring a higher income into the home in order to reduce her need to work full-time or, if she does need to work, are demanding that he participates in the upkeep of home and with childcare.

White women's liberation ideology included a demand to be treated equally in the home. Black women find this concept hard to implement with black men because black men expect to be treated as kings in the home. Household tasks are not generally regarded by black men as duties of a king, but some tasks will be undertaken intermittently. Black women have had to accept that the process of change in their family will be slow and arduous, or reject the man's kingship as an unnecessary burden. Within the group of economically independent black women there is an abundance of successful women raising their families single-handedly. It is not experienced as an ideal situation, but as the best they can do in the circumstances.

The problems of the state dependent black woman

Not all black women have been successful in their careers, for a variety of reasons. Their lack of progress could be due to a combination of the following sorts of reasons. They did not leave school literate and numerate. They did not have confidence in their skills. Their home life was less than happy and stable. Many of them came to Britain as teenagers in the 1970s to join their parents in established family units. They found it difficult to adjust and may not have felt valued or appreciated. Because of this they found themselves in pursuit of love rather than a job. They sometimes had jobs, but these were often short-term and unskilled, with poor terms and conditions, and if they became pregnant, they often lost them. The pregnancy may have been unplanned and not the fruit of a stable, fulfilling and loving relationship. The father may have been absent, both at the birth and throughout the child's life.

Where the state provided a regular income, these women became state dependants, living on the poverty line. Their income barely matched their expenditure. In the 1990s there are many black women like this, in a state benefit low income trap. Equal opportunities initiatives have not emancipated them. Although caught in this trap they still have the aspiration to be treated as an equal in their relationship with potential or actual partners, and a desire to improve themselves through training or a career. They are not content being single parents living on the state, but a lively social life and family life can occupy most of their time.

The stress and strain of trying to survive on a small income cause severe problems in relationships. Single parent women who are state dependent tend to attract men who are also state dependent; and this makes marriage difficult. To declare to the state that you have a partner, by marrying him, will end a reliable income in a time when relationships are *un*reliable. One in four marriages now end in divorce. So this is something that most women will not do, and marriage is much less popular - as it is in society in general.

The oppression of African-Caribbean men

In the 1950s, 60s and 70s African-Caribbean men were fundamentally family men. Marriage was important to them. They worked many hours in two or three low-paid jobs in order to support their family. They were the key breadwinners, and felt needed by their wives. Racism was rife, but they humbled themselves to pave the way for their children. Black men made sure the house was maintained, doing all the repairs, though it was rare for them to do any chores around the house. Their family waited upon them. They often ruled with a rod of iron, to maintain discipline and keep their position as king in the family home - though sometimes the wife had the role of disciplining the children. The sons were to inherit their father's position, and they too were waited upon if they had sisters living at home. Those who did not have a sister to take on the role of mother's helper might have had to help in the home.

When these boys left school, they had positive attitudes like their fathers. They were special; in the home they were boy kings. But they did not want to work at two or three jobs for low wages like their fathers, nor did they want a job where their boss ruled with the rod of correction. That was something they would take from their fathers, but not from anyone else. At school they had learned much: they were articulate and numerate and had achieved qualifications. They were determined, disciplined and felt valued.

There were lots of jobs in the 1970s and some were secured by able black men. These were mostly in large government institutions such as the Post Office and London Transport, or private industries including British Leyland, Ford and British Gas. They were able to undertake apprenticeships and learn trades such as plumbing and car mechanics whilst working for these industries.

Within the first few years of work, black men also began to learn more about institutionalised racism. Their white male boss was hard on them compared with their white colleagues. Their wages were lower than their colleagues. Black men were being discriminated against in the workplace, and only the lower pay and status jobs were available to them. They could be operatives but not supervisors, they could be officers but not managers. This finding has been substantiated by many reports, most recently the TUC report of June 1997.

There were other problems. Access to education was limited and exclusive. In their personal life they could only get housing in a poor condition. The immense pressure this created made a lot of men fight back against racism, in riots and political activity. The equal opportunities initiatives in the 1980s were influenced, by the black man's resistance, into addressing issues of discrimination. Projects were set up in the community to help enable black people to gain access to high quality employment, housing and education.

However, while these courses would have an abundance of black women in attendance, many black men did not embrace opportunities to gain new skills through retraining or further education. Furthermore, equal opportunity programmes were not helping the black man as much as the black woman anyway. This was in part because hiring or promoting black women enabled employers to meet the requirements and achieve *two* goals - one to do with race and one with gender - with *one* move. So there were skilled black men who became successful as white collar workers, but it was black *women* who progressed in larger numbers.

Those skilled black men who left unsatisfactory employment to become self-employed found difficulties accessing private finance and premises from mainstream British institutions. They often had to develop enterprises relying on their own family and community resources. These small enterprises were stable, and would bring in a modest income while remaining financially independent.

Such men have tended to be in long-term relationships and have been able to develop and maintain a secure home environment. They also tend to be responsible parents, even when the relationship with their children's mother has broken down. This can be attributed to their place in the socio-economic strata as well as to being financially independent of the state. This enhances self-respect, self-esteem and a man's ability to relate with and attract his prospective partner - the emancipated black female. In these circumstances, respect and trust are being fostered between two intelligent and communicative individuals who can embrace the new gender roles as depicted in the media.

Changes to the black man's role in the family

But fundamentally, and more often, the gender roles within African-Caribbean relationships remain the same. He is striving to be king and she to be his queen, equal but different. He has always needed this elevation in the home as this is an African tradition, and this is added to by the oppression he experiences outside of the home. This is making black men slower to change. Black women in relationships with them can appreciate this and support them. She will encourage him to work within the home, and many men will participate in the running of the home as a way to show their love for their wife and family - but not necessarily as a regular activity.

When African-Caribbean families first came to Britain it was agreed that both parents had to work because of financial necessity. Most planned to return to their country of origin and to the traditional gender roles in the home. However, many families have stayed and the children of such families are now living in family structures where both parents work outside the home. Conflicts about household tasks arise, due to the pressure of having two working parents. Black men accept there are changes to their family structure, and to their role as providers. The necessity for the black woman to earn income to supplement the man's income has changed their roles economically. The black man is striving for the role of provider once again and in the meantime resists the attempts by black women to domesticate him.

Hindering factors

The market for unskilled black men has diminished over the years as the rise of technology has taken its toll. This group includes the most vulnerable to racism and is the most prone to be stopped by the police. Institutional racism makes it difficult for them to make a living.

This is the most visible black male group in this society today. Unemployment figures contain a disproportionately high number of these men, as do prisons and mental institutions. Unemployment is still rising among unskilled black men, and there are disproportionately more black men in long term unemployment than white men. It is a well researched fact that, if a black man and a white man were facing a penalty for the same crime the black man is more likely to receive a prison sentence than the white man. It is also true that black men are being diagnosed in high numbers as having a mental illness.

As a coping strategy black men have developed a successful street culture to which many black youth aspire today. This includes designer clothing, street language, a hustling economy, fast cars, mobile phones and pretty women as icons of their male culture. They have decided that because of the pressures they bear within British society they will operate outside the system and not work for anyone but themselves - with the hope that the culture they have created will rise as other cultures have. The development of the England language over the years has included street language originating from this group of men.

Where African-Caribbean men have been able to become successful in their chosen career, having a good education has often been a catalyst to this success. In the 1990s many studies have shown that black boys are more likely to be excluded from the school system than any other boys. These factors are hindering the progress of black men in British society today.

The way forward

The economic climate in Britain is such that in order to achieve the basic life goals such as a house, car and annual holidays, it has become necessary for most households in the black community to have two income-generating parents. This has put a huge emphasis on the male's economic role, as the measure of his ability to provide.

But institutionalised racism in British society is hindering the black man's ability to provide for his family. Black women expect to have a comfortable life, and look to the black man to assist in achieving this. The future success of the black community relies upon the children, and they need secure family units with positive male and female role models. It is difficult for black males to be positive role models when the society in which they live actively disempowers them.

The state has done much to help black women to succeed economically; but now it needs to look at the problems of *black families*, and to stop assuming that black women are happy to be single parents, or *want* to be independent from men in this way.

British society must address the racism which is oppressing black men and boys, and tackle the issues to do with long-term unemployment, unfair legal processes, medical diagnoses and the exclusion of black boys from school. These are the urgent issues which need to be addressed, and resources must be found to give active support to black men. For example, realistic and achievable self-employment projects, with the development of business skills, offer the best methods of dealing with long-term unemployment among black men. To include black male teachers as role models within schools with a large number of black boys will help the boys' development and reduce exclusions. And setting up projects which train excluded boys in vocational skills must be better than leaving them on the streets.

There are many issues for black men themselves to address. Foremostly they need to accept that a man can participate in the smooth running of the home and still be king. Secondly they need to appreciate how empowering it is to take the initiative in their own development. Many black men have recognised this and are working to improve themselves - as reflected in the rise in recent years of black men attending places of worship, and of further education, and setting up their own business and support groups, and in the rise of black self-help books promoting self-love and traditional family values. The number of black men who participate fully in the home is also rising.

Black women need to acknowledge this and continue assisting black men in their endeavours. They also need to adjust their expectations, and place equal value on all the components of the provider's role, such as carer, protector, companion and confidant which black men bring or can bring into a relationship and family. Black women have had to take on the role of man and woman in some African-Caribbean homes. Relationships will improve when couples cultivate self acceptance and love, and see that life in Britain does not have to result in broken family units.

The various religions within the black community must facilitate the reunion of modern black men and women. Women were not the main or shared breadwinners in traditional roles. But the need for women to work has changed female roles. In order for black women to achieve the marital stability which their mothers enjoyed in the 60s and 70s they will have to adopt the level of faith which was employed then on a daily basis. Many black women today have left the church and rely on their own resources. The black community though has always survived, through all the adverse experiences in our history, because of the abundance of faith in the Creator. Such faith, if held by the masses, will help reduce the number of families led by a single parent.

Fundamentally, black families are the cornerstone of the African-Caribbean community. They provide each member with the love, understanding and firm belief in their shared purpose which they need in order to survive the pressures which institutionalised racism puts on them in British society.

Black women have learned that their liberation means nothing when it alienates the black man, and that black women have to unite in love with black men in order to rebuild the black family.

Back to Basics and the Search for Love

Dame Barbara Cartland

The coming of Women's Lib

Many of the problems which now afflict our society have developed as a result of Women's Lib, which does not understand either how society works or what most women want. I have lived most of my life before Women's Lib began, so I have seen for myself what effect it has had.

In 1970 they said it was the beginning of the Romantic Era. The Royal Philharmonic Orchestra asked me what songs they should play of the twenties and thirties, while in America I sold a million copies of each novel I wrote. Then two years later the publishers woke up, and said to their authors: "Write like Barbara Cartland but *with* pornography." This was the beginning of the Permissive Era which produced Aids.

In England 'Women's Libbers' were fighting even more violently to prove themselves, not the equal of men, but the superior. What they succeeded in doing was in getting rid of religion. Since the very start of civilisation the guidelines for mankind have always been through religion. From the Totem poles and the Witchdoctors, up to the gods of Ancient Greece and Rome, to Mohammedanism, Buddhism and Christianity. The only guidelines given to children today seem to be: "Don't get caught by the police - they are your enemy!"

In this country, all through the ages, the aristocrats were always supposed to be immoral and so were the peasants. The great Middle Class was strictly moral and never, in any way, discussed or talked about 'sex'. It was they who made the great British Empire over one quarter of the world's surface, and it was said of them that 'the man carried the sword and the woman the Bible'. What 'Women's Lib' achieved was to make the Woman throw away the Bible.

Where we had morality in the home, the village, the town and over most of England, we now have wife swapping in small towns and many other unpleasant sexual pastimes. It has even resulted in the prayers being taken out of State Schools. So for many years if you wanted your child taught about God you had to pay for him to go to Eton or Harrow, or for a girl to go to some equally expensive school. No objection was made by the Archbishop of Canterbury, nor any Bishop. The majority of people did not even know it had happened.

It was only finally in 1990, with the assistance of a newspaper, that I managed to bring to the attention of every Member of Parliament what was happening. I received one hundred and fifty letters in return saying that they agreed with me that it was horrifying. The majority admitted they had no idea that prayers had been missing for many years.

The House of Commons and the House of Lords agreed just before Christmas that there should be both prayers and religious education in state schools. But the damage done over those lost years is horrifying, and will take a long time to repair. We now have, at this moment, the worst child abuse of any country in the world. In London the stations at night are where the children go who have run away from home. They are mostly under fifteen years of age, and wait to be accosted by perverts.

Paying the moral price

Women's Lib is directly responsible for much that has happened in Britain. They have demanded that women should go back down the mines, when we took a century to get them out of them! They have made it more important for a woman to have a career rather than a happy marriage. The more advanced of Women's Libbers want to do away with marriage altogether, and write in their much-publicised books that "marriage has failed and should be abolished altogether. Love has failed and the only real way to obtain 'good sex' is to have a variety of partners." This has resulted in little girls of fifteen being bullied at school because they have not had 'sex', and the same applies to boys.

As it is, in this country a majority of marriages now fail - both

Protestant and Catholic. The Divorce Law, known as the 'Adulteress's Charter', is so appalling in that whatever a man's wife does, he has to give her half of everything he possesses. What is more, she can go on applying for more every year by not agreeing to a Decree Nisi.

It is only surprising that *any* man proposes marriage - promiscuity as advocated by Women's Lib is much easier.

Any policeman or judge will tell you that the young trouble-makers and the hooligans who smash up football grounds are from broken homes. They have been denied love, they hate the world and want to smash it up. Also the ghastly crimes inflicted on children are usually done by the stepfather or the live-in lover.

Apart from this, crime is worse than it has ever been in the whole history of the country. Only one criminal in seven gets caught. Even so, prisons are over-flowing and it has become unsafe for any child or young woman to walk the streets either in a town or in the country.

Going back to basics

What we have to do now is to go back to morality. The prime minister of practically every country in Europe has said it is necessary, and so have the Americans. It is going to be a long and hard task to undo the terrible harm which has been done by Women's Lib and the permissive era.

It is only women, whose job it has been to hold the Bible, who can get us back to anything like normality. A real woman wants to have a man who loves her, protects her, works for her and is determined that His Home and His Family are better than anybody else's in the world. This is as true now for most women as it has even been. But it is more difficult for them to say it.

It is an impossible situation as long as women are told that it is more important to have a career than to look after their husbands and children. In nine cases out of ten the children are neglected and eventually take to drugs. Women should stop taking the jobs which are essential for men. For instance, on television women read out the sports' news and results, which are much better read by men.

The first step, in my opinion - and I have been fighting for years for this - is to have 'wages for wives'. This means that the mother will stay at home with her young children for at least five years, loving them and bringing them up in the right way, before they start school. For this, she should be given the national average wage, which at the moment is about £130 a week.

This would help her and her husband to afford to pay the mortgage, and all the other vast bills which today confront a young married couple. 'Wages for wives' were brought in by the Prime Minister of France in 1988 and it has been a great success. Sweden brought it in last year.

If they can show the way, we, who have always prided ourselves in the past on standing up for what was right and just for our people, can do the same. This is the only way that we can save the children and bring back Morality and the Guidelines which are the whole basis of a civilised country.

APPENDICES

NOTES

Beyond the sexual contract? [pp1-9]

1 "I believe that their disabilities elsewhere are only clung to in order to maintain their subordination in domestic life; because the generality of the male sex cannot yet tolerate the idea of living with an equal". John Stuart Mill (1869), reprinted in Collini (1989: p166).

Family roles in the New Elizabethan Era [17-39]

1 This is a version of a chapter to be included in a book jointly written with Madeleine Arnot and Gaby Weiner (1998, forthcoming) *Closing the Gender Gap; a study of Educational Success and Moral Panic*, Cambridge, Polity Press.

Nearing full circle in the sexual revolution [40-54]

1 Daily Telegraph, July 2nd 1996

2 For an interpretation of the gender aspects of *The Rise of the Meritocracy* see Dench (1995).

3 As Ferdinand Mount has pointed out, throughout history families have repeatedly needed to fight with centralising states to retain some immunity or autonomy. We are now entering the stage in such a struggle at which a newly established political elite reluctantly starts to concede the 'strength and value' of the family. See Mount (1982).

4 If for no other reason than the traditional one that it shows them to have their men under proper control.

5 See Ferri & Smith (1996) Table 23, page 43.

Was Feminism wrong about the family [64-72]

1 The argument here is developed further in my forthcoming book, *Sacred Cows: Is Feminism Up to the Nineties?* (HarperCollins, June 1998)

Effects on children of mothers' employment [73-88]

1   Estimated government figures for average earnings in 1996-97 are that single full-time employees will earn £250 per week, but that female full-time employees will earn £287 per week and that, on average, men will earn £397 per week. This suggests that single men are earning less than women and family men considerably more than both. *Source*: Budget Press Release 28th November 1995.

2   Report 'Women still lag behind in pay and job stakes' *The Daily Telegraph* 16. Sept 1997 and *Facts About Women and Men* Equal Opportunities Commission 1997

3   See Joshi H and Davies H 'Mothers' Human Capital and Childcare in Britain', Employment Committee, *Mothers in Employment*, Vol 3, Appendices to the Minutes of Evidence, pp.507

4   Memorandum from Save the Children Employment Committee Mothers in Employment First Report Vol 3: Appendices and Minutes of Evidence, p564

5   See Vaughn B, Gove F L & Egeland B (1980) and Egeland B & Hiester M (1995).

6 See Belsky (1990), Farber & Egeland (1982), Schwartz (1983), Jacobson & Wille (1984), Egeland & Hiester (1995), Barglow *et al* (1987), Belsky & Rovine (1988) and Belsky (1988).

7   See Chase-Lansdale & Owen (1987) and Belsky & Rovine (1988).

8   See Erickson, Sroufe & Egeland   (1985) and Lewis, Fiering, McGuffog & Jaskir (1985)

9   See Howes (1987) and Rutter (1995).

10 See Lutkenhaus, Grossman & Grossman (1985), Matas, Arend & Stroufe (1978) Stroupe, Fox & Pancake (1983), Pettit & Bates (1989), Bradley, Caldwell & Rock (1988), Estreada, Arsenio, Hess & Holloway (1987) and Lewis *et al* (1984).

11 See Gold & Andres (1978a; 1978b) and Hoffman (1979).

12 A notable example was Dr Ian Roberts from the Child Health Monitoring Unit, at the Institute of Child Health, who asserted that

'There isn't a scrap of evidence that putting children in day-care while mothers go to work is bad for health or education'. He claimed that the 'body of evidence was positive' and seemed to suggest that the 8 studies he had put together represented the sum total of world wide day care research. There are, of course, hundreds of childcare studies and the ones which Roberts had selected were all early intervention projects like 'The Milwaukee project: preventing mental retardation in children at risk' or 'Early intervention for low birth weight, premature infants.' Roberts, I., 'Children at the Centre, Daycare provision and Public Policy: the Health and Welfare Effects of Daycare', Public Policy Seminar, School of Public Policy, University College London. Feb 1997 and report Cooper, G., 'War of words over childcare' *The Independent* 4.2.1997. See also Morgan (1996) for more detail.

13 See Melhuish (1991) and Martin S, Olewis I, McGurk H, Hennessy E & Melhuish E 'Stability in Daycare and Cognitive Development', *unpublished manuscript.*

The fragility of fatherhood [89-102]

1 There are some interesting cases where babies are born to women who did not know they were pregnant until they went into labour. Their situation may be closer to that of some men who cannot face having a child.

2 An interesting and important finding from the Cambridge study is that boys whose fathers have a criminal record are significantly less likely to follow them into crime if these fathers have spent leisure time with them at around the age of 11 (Farrington & Hawkins, 1991).

3 The new Labour government is committed to the EU Social Chapter, which obliges member states to give a minimum of 3 months unpaid leave to each parent. This is likely to come into force in Britain by 1999, but it will not be enough. Young families need money. The benefits of paid leave outweigh the costs (Wilkinson, 1997).

Families after separation [111-22]

1 The most commonly quoted figure is one half, although research by Jonathan Bradshaw (1997) suggests a much lower figure.

2 This is one instance of a far wider problem - the whole discourse in

the Child Support world equates 'responsibility' with funding, not with caring.

Change in gender-role attitudes [126-140]

1 This chapter is an adaptation and extension of a paper that I co-authored with Duane Alwin and Michael Braun, (Scott, Alwin & Braun, 1996). My co-authors bear no responsibility for the interpretations and policy preferences that are expressed here. This work forms part of research funded by the ESRC's Population and Household Change Initiative (#L315253024)

New ties to bind [153-162]

1 The Baby Naming Society is at 66 High Street, Pershore, Worcestershire, WR10 1DU.

Promoting women's economic independence [180-191]

1 I would like to thank Fran Bennett for her helpful comments on the first draft of this chapter.

2 For an account of the importance of autonomy, see Weale (1983) and Taylor-Gooby (1991). I explore its relationship to citizenship in greater depth in Lister (1997).

3 Jonathan Bradshaw and Jane Millar's DSS study (1991) of lone parents found that violence was a factor in the reasons for relationship break-up in a fifth of responses. A more recent study similarly indicated that domestic violence was a key factor leading to lone parenthood in a number of cases (McKay & Rowlingson, 1997).

4 Harriet Harman in a speech to Kids Club Network conference, Church House, London, 1 July 1997.

5 For a discussion of policies that would support working carers, see Phillips (1995).

6 See Roll (1991). Australia has, nevertheless, introduced partial individualisation of means-tested benefits for unemployed couples as a way of promoting work incentives for both partners.

7 Duncan *et al* (1994) modelled a straight split of the income support

payment. An alternative suggestion has been that mothers should receive payment for the children in recognition of the fact that they are normally responsible for meeting children's daily needs.

8   Categorical benefits are paid without either means or contribution test; examples are invalid care allowance and severe disablement allowance.

9   The Commission on Social Justice recommended that lone parents should be required to register for part-time work once their youngest children had reached school age (or possibly older), subject to a number of safeguards and to the prior introduction of a jobs, education and training package modelled on the Australian example.

10 An example is Michael Young and A H Halsey's proposal for a parental wage, although in this version it would be means-tested on the partner's wage. Although they stress that the payment would be available to either parent, they acknowledge that more women than men would probably claim it, regarding this as an advantage, as it would mean 'more jobs for men' which 'would have nothing but favourable effects on the position of men in the family' (Young & Halsey, 1995: p21).

11 The Conservative Government did not implement its original proposal of a system of transferable tax allowances, under which a non-earning partner could transfer her or his tax allowance to an earning partner. The proposal was, however, revived in its 1997 Election Manifesto and has been advocated by Pam Meadows, head of the Policy Studies Institute. The proposal has faced considerable opposition, partly because it would not channel money directly into the hands of those at home providing care.

12 *Women of Europe Newsletter*, No 71, June 1997.

13 Council Recommendation on Child Care, 92/*241*/EEC 1992, art. 6.

The case for a Ministry of the Family [192-206]

1   This figure is estimated from data contained in Laurie (1993).

2   Dex & McCulloch (1995) cite the Labour Force Survey and other statistics showing that part-timers would prefer to work longer hours and feel constrained from doing so by domestic commitments.

However, it is not clear whether this desire is motivated by financial difficulties.

3   These arguments and evidence are examined in more detail in Dex (1996).

4   Under present conditions of high unemployment, the entry of more lone parents into the labour market is likely to intensify competition at the lower end of the market. This could force down the wages of those who are already low paid and put some of them out of work altogether. This may negate any improvement in government revenue which derives from getting lone parents into work.

5   We set out to obtain accurate information for this table from time budget studies. Unfortunately, these studies are fragmentary and the information is not usually presented in a fashion suitable for our needs. The figures we were able to obtain indicate large variations in hours, depending upon which activities are classified as 'domestic housework'. Moreover, in most of these studies, the estimated number of hours spent on housework seem to be very low. We conclude, therefore, that there are conceptual problems attached to the use of time budget studies to indicate the precise numbers of hours devoted to housework by different partners.

6   The figures refer to an average family with two children under 5. Child care figures are based on Swedish guidelines, which stipulate the ratio of carers to children as 1:3 for children under two and 1:4 for children between two and five. Other assumptions are: buildings, equipment, supplies, electricity etc. account for one sixth of total child care costs; to produce one week's supply of additional means of transportation (buses, cars or trains), convenience foods and other work-related items requires three hours of labour. It is also assumed that the entry of seven additional mothers into full-time employment displaces one existing full-time worker who has no children in professional child care.

Politics of the family   [214-221]

1   Report published by All Party Parliamentary Group on Parenting, 1994, ISBN 1899140 03 1. Limited copies available from *Exploring Parenthood* 20a, Treadgold St. London, W11 4PB.

A manifesto for men [226-231]

1 This was first published in the *New Statesman* on 28th February 1997.

The androgynous generation [238-246]

1 Helen Wilkinson is on sabbatical from Demos where she is Project Director. She has been awarded a Harkness Fellowship by the Commonwealth Fund and is a visiting fellow at the Families and Work Institute in New York.

2 Two books from Demos which document this change are Wilkinson & Mulgan, 1995, and Wilkinson & Howard, 1997.

3 See Wilkinson 1994, plus Families and Work Institute, *Women: The New Providers*, Benton Harbour:Whirlpool Foundation.

4 For data and details on this see Wilkinson 1994, Wilkinson & Mulgan 1995, and Wilkinson & Howard, 1997.

5 For generational data, see Wilkinson & Mulgan, 1995.

6 See for example, Wilkinson 1997b.

7 See Wilkinson *et al* 1997.

Rebuilding the African-Caribbean family in Britain [247-256]

1 I am very grateful to the many members of *Ajowa-Ebi* who have given their time in helping to produce this chapter, by expressing their views to me and taking part in discussion groups.

REFERENCES

Acker S (1995) *Gendered Education: Sociological Reflections on Women Teaching and Feminism*, London: Open University Press.

Alwin D F, Braun M and Scott J (1992) 'The separation of work and family: attitudes towards women's labour-force participation in Germany, Great Britain and the United States', *European Sociological Review*, 8: 13-37.

Atkinson A B (1991) *Poverty, Statistics and Progress in Europe*, London: STICERD/LSE.

Banks O (1985) *Two Faces of Feminism*, London: Wheatsheaf.

Barglow P, Vaughn B and Molitor N (1987) 'Effects of maternal absence due to employment on the quality of infant-attachment in a low risk sample', *Child Development*, 58: 945-54.

Baring A and Cashford J (1991) *The Myth of the Goddess: Evolution of an Image*, London: Viking.

Batten M (1994) *Sexual Strategies: How Females Choose their Mates*, New York: Putnam Books.

Bayler N and Brooks-Gunn J (1991) 'Effects of maternal employment and child-care arrangements on preschoolers' cognitive and behavioural outcomes: Evidence from the children of the National Longitudinal Survey of Youth' *Developmental Psychology*, 27, no.6: 932-945.

Becker G (1991) *A Treatise on the Family*, London: Harvard University Press.

Belsky J (1988a) 'Infant day care and socioemotional development: The United States', *Journal of Child Psychology* 29: 398-40.

Belsky J (1988b) 'The "effects" of infant day care reconsidered', *Early Childhood Research Quarterly* 3, 235-272.

Belsky J and Rovine M J (1988) 'Non-maternal care in the first year of life and security of the infant parent attachment', *Child Development*, 59: 157-67.

Belsky J (1990) 'Parental and Non Parental Child Care and Children's Socioemotional Development: A Decade in Review' *Journal of Marriage and the Family*, 52: 885-903.

Belsky J and Eggebeen D (1991) 'Early and extensive maternal employment and young children's socioemotional development; children of the National Longitudinal Survey of Youth', *Journal of Marriage and the Family*, 53: 1083-1110.

Blossfeld H-P and Hakim C (eds) (1997) *Between Equalisation and Marginalisation: Women Working Part-Time in Europe and the USA*, Oxford: Oxford University Press.

Blumberg R L (ed) (1991) *Gender, Family and Economy: The Triple Overlap*, Sage.

Bradley R H, Caldwell B M and Rock S L (1988) 'Home environment and school performance: A ten-year follow-up and examination of three models of environmental action', *Child Development*, 59: 852 - 867.

Bradshaw J and Millar J (1991) *Lone Parent Families in the UK*, DSS/HMS0.

Bradshaw J *et al* (1996) *The Employment of Lone Parents: A Comparison of Policy in 20 countries*, London: Family Policy Studies Centre.

Bradshaw J (1997) *Non-Residential Fathers in Britain*, York: SPRU.

Brah A (1996) *Cartographies of Diaspora*, London: Routledge.

Brannen J *et al* (1994) *Employment and Family Life: A Review of Research in the UK 1980-94*, Research Series No.41, Employment Department.

Brannen J, Moss P, Owen C and Wale C (1997*a) Mothers Fathers and Employment: Parents and the Labour Market in Britain 1984-94*, DfEE Research Report No.10.

Brannen J, Moss P, Owen C and Wale C (1997b) 'Working Fathers', *Labour Market Trends*, 105, No.7: 259-67.

Braun M, Scott J and Alwin D F (1994) 'Economic necessity or self-actualisation? Attitudes towards women's labour force participation in East and West Germany', *European Sociological Review*, 10: 29-47.

Burchinal M R, Roberts J E, Nabors L A and Bryant D M (1996) 'Quality of center child care and infant cognitive and language development', *Child Development* 67: 617.

Burgess A and Rushton S (1996) *Men and Their Children*, London: IPPR.

Burgess A (1997) *Fatherhood Reclaimed: The Making of the Modern Father*, London: Vermilion.

Burghes L (1994) *Lone Parenthood and Marital Disruption: the Outcomes for Children*, London: Family Policy Studies Centre.

Burgoyne C B (1990) 'Money in marriage: how patterns of allocation both reflect and conceal power', *Sociological Review*, 38: 634-665.

Burns S (1995) *Time, Work and the Family*, Parents at Work.

Buss D M (1994) *The Evolution of Desire: Strategies of Human Mating*, New York: Basic Books.

Campbell B (1993) Goliath, London: Methuen.

Campbell B (1994) *Iron Ladies*, London: Virago.

Cass B (1994) 'Citizenship, work and welfare: the dilemma for Australian women', *Social Politics*, 1(1): 106-24.

Chase-Lansdale P L and Owen M T (1987) 'Maternal employment in a family context: Effects on infant-mother and infant-father attachments', *Child Development*, 58: 1505-1512.

Clarke-Stewart A K (1988) '"The 'effects' of infant day care reconsidered" reconsidered'. *Early Childhood Research Quarterly*, 3: 293.

Clarke-Stewart A K (1989) 'Maligned or Malignant?', *American Psychologist*, Feb, p269.

Commission on Social Justice (1994), *Social Justice: A Strategy for National Renewal*, London: Vintage.

Coote A and Campbell B (1982) *Sweet Freedom*, London: Fontana.

Corti L (1994) 'Changes in smoking, self-assessed health and subjective well-being' in N Buck, J Gershuny, D Rose and J Scott (eds) (1994) *Changing Households: The British Household Panel Survey 1990-1992*, ESRC Research Centre on Micro-Social Change, University of Essex.

Corti L, Laurie H and Dex S (1995) *Highly Qualified Women*, Research Series No. 50, London: Employment Department.

Cox M J, Margand N A, Owen M T and Henderson V K (1992) 'Prediction of infant-father and infant-mother attachment', *Developmental Psychology*, Vol. 28, No.3: 474-483.

Crosland A (1956) *The Road to Socialism*, London: Nicholson.

Cucchiari S (1981) 'The gender revolution and the transition from bisexual horde to patrilocal band: the origins of gender hierarchy', in S Ortner and H Whitehead (eds) *Sexual Meanings: The Cultural Construction of Gender and Sexuality*, Cambridge, England: Cambridge University Press.

Dahl T S (1987) *Women's Law*, Norwegian University Press.

Daniels P and Weingarten K (1982) *Sooner or Later*, W Norton & Co.

David M E (1980) *The State, the Family and Education*, London: Routledge.

David M E (1993) *Parents, Gender and Education Reform*, Cambridge: Polity Press.

David M E, Davies J, Edwards R, Reay D and Standing K (1996) 'Mothering, reflexivity and feminist methodology' in V Walsh and L Morley (eds) *Breaking Boundaries: Women and Higher Education*, London: Taylor and Francis.

Dench G (1994) *Reviewing Sexual Contracts*, Centre for Community Studies, Middlesex University.

Dench G (1995) 'Tracking the Demeter tie', in G Dench, T Flower and K Gavron (eds) *Young at Eighty*, Manchester: Carcanet.

Dench G (1996a) *Transforming Men*, New Brunswick, Transaction Books.

Dench G (1996b) *The Place of Men in Changing Family Cultures*, London: Institute of Community Studies.

Desai S, Chase-Lonsdale P L and Micheal R T (1989) 'Mother or market? Effects of maternal employment on the intellectual ability of four-year-old children', *Demography*, 24: 545-61.

De Waal F (1991) *Peacemaking Among Primates*, London: Penguin.

DfEE (1997) *Work and Family: Ideas and Options for Childcare*, London: HMSO.

Dex S (1988) *Women's Attitudes towards Work*, London: Macmillan.

Dex S (1996) 'Employment and caring within households' in N Baker (ed) *Building a Relational Society: New Priorities for Public Policy*, Aldershot: Arena.

Dex S, Clark A and Taylor M (1995) *Household Labour Supply*, Research Series No. 43, Employment Department.

Dex S and McCulloch A (1995) *Flexible Employment in Britain: A Statistical Analysis*, Research Series No.15, Equal Opportunities Commission.

Dunbar R (1996) *Grooming, Gossip and the Evolution of Language*, London: Faber & Faber.

Duncan A, Giles C and Webb S (1994) *Social Security Reform and Women's Independent Incomes*, Equal Opportunities Commission.

Egeland B and Hiester M (1995) 'The long-term consequences of infant day-care and mother-infant attachments', *Child Development*, 66: 474-485.

Eichenbaum L and Orbach S (1990) *What Do Women Want?*, London: Fontana.

Eisenstein Z (1983) *The Radical Future of Liberal Feminism*, London: Sage.

England P (1992) *Comparable Worth*, New York: Aldine de Gruyter.

Erickson M F, Sroufe A and Egeland B (1985) 'The relationship between quality of attachment and behaviour problems in pre-school in a high-risk sample', in Bretherton I and Waters E (eds) *Growing Points of Attachment Theory and Research: Monographs of the Society for Research in Child Development*, Serial No. 209, nos. 1-2.

Estrada P, Arsenio W F, Hess R D and Holloway S D (1987) 'Affective quality of the mother-child relationship: Longitudinal consequences for children's school relevant cognitive functioning", *Developmental Psychology*, 23: 210 - 215.

Equal Opportunities Commission (1990) *The key to Real Choice; An Action Plan for Childcare*, Manchester.

European Commission (1984) *European Men and Women 1983*, Luxembourg: Office for the Official Publications of the European Communities.

European Commission (1991) 'Family and Employment within the Twelve', *Special report on Eurobarometer*, No. 34, Brussels: DGV.

European Commission (1995) *Social Protection in Europe*, Luxembourg: Office for the Official Publications of the European Communities.

European Commission (1997) 'Modernising and Improving Social Protection in the European Union', Communication from the Commission, COM(97)102.

Everson M D, Sarnat L, and Ambron S R, (1984) 'Day care and early socialisation: The role of maternal attitudes' in R C Ainslie (ed) *The Child and the Day Care Setting: Qualitative Variations and Development*, New York: Praeger.

Farber E and Egeland B (1982) 'Developmental consequences of out-of-home care for infants in a low income population'. in E Zigler and E Gordon, *Day Care: Scientific and Social Policy Issues* Boston: Auburn House.

Farrington D P and Hawkins J D (1991) 'Predicting participation, early onset and later persistence in officially recorded offending', *Criminal Behaviour and Mental Health*, 1: 1-33.

Ferri E (1993) *Life at 33*, National Children's Bureau.

Ferri E and Smith K (1996) *Parenting in the 1990s*, London: Family Policy Studies Centre.

Ford R (1996) *Child Care in the Balance*, London: Policy Studies Institute.

Franks S (1997) 'The Great Experiment', *Prospect*, April, 10-11.

Gardiner J (1997) *Gender, Care and Economics*, Basingstoke: Macmillan.

Garner L (1988) 'The price of taking home a pay packet' in *The Daily Telegraph*, 6 July.

Gershuny J and Robinson J (1994) 'Measuring hours of paid work: time-diary versus estimate questions', *Bulletin of Labour Statistics*, 1994.1.

Gilder G (1973) *Sexual Suicide*, New York: Quadrangle.

Gilmore D D (1990) *Manhood in the Making: Cultural Concepts of Masculinity*, New Haven: Yale University Press.

Gold D and Andres D, (1978a) 'Relations between maternal employment and the development of nursery school children', *Canadian Journal of Behavioural Science*, 10(2).

Gold D and Andres D, (1978b) 'Developmental comparisons between 10-year-old children with employed and non-employed mothers', *Child Development*, 47: 75-84.

Gottfried A E, Gottfried A W and Bathurst K (1988) *Maternal Employment, Family Environment and Children's Development: Infancy Through the School Years*, Plenum Press.

Graham H (1987) 'Being poor: perceptions of coping strategies of lone mothers' in J Brannen and G Wilson (eds) *Give and Take in Families*, London: Allen & Unwin.

Gregg, P (1994) *Work Rich and Poor Households*, National Institute of Economic and Social Research, Discussion Paper No. 65.

Griffiths J (1997) *Fathercare*, Cambridge: Colt Books.

Hakim C (1991) 'Grateful slaves and self-made women: fact and fantasy in women's work orientations', *European Sociological Review*, 7: 101-121.

Hakim C (1992) 'Explaining trends in occupational segregation: the measurement, causes and consequences of the sexual division of labour', *European Sociological Review*, 8: 127-152.

Hakim C (1994) 'A century of change in occupational segregation 1891-1991', *Journal of Historical Sociology*, 7: 435-454.

Hakim C (1995) 'Five feminist myths about women's employment', *British Journal of Sociology*, 46: 429-455.

Hakim C (1996a) *Key Issues in Women's Work: Female Heterogeneity and the Polarisation of Women's Employment*, London: Athlone Press.

Hakim C (1996b) 'Labour mobility and employment stability: rhetoric and reality on the sex differential in labour market behaviour',

European Sociological Review, 12: 1-31.

Hakim C (1996c) 'The sexual division of labour and women's heterogeneity', *British Journal of Sociology*, 47: 178-188.

Hakim C (1997) 'A sociological perspective on part-time work', in Blossfeld and Hakim, *q. v.*

Hakim C and Jacobs S (1997) 'Sex-Role Preferences and Work Histories: Is There a Link?', Working Paper No. 16, London School of Economics Department of Sociology.

Haller M and Hoellinger F (1994) 'Female employment and the change of gender roles: the conflictual relationship between participation and attitudes in international comparison', *International Sociology*, 9: 87-112.

Hantrais L and Letablier M-T (1996) *Families and Family Policies in Europe*, Harlow: Addison Wesley Longman.

Harkness S, Machin S and Waldfogel J (1995) 'Evaluating the pin money hypothesis: the relationship between women's labour market activity, family income and poverty in Britain', Discussion Paper WSP/108, London: STICERD/LSE.

Harman H (1993) *The Century Gap*, London: Vermilion.

Harris M (1993) 'The evolution of human gender hierarchies: a trial formulation', in B Miller (ed) *Sex and Gender Hierarchies*, Cambridge, England: Cambridge University Press.

Hawton K (1992) 'By their own young hand', *British Medical Journal*, 304: 1000.

Hewitt P (1993) *About Time*, London: Rivers Oram.

Hewitt P and Leach P (1993) *Social Justice, Children and Families*, Report to Commission on Social Justice.

Hewlett B (1987) 'Intimate Fathers: Patterns of Paternal Holding Among Aka Pygmies', in M Lamb (ed) *The Father's Role; Cross Cultural Perspectives*, Hillsdale, New Jersey: Lawrence Erlbaum Associates.

Hewlett B (1992) 'Husband-Wife Reciprocity and the Father-Infant Relationship among Aka Pygmies', in Hewlett (ed) *Father-Child Relations: Cultural and Biosocial Contexts*, New York: Aldine de Gruyter.

Hobson B (1990) 'No exit, no voice: women's economic dependency and the welfare state', *Acta Sociologica*, 33(3), 235-50.

Hochschild A (1990) *The Second Shift*, London: Piatkus.

Hoem B (1995) 'The way to the gender-segregated Swedish labour market', in K Mason and A-M Jenson (eds) *Gender and Family Change in Industrialised Countries*, Oxford: Clarendon Press.

Hoffman L W (1979) 'Maternal Employment', *American Psychologist*, 34: 859 - 865.

Hoffman L W (1989) 'Effects of maternal employment in the two-parent family', *American Psychologist*, Feb, p284.

Holtermann S *(1995) All Our Futures; The Impact of Public Expenditure and Fiscal Policies on Britain's Children and Young People,* Ilford, Essex: Barnardos.

Howes C (1987) 'Social competency with peers: Contributions from child care', *Early Childhood Research Quarterly* 34, 2: 155-167.

Hughes D and Galinsky E (1988) 'Balancing work and family lives: Research and corporate applications' in Gottfried A E, Gottfried A W and Bathurst K *q. v.*

Humphries S and Gordon P (1996) *A Man's World: From Boyhood to Manhood 1900-1960,* London: BBC Books.

Jacobson J l and Wille D E (1984) 'Attachment and separation experience on separation distress at 18 months', *Developmental Psychology*, Vol 20, No.3: 477-484.

Jenkins S (1991) 'Poverty measurement and the within-household distribution: agenda for action', *Journal of Social Policy*, 20(4): 457-83.

Joshi H, Dale A, Ward C and Davies H (1995) *Dependence and Independence in the Finance of Women Aged 33*, London: Family Policy Studies Centre.

Kiernan K (1992) 'Men and women at work and at home', in R Jowell *et al* (eds) *British Social Attitudes - the 9th Report,* Aldershot, Hants: Gower.

Klein U (1995) 'Returning to work: A challenge for women', *World of Work*, International Labour Office, No 12 May/June.

Kon A (1992) 'How We're Learning the Creche Lesson', *The Sunday Express* 1 March.

Kraemer S (1991) 'The origins of fatherhood: an ancient family process', *Family Process*, 30, 377-392.

Kraemer S (1995) 'What are fathers for?' in C Burck and B Speed (eds) *Gender, Power and Relationships: New Developments,* London: Routledge.

Kraemer S (1997) 'Parenting Yesterday Today and Tomorrow', in K N Dwivedi (ed) *A Professional Handbook for Enhancing Parenting,* Chichester: Wiley & Sons.

Krugman S (1995) 'Male Development and the Transformation of Shame' in R Levant and W Pollack, *A New Psychology of Men,* New

York: Basic Books.

Lamb M (1986) *Father's Role, the Applied Perspectives*, Chichester: Wiley.

Lamb M and Oppenheim D (1989) 'Fatherhood and father-child relationships: five years of research' in S Cath, A Gurwitt and L Gunsberg (eds) *Fathers and their Families*, Hillsdale NJ: The Analytic Press.

Lamb M, Sternberg K, and Prodromidis, M (1992) 'Nonmaternal care and the security of infant-mother attachment: A reanalysis of the data', *Infant Behaviour and Development* 15: 71-83.

Land H, Hall P, Parker R and Webb A (eds) *Change, Choice and Conflict*, London: Macmillan.

Laurie H (1993) 'A woman's choice? Household contexts and women's labour market decisions', paper given at the British Sociological Association Conference, University of Essex.

Leach P (1994) *Children First*, Harmondsworth: Penguin Books.

Lewis M *et al* (1984) 'Predicting psychopathology in six-year-olds from early social relations', *Child Development* 55: 123-36.

Lewis M, Fiering C, McGuffog C and Jaskir J (1985) 'Infant-mother attachment at twelve months and style of interaction at twelve months and style of interaction with a stranger at the age of three years', *Child Development*, 56: 1538 - 1542.

Lewis S N C and Cooper C L (1987) 'Stress in two-earner couples and stage in the life cycle', *Journal of Occupational Psychology*, 60: 289 - 303.

Lister R (1992) *Women's Economic Dependency and Social Security*, Equal Opportunities Commission.

Lister R (1997) *Citizenship: Feminist Perspectives*, Macmillan.

Lutkenhaus P, Grossman K E and Grossman K (1985) 'Infant-mother attachment at twelve months and style of interaction with a stranger at the age of three years", *Child Development* 56: 1538 - 1542.

Ma Y, Wang Z, Sheng X and Shinozaki M (1994) *A Study of Life and Consciousness in the Contemporary Urban Family in China - Research Report on Beijing with Comparisons with Bangkok, Seoul and Fukuoka*, Beijing: Chinese Academy of Social Sciences and Kitakyushu Forum on Asian Women.

McKay S and Rowlingson K (1997) 'Choosing lone parenthood? The dynamics of family change', paper presented at seminar 'Private lives and public responses: lone parenthood and future policy in the UK', University of Bath, June.

Martin J and Roberts C (1994) *Women and Employment: A Lifetime Perspective,* DE/OPCS, HMSO.

Mason K and Lu (1988) 'Attitudes towards women's familial roles: changes in the United States, 1977-1985', *Gender and Society* 2: 39-57.

Matas L, Arend R A and Sroufe A (1978) 'Continuity of adaptation in the second year: the relationship between quality of attachment and later competence", *Child Development*, 49: 547 -556.

Melhuish E C (1991) 'Research on day care for young children in the United Kingdom', in E C Melhuish and P Moss, *Day Care for Young Children: International Perspectives*, Routledge.

Mill J S (1869) 'The Subjection of Women' reproduced in S Collini (1989) *On Liberty and Other Essays,* Oxford: Oxford University Press.

Milne A M, Myers D E, Rosenthal A S and Ginsburg A (1986) 'Single parents, working mothers and the educational achievement of school children', *Sociology of Education*, 59: 125-39.

Mishra R (1976) *The Welfare State in Crisis,* London: Wheatsheaf.

Mooney B (1993) 'The year that sex began for me', *Sunday Times*, 21st March. [12]

Morgan P (1995) *Farewell to the Family? Public Policy and Family Breakdown in Britain and the USA*, London: Institute of Economic Affairs.

Morgan P (1996) *Who Needs Parents? The effects of Childcare and Early Education on Children in Britain and the USA*, London: Institute of Economic Affairs.

Morris L (1990) *The Workings of the Household*, Cambridge: Polity.

Moss P (1988) *Childcare and Equality of Opportunity*, Consolidated Report to the European Commission.

Moss P (1990) 'Childcare in the European Communities 1985-1990', *Women of Europe Supplement*, 31, European Commision Childcare Network\Commission of the European Communities.

Moss P (1995) 'Introduction' in Moss P (ed) *Father Figures: Fathers in the Families of the 1990s,* Edinburgh: HMSO.

Mount F (1982) *The Subversive Family*, London: Cape.

Murray C (1993) 'Keep it in the Family' in *The Sunday Times*, 14th November.

Murray C (1994) *Underclass: The Crisis Deepens*, Choice in Welfare series No. 20 (in association with *The Sunday Times)*, London: Institute of Economic Affairs.

National Council for One parent Families (1996) *Key Facts*, London: NCOPF.

New C and David M E (1985) *For the Children's Sake: Making Child Care More Than Women's Business*, Harmondsworth: Penguin.

O'Brien M and Jones D (1997) 'Locality, family cultures and educational disadvantage: the case of Barking and Dagenham', paper for European Sociological Association Conference August.

O'Brien Caughy M, DiPietro J A and Strobino D M (1994) 'Day-care participation as a protective factor in the cognitive development of low-income children', *Child Development 65*: 457-471.

Okin S M (1989) *Justice, Gender and the Family*, New York: Basic Books.

O'Neil R and Green Berger E, (1994) 'Patterns of commitment to work and parenting: Implications for role strain', *Journal of Marriage and the Family*, 56: 101-118.

Osborn A F, Butler N R and Morris A C (1984) '*The Social Life of Britain's Five Year Olds*', London: Routledge and Kegan Paul.

Owen M T and Cox M J (1988) 'The transition to parenthood' in Gottfried, Gottfried and Bathurst.

Pahl J (1989) *Money and Marriage*, Macmillan.

Paige K and Paige J (1981) *The Politics of Reproductive Ritual*, Berkeley: University of California Press.

Parke R (1981) *Fathering*, Fontana.

Parker H and Parker S (1986) 'Father-daughter sexual abuse: an emerging perspective', *American Journal of Orthopsychiatry*, 56 (4): 531-549.

Parker H (1991) *Basic Income and the Labour Market*, Basic Income Research Group.

Pateman C (1988) *The Sexual Contract*, Cambridge: Polity.

Pateman C (1989) *The Disorder of Women*, Cambridge: Polity.

Pettit G S and Bates J E (1989) 'Family interaction patterns and children's behaviour problems from infancy to 4 years", *Developmental Psychology*, 23: 413 - 420.

Phillips C and Anzalone J (1982) *Fathering*, Mosby.

Phillips A (1997) 'What has socialism to do with sexual equality?' in J Franklin (ed) *Equality*, London: IPPR.

Phillips J (ed) (1995) *Working Carers*, Avebury.

Presser H (1995) 'Are the interests of women inherently at odds with the interests of children or the family? A viewpoint', in K Mason and A-M Jensen (eds) *Gender and Family Change in Industrialised*

Countries, Oxford: Clarendon Press.

Pruett K (1993) 'The Paternal Presence, Families in Society', *The Journal of Contemporary Human Services*, 74 (1): 46-50.

Quest C and Conway D (1997, *forthcoming) Free Market Feminism*, London: Institute of Economic Affairs.

Ridley M (1994) *The Red Queen*, New York: Viking.

Ridley M (1996) *The Origins of Virtue*, New York: Viking.

Riley D (1983) *War in the Nursery*, London, Fontana.

Roberts C and Cronin N for the Family Policy Studies Centre and Dodd T and Kelly M for the Office of Population and Census Surveys (1995) *National Study of Parents and Parenting Problems*, London: Family Policy Studies Centre.

Robinson J and Godbey G (1995) *Time for Life*, Penn. State Univ. Press.

Roll J (1991) *What is a Family? Benefit Models and Social Realities*, London: Family Policy Studies Centre.

Rubery J and Fagan C (1993) 'Occupational Segregation of Women and Men in the European Community', *Social Europe*, Supplement 3/93, Luxembourg: Office for the Official Publications of the European Communities.

Russell G and Radejovic M (1992) 'The changing role of fathers? Current understandings and future directions for research and practice', *Infant Mental Health Journal*, 13 (4): 296-311.

Rutter M (1972) *Maternal Deprivation Reassessed*, Penguin.

Rutter M (1995) 'Clinical implications of attachment concepts: Retrospect and prospect', *Journal of Child Psychology and Psychiatry*, pp549-568.

Sanger S and Kelly J (1988) *The Woman who Works: the Parent who Cares*, Bantam Books.

Scarr S and Eisenberg M (1993) 'Child care research: issues, perspectives and results', *Annual Review of Psychology*, 44: 613-44.

Schwartz P (1983) 'Length of day-care attendance and attachment behaviour in eighteen month old infants', *Child Development* 54, 1073-1078.

Schweinhart L J and Weikart D (1993) *A Summary of Significant Benefits: the High/Scope Perry Preschool Study through Age 2*, Michigan: High/Scope Ypsilanti.

Scott J (1990) 'Women and the family' in R Jowell *et al* (eds) *British Social Attitudes: the 7th Report*, Aldershot, Hants: Gower.

Scott J and Duncombe J (1992) 'Gender role attitudes in Britain and the

USA', in S Arber and N Gilbert (eds) *Women and Working Lives: Divisions and Change*, Basingstoke: Macmillan.

Scott J, Braun M and Alwin D (1993) 'The family way' in R Jowell *et al* (eds) *International Social Attitudes: the 10th BSA Report*, Aldershot, Hants: Gower.

Scott J, Alwin D F and Braun M (1996) 'Generational changes in gender-role attitudes: Britain in a cross-national perspective', *Sociology*, No. 3: 471-492.

Service E R (1975) *Origins of the State and Civilization: The Process of Cultural Evolution*, New York: W W Norton.

Shapiro L (1997) 'The Myth of Quality Time', *Newsweek*, May 19.

Sharp D *et al* (1985) 'The impact of postnatal depression on boys intellectual development', *Journal of Child Psychology and Psychiatry*, Vol 36, No.8: 1315-1336.

Silk J B (1993) 'Primatological perspectives on gender hierarchies' in B Miller (ed) *Sex and Gender Hierarchies,* Cambridge, England: Cambridge University Press.

Stith S M and Davis A J (1984) 'Employed mothers and family day care substitute caregivers: A comparative analysis of infant care', *Child Development*, 55: 1340-1348

Stockman N, Bonney N and Sheng X (1995) *Women's Work in East and West*, London: UCL Press.

Stroupe A L, Fox N E and Pancake V R (1983) 'Attachment and dependency in developmental perspective", *Child Development*, 54: 1615 -1627.

Taylor-Gooby P (1991) *Social Change, Social Welfare and Social Science*, Harvester Wheatsheaf.

Thatcher C (1996) *Below the Parapet*, London: Harper Collins.

Thatcher M (1993) *The Downing Street Years*, London: Harper Collins.

Thatcher M (1995) *The Path to Power,* London: Harper Collins.

Thomson K (1995) 'Working mothers: choice or circumstance?' in R Jowell *et al* (eds) *British Social Attitudes - the 12th Report*, Aldershot, Hants: Dartmouth.

Tokyo Metropolitan Government, Women and Youth Division (1994) *International Comparative Survey Concerning Issues Confronting Women* (translated by Nomura Research Institute), Tokyo: Tokyo Metropolitan Government.

Toynbee P (1997) 'Scaring mothers? Its Panorama's bit of fun', *The Independent*, 4.February.

Utting D (1996) 'Tough on the Causes of Crime? Social Bonding and

Delinquency Prevention' in S Kraemer and J Roberts (eds) *The Politics of Attachment: Towards a Secure Society*, London: Free Association Books.

Utting D (1996) *Family and Parenthood: Supporting Families, Preventing Breakdown: a Guide to the Debate*, York: Joseph Rowntree Foundation.

Vaughn B, Gove F L and Egeland B (1980) 'The relationship between out-of-home care and the quality of infant-mother attachment in an economically disadvantaged population', *Child Development*, 51: 1203-1214.

Violata C and Russell C (1994) 'Effects of nonmaternal care on child development: A meta-analysis of published research', *Paper presented at the 55th annual convention of the Canadian Psychological Association*, Penticton, British Columbia: Canada.

Vogler C (1994a) 'Money in the household' in M Anderson, F Bechhofer and J Gershuny (eds) *The Social and Political Economy of the Household*, Oxford University Press.

Vogler C (1994b) 'Segregation, sexism and labour', in A M Scott (ed) *Gender Segregation and Social Change*, Oxford: Oxford University Press.

Ward C, Dale A and Joshi H (1996) 'Combining employment with childcare: An escape from dependence', *Journal of Social Policy*, Vol.25, No.2.

Weale A (1983) *Political Theory and Social Policy*, Macmillan.

Weinraub M and Jaeger E (1991) 'Timing the return to the workplace: Effects on the mother-infant relationship' in J S Hyde and M Essex (eds) *Parental Leave and Child Care*, Phil.:Temple Univ Press.

Whitty G (1993) 'Central control or market forces?' in M Flude and M Hammer (eds) *The Education Reform Act 1988*, Lewes: Falmer Press.

Wilkinson H (1994) *No Turning Back: Generations and the Genderquake*, London: Demos.

Wilkinson H and Mulgan G (1995) *Freedom's Children*, London: Demos.

Wilkinson H [with Radley S, Christie I, Lawson G and Sainsbury J] (1997) *Time Out: The Costs and Benefits of Paid Parental Leave*, London: Demos.

Wilkinson H [with addit. research by Alison Beeney] (1997b) *The Proposal: Giving Marriage back to the People*, London: Demos.

Wilkinson H and Howard M (1997) *Tomorrow's Women*, London:

Demos.

Witherspoon S (1988) 'Interim report: a woman's work', in R Jowell *et al* (eds) *British Social Attitudes: the 5th Report*, Aldershot, Hants: Gower.

Wolcott I and Glezer H (1995) *Work and Family Life: Achieving Integration*, Melbourne: Australian Institute of Family Studies.

Wollstonecraft M (1792/1985) *Vindication of the Rights of Women*, Penguin.

Wright R (1995) *The Moral Animal*, New York: Viking.

Young M (1958) *The Rise of the Meritocracy*, London: Thames & Hudson.

Young M and Willmott P (1973) *The Symmetrical Family*, London: Routledge & Kegan Paul.

Young M and Halsey A H (1995) *Family and Community Socialism*, London: IPPR.

Zaslow M J, Pedersen F A, Suwalsky J T D, Cain R L, and Fivel M (1985) 'The early resumption of employment by mothers: Implications for parent-infant interaction', *Journal of Applied Developmental Psychology*, 6: 1-16.

Zeldin T (1994) *An Intimate History of Humanity*, London: Sinclair-Stevenson.

CONTRIBUTORS

John Baker is editor of *Access*, the journal of the self-help group for contact parents, *Families Need Fathers*. A former member of ICS, he is now Senior Lecturer in Social Policy Studies at the University of Brighton. He is the father of two children mainly living in France, and of two living with himself and his wife.

Dame Barbara Cartland has written more than 600 books, with worldwide sales of well over 650 million. Her first novel, published in 1923 when she was twenty-two, ran to six editions and was translated into five languages. During the 1920s she became known as one of the Bright Young People.

Ros Coward is a columnist for The Guardian and is Senior Research Fellow at Nene College, Northampton. She is author of *Female Desire, Our Treacherous Hearts: Why Women Let Men Get their Way,* and (forthcoming, HarperCollins, 1998) *Sacred Cows.*

Miriam E David is Dean of Research at the London Institute. Previously she was Professor of Social Sciences and Director of the SSRC Centre at South Bank University. She has written extensively on families, gender, education and social policy, and her next book will be *Closing the Gender Gap* (with Madeleine Arnot and Gaby Weiner, 1998, Polity Press).

Geoff Dench is a senior research fellow at the Institute of Community Studies and a visiting professor at Middlesex University, where he was formerly Head of Sociology and Social Policy. He has worked mainly in ethnic relations (last book *Minorities in the Open Society*) and more recently in sex and gender (latest book *Transforming Men*).

Shirley Dex is the author of eight books and many academic journal articles on women's employment, flexible work, low pay, and the effects of social policies on women's employment and status. Since 1996 she has been a Lecturer in Management Studies at the Judge Institute for Management Studies at the University of Cambridge. Previously she was a Research Professor at Essex University.

Jonathan Gershuny is now Professor of Sociology at the University of Essex and Director of the ESRC Research Centre on Micro-Social Change in Britain, where he directs the British Household Panel Study. He was previously a fellow of Nuffield College, Oxford, and also Head of the School of Social Sciences at Bath University. His books include *After Industrial Society* and (jointly edited with Frank Bechofer and Michael Anderson) *The Political Economy of the Household*

John Griffiths was once Britain's youngest JP and reckons he is now probably, at 63, its oldest single father. He runs an independent TV production company, Minerva Vision, and was founder in 1985 of Europe's first satellite Arts Channel. He is a former National President of the Liberal Party, and has written books on a variety of subjects, including *Modern Iceland*, *The Science of Winning Squash*, and *Flashpoint Afghanistan.*

Catherine Hakim is Senior Research Fellow in the London School of Economics Department of Sociology. Her experience includes policy research in the Department of Employment; and her publications include numerous articles and research monographs, and textbooks on labour statistics and research design. Recent books include *Key Issues in Women's Work* and (forthcoming 1998) *Social Change and Innovation in the Labour Market.*

Sharon James-Fergus was born in Britain with Jamaican parents and an African heritage. After taking a Social Science degree she worked as a professional trainer before joining *Ajowa-Ebi*, a family resource centre providing services for disadvantaged families in the North London area. She is now Director of *Ajowa-Ebi*.

Rt. Revd. James Jones was ordained after working as a teacher and as a producer at the Scripture Union. He has been Bishop of Hull since 1994. His books include *Finding God, Why Do People Suffer?* and *A Faith that Touches the World.*

Sebastian Kraemer is a Consultant Child and Family Psychiatrist at the Tavistock Clinic and at the Whittington Hospital, London. Besides clinical and training work in the NHS he has published papers and chapters on fatherhood and is the co-editor of *The Politics of Attachment: Towards a Secure Society.*

Ruth Lister is Professor of Social Policy and Administration at the University of Loughborough. She is a former Director of the Child Poverty Action Group and served on the Commission for Social Justice. She has published widely around poverty, income maintenance and women's citizenship. Her latest book is *Citizenship: Feminist Perspectives* (Macmillan, 1997).

Patricia Morgan is a sociologist and Senior Research Fellow on the Family at the Institute of Economic Affairs Health and Welfare Unit. She is a frequent participant in television and radio programme debates, is author of a number of books, including recently *Farewell to the Family, Are Families Affordable,* and *Who Needs Parents?,* and a contributor to many others.

Jack O'Sullivan, 36, is an associate editor of The Independent and writes on men's issues. He was previously the paper's health and social services correspondent. He is married to Hester Collicutt and, in November 1996, their first child, Sophie, was born.

Carole Pateman was born in Sussex and is currently Professor of Political Science, University of California Los Angeles. She is a fellow of the American Academy of Arts and Sciences and was President of the International Political Science Association from 1991 to 1994. Her publications include *Participation and Democratic Theory* and *The Sexual Contract.*

David Phillips grew up in southeast Asia and South Africa. He trained as a cultural anthropologist, then worked on a number of adult education programmes and refugee resettlement projects in East and North Africa before becoming a journalist. He still lives mainly in Africa.

Robert Rowthorn has written extensively on economic growth, employment and wages. He is a professor of economics at Cambridge University, where he and Shirley Dex direct a research project on Fiscal Policy, Parenting and Business Organisation. This project is located in the ESRC Centre for Business Research and is funded by the Sainsbury Family Charitable Trusts, The Newton Trust and the Esmee Fairbairn Trust.

Rt. Hon. Dame Angela Rumbold was until this year MP for Mitcham and Morden, and Vice-Chairman of the Conservative Party. As such she was responsible for parliamentary candidates and drew up the current selection system. From 1986 to 1990 she was co-chairman of the Women's National Commission.

Jacqueline Scott is in the Faculty of Social and Political Sciences at the University of Cambridge, and a fellow of Queens' College. She was formerly the Director of Research at the ESRC Research Centre on Micro-social Change at the University of Essex.

Roger Scruton is a writer, philosopher, composer and journalist. He founded the Conservative Philosophy Group and edits *The Salisbury Review*. He has written more than twenty books, most recently *Animal Rights and Wrongs* and, due out shortly, *The Aesthetics of Music* (O.U.P).

Clive Soley has been MP for Hammersmith since 1979 and Ealing, Acton and Shepherds' Bush since May 1997. He is now Chairman of the Parliamentary Labour Party, and until recently was Chairman of the All-Party Parliamentary Group on Parenting.

Rosie Styles was born and educated in Oxford. After thirteen years of teaching religious education in Oxfordshire and London, she left the profession for work in the voluntary sector. She became National Secretary for the Townswomen's Guild before taking on directorship of the Baby Naming society in 1994.

Fay Weldon has written numerous television plays, dramatisations, and stage plays. Her novels include *Down Among the Women, The Hearts and Lives of Men* and *Life and Loves of a She Devil.* She has been the chairperson of the Booker Prize judges. Her work is translated into most main world languages. She lives and works in London, is married and has many children.

Helen Wilkinson is Project Director at *Demos*, where she has focused mainly on gender, family policy and generational issues. Before that she has worked in broadcast journalism, in political research roles and policy development in Parliament and Congress, and at the NCC. She has been awarded a Harkness Fellowship by the Commonwealth Fund as is currently a visiting fellow at the Families and Work Institute in New York.

Michael Young, *aka* Lord Young of Dartington, is Director of the Institute of Community Studies. He is the author of many books, including *The Rise of the Meritocracy*, has founded many organisations like the *Consumers' Association*, and has prompted many public initiatives like the ESRC and the Open University.